Glow-in-the-Dark Animals

PLANKTON

Ryan Nagelhout

PowerKiDS press.

New York

Published in 2015 by The Rosen Publishing Group, Inc.
29 East 21st Street, New York, NY 10010

First Edition

Editor: Katie Kawa
Book Design: Katelyn Heinle

Photo Credits: Cover Purestock/Thinkstock.com; cover, pp. 1–24 (background texture) olesya k/Shutterstock.com; pp. 4–5 Alexander S. Kunz/Moment/Getty Images; pp. 6–7 Brandon Rosenblum/Moment Open/Getty Images; p. 6 (phytoplankton) http://commons.wikimedia.org/wiki/File:Diatoms_through_the_microscope.jpg; p. 6 (zooplankton) http://en.wikipedia.org/wiki/Zooplankton#mediaviewer/File:Copepodkils.jpg; pp. 8–9 DuongMinhTien/Shutterstock.com; pp. 10–11 Stocktrek Images/Getty Images; pp. 12–13, 14–15 Visuals Unlimited, Inc./Wim van Egmond./Visuals Unlimited/Getty Images; pp. 16–17 Ethan Daniels/Shutterstock.com; pp. 18–19 © iStockphoto.com/bbsferrari; pp. 20–21 Per-Andre Hoffmann/Picture Press/Getty Images; p. 22 © iStockphoto.com/bjonesmedia.

Library of Congress Cataloging-in-Publication Data

Nagelhout, Ryan, author.
  Plankton / Ryan Nagelhout.
      pages cm. — (Glow-in-the-dark animals)
  Includes bibliographical references and index.
  ISBN 978-1-4994-0177-6 (pbk.)
  ISBN 978-1-4994-0179-0 (6 pack)
  ISBN 978-1-4994-0175-2 (library binding)
  1. Marine plankton—Juvenile literature. 2. Bioluminescence—Juvenile literature. I. Title.
  QH91.8.P5N34 2015
  578.77′6—dc23
                                    2014030408

Manufactured in the United States of America

CPSIA Compliance Information: Batch #CW15PK: For Further Information contact Rosen Publishing, New York, New York at 1-800-237-9932

CONTENTS

GLOWING WAVES

Have you ever stood on the beach at night and watched the water rush to your feet? What would you think if that water was glowing? Would you think something bad was put into the water? Would you worry the water wasn't safe for swimming?

In some parts of the world, water glows because of tiny creatures called plankton. There are more than a million species, or kinds, of plankton. Some special kinds have **chemicals** that cause them to glow at night. Why do they glow? Where can we find this glowing plankton? Read on to find out!

These waves are glowing because they're home to glowing plankton.

PLANT OR ANIMAL?

Plankton are tiny **organisms** that live in the ocean and sometimes in freshwater. "Plankton" is a general term for different organisms, such as **algae**, bacteria, and other tiny animals. Because they're too small or too weak to swim, they float and drift with the water's current.

Plantlike plankton are called phytoplankton. Animallike plankton are zooplankton. Glowing plankton live in oceans, usually in warmer waters. The glowing plankton we see from beaches live close to shore in **shallow** waters, but glowing plankton live throughout the oceans as well.

phytoplankton

zooplankton

Most plankton can't be seen unless they glow.

NEWS FLASH!

Scientists don't know why there aren't any freshwater glowing plankton. Some think freshwater plankton don't have certain chemicals that cause the glowing.

HOW SMALL ARE THEY?

Just how tiny are plankton? They're tiny enough that thousands of them fit inside a single drop of water! Many are so small they can't even be seen without a **microscope**. There are three basic sizes of plankton. The largest, called macroplankton, can be over 0.04 inch (1 mm) long and can be caught in nets.

Some plankton can be caught in fishing nets. Nannoplankton can't be caught in any kind of net.

Plankton from 0.002 to 0.04 inch (0.05 to 1 mm) long are called microplankton, a group that includes both phytoplankton and zooplankton. The smallest plankton, called nannoplankton or dwarf plankton, are less than 0.002 inch (0.05 mm) long. Most nannoplankton are plantlike.

NEWS FLASH!

Phytoplankton are too small to be considered macroplankton.

HOW DO THEY GLOW?

Plankton glow because of a **process** called bioluminescence (by-oh-loo-muh-NEH-suhns). The word comes from "bio," which means "life," and "lumen," which means "light." A bioluminescent animal is one that makes its own light! It does this with the help of special chemicals in its body.

Many different kinds of plankton make their own light. Plankton usually make blue or green light. Scientists think plankton only create light at night because they only use their ability to create light when it's needed. They don't need light often during the day.

During the day, some kinds of algae can turn the water red. At night, these same plankton make the water glow!

11

WHY SO BRIGHT?

Plankton glow to stay safe. Many animals that live in oceans eat plankton. Plankton can feel when the water around them moves. They think the motion is caused by a predator, so they create a flash of light with their body. Plankton use their light flashes to scare off animals that are trying to eat them.

Scientists also think plankton's flashes could actually be used to **attract** fish larger than the ones hunting them. These larger predators would eat the fish hunting the plankton.

Bioluminescence is a common way ocean creatures keep themselves safe from predators.

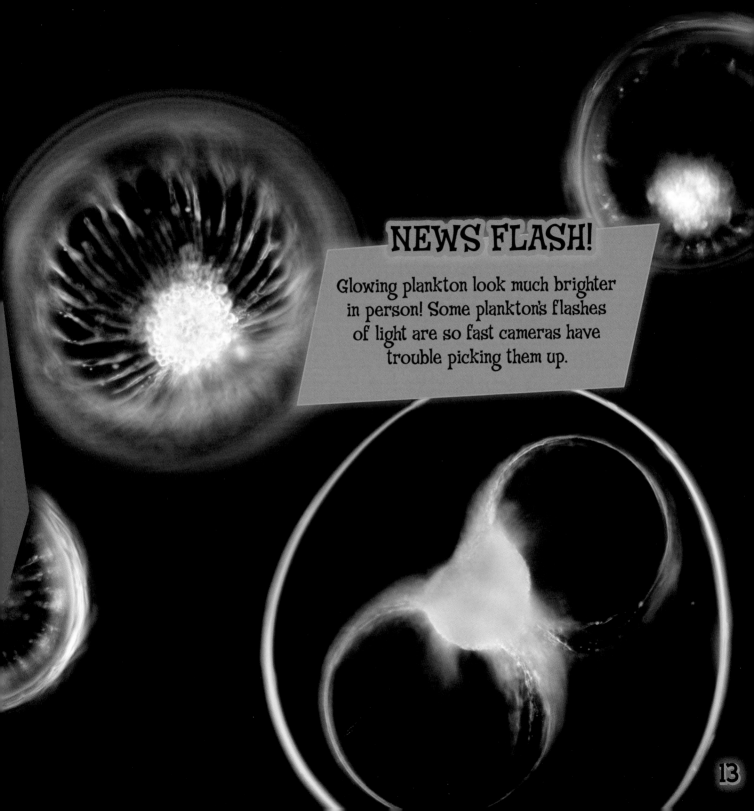

NEWS FLASH!

Glowing plankton look much brighter in person! Some plankton's flashes of light are so fast cameras have trouble picking them up.

13

SPARKLING AND SHOOTING GOO

Many glowing plankton are a type of algae called dinoflagellates. Because dinoflagellates are a kind of algae, they're considered a phytoplankton. Dinoflagellates are the most common form of bioluminescent plankton. One kind of dinoflagellate called a sea sparkle glows when it's moved by waves or other things in the water.

Some plankton can't make themselves glow, but they have another defense from predators. They shoot glowing goo into the water when predators are nearby. These gobs of goo confuse fish wanting to eat plankton.

Dinoflagellates, such as the sea sparkles shown here, are the most common bioluminescent creatures in the open ocean.

NEWS FLASH!

Dinoflagellates have two flagella, which are thin, movable body parts that help them swim. These help dinoflagellates spin as they move forward.

HUNGRY PLANKTON

What do plankton eat? It depends on the kind of plankton. Zooplankton commonly eat single-**celled** organisms or tiny plants.

Many phytoplankton make their own food. They do this through a process called photosynthesis, which takes energy from the sun and uses it to make food. These types of plankton include algae. Like plants, phytoplankton let out oxygen during photosynthesis. Animals need this gas to live.

Plankton are at the bottom of the food chain in ocean **habitats**. They're eaten by many different fish, which means they're important to many different animals, including people who eat fish!

Scientists don't think plankton use bioluminescence to help them find food. They use it to keep themselves from getting eaten by animals such as this crab.

MAKING PLANKTON AND SEA FOAM

Different kinds of plankton reproduce, or make more plankton, in different ways. Some reproduce on their own by putting **spores** into the water. Some split in half to make two plankton. Others need male and female plankton to come together and make babies. Most plankton can reproduce very quickly.

When plankton die, their bodies break down in the water. The dead plankton clump together to make sea foam. Sea foam forms when the wind and waves churn and whip the water around to create floating, soap-like bubbles. The sea foam sits on top of the water and is blown around by the wind.

NEWS FLASH!

A very quick increase in a plankton population is called a bloom.

Sea foam is so light that it can be blown onto land.

SEEING THE LIGHTS

People travel many miles to see glowing plankton on beaches at night. Bioluminescent Bay in Puerto Rico is famous for giving tours of its glowing shorelines. It's believed that up to 720,000 glowing plankton are in a single gallon of water from Bioluminescent Bay!

All around the world, people take pictures of glowing waters and watch the ocean light up as they go for a moonlight swim. Many people even take underwater dives in the dark to get a better view of bioluminescent plankton glowing in deeper waters.

Looking for glowing plankton has become a popular thing to do in many places around the world.

NEWS FLASH!

Some people go surfing or kayaking in waters where glowing plankton live. The movement of the surfboard or boat in the water makes the plankton glow!

21

FUN PLANKTON FACTS

1. Plankton are hunted by some predators that are also bioluminescent, such as lantern fish.

2. Some species of plankton go closer to the surface of the water at night and go deeper when the sun is out. This is called vertical migration.

3. Plankton glow blue and green because those colors of light are seen best in water.

4. In very deep parts of the ocean, bioluminescence is the only kind of light.

5. Phytoplankton populations decrease when the water's surface gets warmer.

GLOSSARY

algae: Small, plantlike organisms that grow in water.

attract: To bring close.

cell: The smallest basic part of a living thing.

chemical: Matter mixed with other matter to create change.

habitat: A place or type of place where a plant or animal usually lives.

microscope: An instrument that uses lenses to show detail in very small objects.

organism: A living thing.

process: A series of actions or changes.

shallow: Not deep.

spore: A small, seedlike body that can grow into a new organism.

INDEX

WEBSITES

Due to the changing nature of Internet links, PowerKids Press has developed an online list of websites related to the subject of this book. This site is updated regularly. Please use this link to access the list: www.powerkidslinks.com/gitda/plank

THE
WESTERNERS

A ROUNDUP
OF PIONEER
REMINISCENCES

COMPILED AND ANNOTATED

JOHN
MYERS MYERS

UNIVERSITY OF NEBRASKA PRESS, LINCOLN AND LONDON

⊗ The paper in this book meets the minimum requirements of American
National Standard for Information Sciences—Permanence of Paper for
Printed Library Materials, ANSI Z39.48-1984.

First Bison Books printing: 1997
Most recent printing indicated by the last digit below:
10   9   8   7   6   5   4   3   2   1

Library of Congress Cataloging-in-Publication Data
The westerners: a roundup of pioneer reminiscences / compiled and annotated
[by] John Myers Myers.
p.   cm.
Originally published: Englewood Cliffs, N.J.: Prentice Hall, 1969.
Includes index.
ISBN 0-8032-8236-2 (pbk.: alk. paper)
1. Frontier and pioneer life—West (U.S.)   2. West (U.S.)—Biography.
I. Myers, John Myers, 1906–
F596.W513   1997
978'.02'0922—dc21
[B]
97-1510   CIP

The attitudes expressed in the here collected reminiscences are solely those of
the venerable contributors, as are the statements concerning people, places,
events and institutions.

Reprinted from the original 1969 edition by Prentice-Hall, Inc., Englewood
Cliffs, New Jersey.

To
C. M. VANDEBURG

Parked across the night that parts
Past from present tense
Lay a hunting range of hearts
Never under fence:
Antipode to Paradise
Nothing easy marred
Furnished errands to suffice
Lads released from guard.

When the fences rose, it fell
Into yesterday,
Double-eagle down a well
Careless to repay;
Luster lost in such a nook
Few reatas snare,
Bringing rather back to book
Tin in ill repair.

Only when the compass point
Rallies to the lode
Dare we judge the seeker joint
With the precious node;
Westaway the weather vane
Crows that here is true
Bullion, smuggled from a main
Close at home to you.

THE AUTHORS OF THIS BOOK
An Introduction

THE BODY OF this volume is made up of tape-recorded reports on the West by people old enough to have been active there during the closing decades of the nineteenth century and the opening ones of the twentieth. Ranging in age from the mid-seventies to the early nineties, they were asked to look back at the final phase of America's pioneer era and enlarge history by telling what it was like to live at that time.

The two dozen spokesmen included here may seem few for a generation hailing from some of the largest of the United States. Yet they stand for a respectable percentage of those yet competent to give vivid descriptions of the period of their youth. For these frontier holdovers represent the elite of a never extensive field.

"So many people today don't know how few of us there were," as one contributor said of turn-of-the-century pioneers. The young people of that day were never numerous, and they were born at a time when life expectancy was considerably shorter than is true of today.

Only a small percent of a sparse population could be expected to live for three-quarters of a century or better. Only a fraction of these, moreover, could be counted on to go the distance possessed of sound faculties. A person who works clinically with advanced age told me that only one in twenty-five reaches that stage without either suffering a loss of memory or developing a bent for invention. And from the responsible residue must be subtracted the diffident, the sour, and the unaware, who wouldn't make good interview material encountered at whatever age.

At that the task of finding sharp longevity would have been many times easier had the search commenced a few years earlier. In the course of studying Western lore I had run across quite a sprinkling of colorful old-timers. Yet, by the time this project was begun I found that I knew but one man who could still be of help to me. The rest had died or had lost their power of recall. Application to fellows in the field of Western Americana elsewhere turned up the news that the local Arizona picture was widely duplicated. The last lustrum had either killed or incapacitated most suitable candidates.

But with the aid of the numerous people cited in my list of acknowledgments, I at length found the people I was looking for, and some besides. For various reasons certain interviews did not turn out as well as had been hoped. A few, satisfactory in themselves, were scratched because of livelier ones covering much the same subjects. Emerging were the contributions of the twenty-four highly articulate and aware authors of this book.

Individually and as a group they are remarkable. Some have attained a legendary renown. Quite a few are regional notables or have won national recognition. All are looked upon, and by people well qualified to know, as authoritative and reliable spokesmen for their respective areas and spheres of pioneer action.

Between them they speak for the frontier on an admirably wide scale, whether the standard is geography or lines of endeavor. The two yardsticks will be dealt with in the order of mention.

The original idea called for reminiscences garnered by scouring the entire West for contributors. As that seemed too large an undertaking, the field of exploration was narrowed to parts neighboring my Arizona base of operations. Theoretically the zone dealt with by the interviewed was restricted, too. In practice it didn't work out that way, because where an old-timer lived in the nineteen sixties was no clue to what he would talk about when asked to review days more than half a century ago.

A spread of men consulted in the Arizona Pioneers Home at Prescott told me of matters taking in the breadth of Texas and stretching from the Mexican border to the Canadian one. The Atlantic was spanned, too, for one of the contributors had been in England with a Wild West show. And a Colorado pioneer took me across the Pacific, besides. In terms of states the reminiscences covered, with varying degrees of emphasis, more than I had bargained for: Texas, New Mexico, Arizona, California, Nevada, Utah, Colorado, Wyoming, Montana, Idaho, and Oklahoma as represented by the Indian Territory.

Well, wherever the contributors roamed, they remained among The Westerners. I asked questions of people who had been young in a young country, and the recorder stored their amazing variety of answers.

If the contributors did not collectively visit all Western points, they tell of every kind of Western terrain. Mountains, plains, river valleys, deserts neat and irrigated, forests of various sorts, grasslands parched as well as snow-refreshed—all are paraded here.

As for the range of topics, it can fairly be called encyclopedic. If a profession or a roguery was practiced in the West, these people describe it. They relate a wealth of regional lore, passed to them by the generation to which their parents belonged. And they knew, or knew of, numberless famous Western characters—concerning whom they sometimes spring news not elsewhere on record.

If only four of the two dozen are women, that roughly reflects the actual disproportion between the sexes in the West of their youth. In and out of towns stags predominated, and only in the occasional farming districts was domesticity anything like the norm.

Unlike most of their parents, the contributors were born on the Western frontier or spent their forty-five years there. So as a group they are of the West in a sense that was not true of the majority of earlier pioneers. Growing up elsewhere, these arrived with bents developed in other sections of the country. But the people of this book were no mature migrators who had left one foot where they came from. At the latest they reached the West as striplings eager to merge with the people and attitudes of a region which was often without so much as communication with other American parts. To use the words of one contributor, "We never knowed what was goin' on in the rest of the country; heck, no."

In youth, then, they were totally of the West, and at a period when it differed from the national norm as no region could by the time they were in or nearing middle age. What started the merger with the rest of the country was America's entry into World War I. The need for supplying the European allies of the United States, as well as its own war machine, made the West's resources of crucial importance.

More forceful of change, though, was the shift in points of view brought about by the conflict. People who had been cheerfully indifferent to what was going on in the rest of the nation now craned necks eastward—for news, among other things, of young kinsmen and neighbors on duty in the armed services.

When these came home from foreign as well as Eastern parts, the outside world closed in on isolation, flattening the key factor in the West's previous history. Embracing the Industrial Age reversed the urge to be separate from it, which had been largely responsible for settling the region. With the drive for material parity with the East which then began, the frontier wilted as a distinctive shaper of character even more rapidly than it did as a physical entity. So the gap dividing the contributors' generation from the following ones is far wider than most such chasms. Certainly the Westerners who today revel in luxurious homes and offices differ in outlook from sires who by preference did not live indoors at all when young. And surely these folk inured to glad-handing strangers today have a separate concept of man's relation to man from that of forebears who were affronted if so much as asked their names.

That extreme of individuality found modification in the little towns which called themselves cities, of course; but life in them did not pair with counterparts in other sections of the country. Nor were booming camps the only swervers from rural placidity. "In all the villages," as one contributor pointed out, "the main industry was saloons. And every saloon had gambling in the rear."

But those same wide-open burgs were ones in which a woman could walk unmolested, for the man who didn't heed decorum in this respect was "gentled" by having "something put over his head." Now in many of the same towns that have since become urban a poker game is hard to find and women have ceased to be off-limits for the lawless.

The prevailing violence of the frontier was more channeled than that of today, and was carried out largely by men in the class with the felons cited in Gilbert's *Pirates of Penzance:* counted on to mind the amenities, that is to say, when not on duty as criminals. "They'd never bother nothin' but only a bank or a train," one contributor said of a widely famed group of outlaws.

"It was an altogether different world," as another observed when comparing the era of his youth to the present one, "and the people was different." To that contention his reminiscences and its companion pieces stand as fascinating monuments.

John Myers Myers

CONTENTS

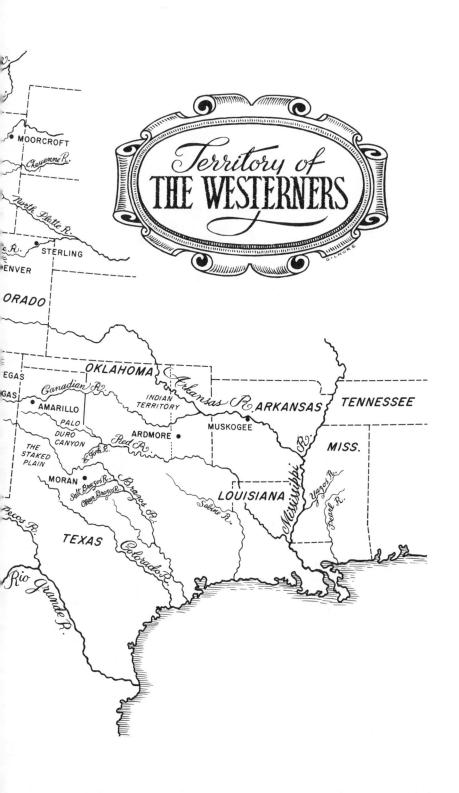

MAINLY OF VARIOUS RANGES

I
THE PANHANDLE AND
THE PECOS

"Nobody asked anybody's name in them days: it wasn't courtesy."

PAUL GRAY, Prescott, Arizona

Many years ago Carlsbad, New Mexico, was not the seat of an internationally known tourist attraction; in fact it wasn't even called Carlsbad. It was an uncelebrated cow town known as Eddy, whose other industry was digging out the fertilizer which bats had deposited in a nearby cavern. Mr. Gray recalls that Pecos Valley era, together with old ranching days in west-central Texas before he rode the cattle trails of the Panhandle, the Staked Plain, and points adjacent.

Prairie fires were one of the stock-raising hazards of regions where irrigation was then unknown, and ingenious means for coping with them were devised by men who had no public utilities or chemicals to call upon. But if the country was dry, the rivers were wet before they had been dammed in the name of agriculture and hydroelectric power, and there were treacherous spots in them where thirsty cows would sink. Still there were ways of meeting this problem, too, by a rider who couldn't pull a tractor or a derrick out of his pocket, and Mr. Gray recalls them. He also remembers the fate of the last footloose Western buffalo and the day when he and his pony—neither psychologically prepared for the encounter—beheld their first horseless carriage.

A well-known Southwestern cowman, Mr. Gray was an early associate of Messrs. Higgins and Powell, the authors respectively of contributions 8 and 24.

HIS CONTRIBUTION

I was born in Texas, somewhere near Llano, in 1880. My mother didn't like moonlight nights—no-o-o-h! She said, "People always rave about moonlight nights, but I hate 'em." The Indians always raided on moonlight nights, you see. The Comanches'd come on moonlight nights to steal horses and scalp people.

4

I remember she said the Indians'd hide along the trail when the kids was going to school, and they'd jump out and try to get hold of the bridle reins. So the kids'd have to outrun the Indians. That was in San Saba County. She said when her father moved up there he traded most of his horses off for oxen, because the Indians'd take horses but wouldn't steal oxen. He kept the horses he did bring along in a barn of nights, and he had two boys upstairs with muzzle-loading shotguns, right over 'em. So he didn't lose any horses; he got along with the Indians all right.

My grandfather had a rifle—a lever-action brass-jawed thing, and he used to tell me about it. He said that he and Newt Jackson used to go down to Austin to get a load of groceries. They'd haul deer hides and beef hides and one thing and another, and trade 'em for flour and sugar and shotgun powder and bullets.

They got down to Austin one time, and there was a fellow with a rifle, and he was just aloading and ashooting. Well, all they had was muzzle-loaders that you'd put one bullet in at a time, and here was a fellow with a gun that you'd pump the lever and it'd shoot ten or fifteen bullets in a string.

My grandfather said, "I traded about my whole wagon load for two of them rifles and a lot of cartridges." He said, "Going back home, Newt and I was spoiling for a fight, but, you know, them Indians wouldn't come close to us."

The gun was the first repeater to come out West—the old Henry rifle. It shot a short .44 cartridge, rim fire. But it'd shoot a hundred or a hundred and fifty yards pretty good, and that was too long a range for Indians with bows and arrows.

I remember the first stove—before that we cooked on a fireplace or in Dutch ovens—that come into that country. It was a big old iron thing, and there was a place on the back side of it that held ten gallons of water.

Everybody in the county come to see that stove. "Goodness alive! Tom Barker's family have a wood stove, and they got *hot* water." That was in the eighties, probably about '85; because I was born in 1880, and I was five or six years old when that happened.

We come to New Mexico the first time in '87 in a covered wagon and settled at Rock Arroyo, about seven or eight miles out of Seven Rivers. I didn't go to it myself, but the first school I ever visited as a little kid had logs with pegs drove in 'em to hold 'em up for seats. I went to school in Eddy—it's Carlsbad now—when I was about eight years old. It was a one-room school, but they finally built another on it called a kindergarten. They had benches; it wasn't like the old ones that had log pews.

Then we moved back to Texas, and I went to school at what was called the West Texas Normal and Business College. It was located in Cherokee, about halfway between Llano and San Saba.

There was about twenty-five pupils in the school at Eddy, but the school I went to there in Cherokee must have had fifty. A fellow come in there by the name of Burns, and he was a Yale man. He got a pretty good school going, and they built this college out of rock. That was about '94, I guess; and I went to school there till '97.

We moved back to New Mexico that year, and I remember when Dave Kemp killed Les Dow on the street there in Eddy. Les had a hard gang and was kind of making it rough for people. So Dave decided to kill him, and he did, right in front of the post office.

Les always carried his six-shooter in a paper sack, and Kemp knew it. Well, when Dow went into the post office to get his mail, Dave just backed up there and waited for him to come out. Of course, Les had his six-shooter in his right hand, which was in that sack. The other fellow knew it, so he was on Dow's left side. And he said, "Why hello, Les," and shot him. Les didn't die right then, but he did a few days later.

There was too many witnesses, and Dow's gang was too strong around there, so Dave died first. Let's see; there was one fellow standing right out in the street there, and another was hid behind a tree; and there wasn't either one of 'em over twenty feet from Dave. He didn't have a chance. I don't remember what year that was, but it was a long time ago.

They changed the name of Eddy to Carlsbad in about '97. I've been in the *old* cave there—they used to call it the Bat Cave. They used to haul guano from there and ship it to California. That was before they knew about the cave that's such a big attraction now. Jim White, an old-timer from around there, discovered it.

About '98 I was working for an outfit farther down the Pecos, and we couldn't sell our steers or calf crop anywhere around there, so we shipped 'em to Kansas. We shipped from a little place called Riverton, about thirty miles from Pecos City. I had nine steers in that bunch, but they didn't do any good in Kansas.

But I didn't know about that, so I said to the boss, "What about my check for them steers? I got to buy a new saddle. A horse bucked me and my saddle off, and it got under his belly, and he tore it all to pieces."

The boss said, "Do I owe you any money on them steers?"

So I said, "Sure, I had nine head in there."

He said, "You owe me six bits a head."

The steers hadn't quite paid for the cost of shipping 'em, so they took it out of my wages. That was my first real experience in the cow business.

The family stayed around Eddy until 1900; then we moved up on the [Staked] Plain above Monument, and I worked on all them outfits around there and up and down the Pecos. And I was on cattle drives. We shipped from Portales, we shipped from Kenna, on the line of the Santa Fe running up through Clovis, and we shipped from Amarillo.

Nobody asked anybody's name in them days; it wasn't courtesy. If a fellow stayed around awhile, somebody'd give him a name— "Slick" or "Skillet" maybe. They mostly called me Paul, but one outfit called me "Lightweight," because I didn't weigh very much. That was up around Fort Sumner in 1901.

I stopped in there and went to work for an outfit that had a lot of steers. I'd had my leg broke, and I was just getting well when I got that job from old man Witherspoon—Carver Witherspoon.

We drove a bunch of cattle from Fort Sumner across to Plemons, on the Canadian; northeast of Amarillo and over two hundred miles by cow trails. And I got that leg broke again; a horse fell on me.

My leg was set right on the trail. We couldn't get a doctor—we didn't know where there was one. We didn't even know where we was, either, but it was on the Chisholm Trail. [One of the successive variants of the original trail, whose course was well east of the Panhandle.]

So they put me on the camp wagon, but it was painful on that

7

old wagon. Still I had a gentle pony, so I'd get on him part of the time. But we finally got to the Canadian and got the herd across and went down the other side to Plemons.

We come back through Amarillo. It was a town with a board sidewalk; and there was mud and snow, because it was in the wintertime. As a matter of fact it was Christmas Day when we come through there. We loaded up the wagon with chuck there and went on back to Fort Sumner.

Well, they couldn't fire me, because the company's check was no good. The boss give me a check, but nobody around there'd cash it. So they give me the freight wagon, and I could handle that on a crutch, driving four gentle ponies. I freighted that winter from Santa Rosa to Sunnyside, carrying grain and hay and chuck for the ranch. When spring come I was all right and went riding again.

There was the funniest thing that happened then. When I got so I could ride again, they put me up the river with another cowpuncher. And there was a little Mexican store up there.

Well, this company—their credit wasn't any good anywheres, so they was feeding us just bacon and beans and spuds and 'lasses. We got burnt out on that stuff. Of course, we had company beef, so my partner killed a beef and hung the hide on a fence. Then he found that the Mexican that was running that store had a lot of cattle around there. So he'd butcher that Mexican's cattle, and he'd take it up there to the store and trade it to him. He'd borrow my saddle and load it with beef and take it up there and trade it for canned goods. Oh, we had everything there was to eat.

And this boss'd come up there and visit our camp. There was eight of 'em around the country within thirty miles, and he'd check 'em all.

I told Bill the first time he come up there, "We're fired, boy."

And he said, "They can't fire us; they ain't got no money to pay us off."

I'm not going to tell Bill's last name; I'll have to take the Fifth Amendment on that, because he's gone. But anyhow the boss come back and visited us twice more, and he'd stay and stay and stay and eat and eat and eat.

I saw that boss about fifteen years later in the southern part of New Mexico, and he said, "You and Bill was the only ones that had any sense. The rest of them fellows eat that old sowbelly and beans and 'lasses all winter, and you fellows eat everything."

We didn't have real trouble with rustlers; but there was beef-eaters, though lots of times nobody cared. You take these big companies—the way it *used* to be—and you took your horse and throwed in with one of them outfits and helped 'em herd cattle and helped 'em brand calves; them outfits worked you the same as if you belonged to 'em, and you was supposed to eat beef. And sometimes it was all right to kill a steer if you didn't work for 'em, if they knew you.

I remember one time when I was a kid in Eddy, a Mexican wood hauler killed a beef and took it in. Well, they had him up before the judge, and he said he was hungry and didn't have anything for his family, so they didn't do anything about it.

The lobo wolves [a largely Mexican species, smaller than the timber wolf] used to be pretty bad, but the cow men put a bounty on 'em. And they're not like the coyote; they're pretty easy to catch.

I never trapped 'em but one time. That was at the head of Black River, that runs into the Pecos about thirty miles below Carlsbad. There was six of 'em come in there. I caught five of 'em, and the other evidently left the country. But about two years after that he come back, or I guess it was the same one, and he was howling around the house before daylight. So I took some bait—some beef poisoned with strychnine—up a hill near the house, and the next day I went there again.

There was a little bit of snow on the ground, and I saw where he hit that trail of bait. He didn't touch the first one, but the second one was gone. I followed his tracks for about two hundred yards, and he commenced going thisaway and thataway. So I got up on a pretty good-sized boulder, and I saw him lying there. I guess he was the last wolf in that part of the country. He was so old that he didn't have any teeth; he was hungry or he wouldn't have took that bait.

Although I never caught one, there was quite a few mountain

lions in the hills, but their favorite dish was colt, not cows. They liked horsemeat better than anything else.

And there was a few bears around. I saw a fellow bring one into the roundup one spring. He roped it and drove it in. It was a brown bear, not too big, and he was pretty poor. I think the fellow give it to somebody in Carlsbad.

I never got to see a buffalo except for one old cow along the Pecos below Carlsbad that was tame and used to graze along with the steers. But some dude come out from New York City, and damned if he didn't kill that old cow; he thought it was wild. He was out there hunting, and he killed him a buffalo—the last one left. It sure made everybody sore.

In the Pecos River there was bad quicksand. A cow'd walk in there to get a drink of water, and she'd get stuck. The only way to get her out was just to pull off your clothes and go in and tromp around a leg. You'd tromp, and the quicksand'd boil out of there, and you could pull that leg out with a rope. Then you'd get the other legs out.

Well, when you turned the cow loose, she'd take after you every time. Now that they've put in them dams, there isn't enough of it for the ducks to light on, but the Pecos used to run a lot of water. So when the cow went for you, you'd make a dive out in the river, and she'd follow and bog down again. You just wanted to knock her on the head.

Out on the Plains they used to have prairie fires that'd wipe up a lot of country. Generally if ranchers knew a fire was coming, you could save the cows. You could see one rolling across the prairie from a good ways off most of the time, and you'd get the cattle out of the way.

Once in a while ranchers could fight the things, though, and save a lot of grass. The only way they could quiet a fire was when the wind'd go down. Then they'd kill a cow or yearling and split it open. They'd chop it right down the back and leave the hide on so it would spread out. Then they'd put two men on it with ropes, and they'd drag right down the fire line with this beef and put it out. You see, it'd been burning slow with the wind down, and you could put out a lot of fire with one beef.

But you couldn't handle prairie fires at all when there was a high wind. That was in the trade-wind belt, and sometimes it'd blow fifty or sixty miles an hour.

That was when cattle got caught by the things, and sometimes men, too. I remember that LFD outfit, owned by two brothers, Tom and Phelps. They had a big lot of country toward Paloduro Canyon and Yellowstone Canyon, over in the old XIT range.

They'd had a big fire there, and old Tom was telling us fellows about it. He said, "Phelps was out there with two little mules, and that fire run 'em up against a fence; and you know, it just about burnt all the hair off them poor little old mules." He didn't say nothing about his brother. His brother'd laid down and curled himself up, and the fire went over him and burnt the hide off him pretty bad. But Tom just said, "Them poor little old mules."

When the Plains first began to get settled, there come a few girls into the country. Before that there wasn't any; there was only boys, you know. Well, after the girls was there, they had dances around at different places. And everybody'd go on horseback and stay all night—dance all night and get breakfast, if you was still able to stand, about sunup. We'd ride twenty-five or thirty miles to a dance and then head back to work in the morning.

Cars come in there after 1900. One time I got a grain of sand or something in my eye, and my face swelled up so I couldn't see out of it. I put up with it for two or three days, and then I started for Carlsbad. I had to ride sixty-five miles to get to a doctor there.

Along about the first evening that I headed in toward Carlsbad, I saw a kind of contraption down the road. It looked like a buggy, but I didn't see no horse, and there was two men working around the thing. It was a kind of buggy affair, you see. I got to look at it afterwards, and they had two engines there; one along one way and one the other, flat. It had wheels like a buggy and a bucket chain—chain drive, you know. That was the first one I ever saw; in about 1901 or '02, I guess. After that they got thicker, but we didn't have no roads for automobiles, just wagon trails full of chuck holes.

Well anyhow, I rode on down the road, and I got thirty-five or forty yards from them two fellows; and they cranked the thing, and it went off. And that little old pony of mine headed straight back where I'd come from, and he went a hundred and fifty yards before I could stop him. He didn't want anything to do with that outfit.

2

WHEN THE COLORADO WAS THE GRAND

"If you want to ride this son of a bitch, you put your saddle on him."

JAKE GOSS, Fruita, Colorado

In western Colorado, close to the Utah line, the region in which Mr. Goss grew up, was one of the last areas of the West to be opened for white settlement. This did not take place until after the Ute Indians were moved to reservations in Utah in 1881. Mesa County was then laid out, and in the fall of 1881 the newly surveyed townsite of Grand Junction was recognized as its seat. The junction was that of the Gunnison with the Grand River, as the Colorado above its union with the Green was then known.

Flanking the stream was the Western paradox of desert holding its own beside ample water, and this in turn was and is framed by towering ranges of the Rockies. Into the thus-shaped valley of the Grand, itself forty-five hundred feet high, came settlers such as Goss senior, looking for land to claim along the river or amongst the grasslands in the mountains created by tributary creeks. As Mr. Goss was only two years old when he arrived, he was in effect a native of a region which was but three years away from being pristine when he first drew breath.

Unlike most parts of western Colorado, mining played but a small part in the history of the region here discussed. Over the years irrigation turned an arid region into a very fertile one, hence the prideful name of Fruita. But raising cattle was the vicinity's first industry, as it remains the dominant one, and Mr. Goss was associated with it, together with the allied trade of teaching horses to cooperate for over seventy years.

HIS CONTRIBUTION

My name's plain Jake Goss. I was born in Jefferson County, North Carolina, in 1884. We come to Pueblo, Colorado, in 1885, when I was only a year old. By golly, I come to Mesa County in a covered

14

wagon in 1886, and we drove cattle over the mountains. My father rooted around and moved around and finally settled on a ranch he liked. His last place was right out here, about two miles west of town.

There was seven boys and seven girls of us, and I was right in the middle of 'em. From the first I can remember we all worked. Every time us kids had a chance to make a dime—by picking strawberries or pulling weeds, or anything we could do—we done it. I never did go to school much, but the first time I went was at High Point. After that I went to the Fruitie school here, and I graduated—from the fourth grade.

Then I punched cows, which I done about all my life. I started out with my brother-in-law, when I guess I was ten or twelve years old. He finally got a bunch of cattle in Utah, and I went after 'em with him. We made two or three trips there together.

When I was about thirteen years old, I wrangled horses at a roundup and got fifteen dollars a month. Each man had anywhere from three to seven head of horses in his string. The horses'd herd all together out grazing, and I'd have to take care of 'em. I'd have to bring 'em into camp, as maybe the men'd want to change horses, and I'd have to take 'em out to graze again. Sometimes I'd have to bring 'em in at noon, so the riders could change horses, and sometimes at night.

In the roundup there was three of the men that would catch a night horse. Their job was what was called night hawkin'. The next mornin' they'd bring their horses in, and I'd have to take 'em out to graze again. But I didn't do any night hawkin' myself while I was a horse wrangler. After I brought the horses in at night I was done with 'em.

When I was a knot-headed kid of fifteen or sixteen, I hired out to work on a ranch off in the mountains to cut hay for a man named Turner. He fired his cowpuncher and kept me, after we got the hay up. Then I was by myself there for three months and never seen a white man; and, by God, that took guts!

The Indians'd come down once in a while; probably every week or two weeks. Turner had a little old store there, and they'd come down for coffee or salt or somethin'. They was Utes that was camped at Flat Rock, on the other side of Winter Creek. That was all I'd see, and after a while I got so I'd talk a little Ute.

They was pretty good Utes, and don't think they wasn't. There was one chief that'd come down there, and he'd eat as much in one meal as I would in two days. His name was Saddio, and he wanted oatmeal at every meal. He'd say, "What'sa matter you gottee no oast mew?"

I don't know how many cattle Turner ran there, and I doubt if he did either. But once just we two cut out [of the herd] and branded a hundred and three calves in one day.

He'd market his cattle right here in Fruitie [made a railhead shipping point by the originally narrow-gauge Denver and Rio Grande]. I remember one time a bunch of cows was brought in and sold to a man called Wilcox. They had 'em all cut out and bunched, and just about the time they got 'em all cut out, a train come along and stampeded 'em.

That fellow Wilcox hired me to ride that winter and bring in the damned steers. I had a shepherd dog, and I figured he could find 'em. The fellow I got him from said he'd be no good to me because he was a sheep dog. But I said, "Hell, there's no difference between a sheep dog and cow dog but just the way you train 'em."

I made that dog so kids couldn't play with him. You could hardly point your finger at him but he'd get it. I made a *good* dog out of him.

He'd ride behind my saddle as far as the [irrigation] canal. I could set him just as far away as he could see my hand, and he'd keep goin'. Sometimes he'd bring in one, sometimes two, and sometimes three steers in a day.

When I was seventeen years old, I had twenty-three head of my own. I was workin' for my brother-in-law then, and I got my arm broke; it was hangin' out my sleeve in splinters. A fellow was supposed to stay with the cows in the fall to wean the calves, and as I was all alone I couldn't leave. But after a while three fellows come through there, and one of 'em said he'd stay to feed the calves until I went to town to get my arm fixed.

When I got back—I was in town and on the road three days—that fellow'd gone and'd turned the calves out with the cows. To feed the calves [fodder to start the interrupted weaning process again], I stuck the pitchfork between my legs and worked it left-handed. I couldn't use that other arm, you know.

The same day I got back there, my brother-in-law did, too. When I got to the ranch where he was, and he found that the cows was with the calves, he really come undone. So the next day I quit him and punched cows for Charlie Turner on Willow Creek, out in Utah.

I worked for him there for a little over a year. And when I come back to Colorado, I bought that place of mine out west of here and stayed there until I had to quit work a few years ago on account of my eyes.

After I first got to punchin' cows, sometimes we'd be out for weeks; campin' out, you know. The cows was all turned loose, but we'd catch up the calves and brand 'em. We'd cut the bull calves and ear-mark [as brands could be altered, ranchers used other means of identification, too] all of 'em. Sometimes we'd take a piece of skin off the jaw and cut it loose and let it hang down. They called that a wattle. We didn't give 'em dewlaps [piercing or otherwise cutting the folds of skin at the base of the brisket as well as the dewlaps proper] like some people did, because they might catch on the brush and bleed.

We'd dally [anchor the thrown lariat by twisting the free end around the saddle horn, as opposed to the practice of knotting it there] and rope the other way. Most punchers rode with a tied-down rope, but it depends. With calves I'd tie-down and with big stuff I'd always take dallies.

I lassoed a deer one time. He was goin' up a hill; you can't catch one downhill. They can go three times as fast as a horse downhill; but uphill a horse can catch one, if he gets an even break. So I got this deer, but he went on one side of a tree and I on the other. I cut him loose then; I didn't want to get close to him, because a deer can cut a man all to pieces with his feet.

My brother and another fellow roped a bear one time, but they was sure glad to get rid of him. There was a few bears around, and now and then wolves gave us trouble, too. And there was a lot of rustling going on, *but nobody knowed a thing about it.*

17

I caught wild horses and cattle—the wild horses right out on the desert here. Sometimes you'd set traps for 'em [usually a funnel-shaped fence ending in a corral] and drive 'em into it, and sometimes you'd walk 'em to death. I done both. Then to break 'em, you've just got to take to 'em and stay with 'em until they're gentled down. When they find out what you're goin' to do, and that you're sure goin' to do it, why, they give up then. Once in a while you get one that you can't bring out of it at all, though. Some of 'em never are gentle, while some you can break in a week or two.

I used to break horses to ride, drive, do heavy work—everything. That used to be part of my business. I broke lots of 'em, and they broke me up a little bit, too. I got that arm I was tellin' about broke, and this wrist broke and that wrist broke—all from horses that'd fell down with me. I could ride 'em, if they just bucked, but them stampedin' sons of guns sure scared me. Some of 'em'd just put their heads down and shake 'em, so there was no tellin' what they'd run into.

When I was with another brother-in-law than the one I quit, he'd buy colts. They ran wild with the mares in the wintertime, and their owners'd sell 'em in the spring. These colts that my brother-in-law bought was three-year-olds when I started breakin' 'em. We had five head one time that I remember, and one of 'em was a stampeder. He'd just break and run, and by God! you couldn't do nothin' about it.

One day he started stampedin' with me while I was drivin' a bunch of cattle with my brother-in-law. That son of a gun stampeded, and they was washes there—little canyons leadin' into the crick from the hills. Some of 'em was only two feet wide, but some of 'em was ten feet wide and ten feet deep.

I never did like to use a spur on a horse I was breakin'; I always used a quirt. Well, when that colt stampeded, I started beatin' him over the head with the butt of my quirt, to turn him out of the brush and get him back on the road.

And my brother-in-law told me, "Quit hittin' that horse over the head; quit hittin' that horse!"

I finally got the colt out of the brush up to the road, and got him stopped. Then I got off him. I'd rode with just a hackamore—didn't have no bridle—and I uncinched the saddle and jerked it off. And I told my brother-in-law, "If you want to ride this son of a bitch, you put your saddle on him."

He didn't know what to say, and I asked him, "Do you want to ride him now or shall I turn him loose?"

He said, "Turn him loose."

He didn't think I would, but I just reached up and pulled the hackamore off and let the colt go. It was a good two miles to the ranch from where we was at, and I took off afoot. I had a horse of my own up there, you know—but by God, by the time I got to the ranch and got my horse, it was darker'n pitch. I didn't pull out, because the trail away led over a rough mountain that I was afraid to cross in the dark, and the next day my brother-in-law talked me into stayin'. That was the only words we ever had, but he never tried to ride my horse again.

I rode in rodeos, too. The last one we had in Fruitie was in 1916, and I got a rope on a big old steer by mistake. I had this racehorse, you see. I had to rope him before I could get in the saddle-horse race, and the saddle-horse race brought more money than anything else. I never figured on catchin' a damned steer, but by God I did when I went by him! I got him, and when I hit the end of the rope, both of us piled up in the same pile. I guess it damned near killed me. I didn't know nothin' then, but when I come to, there was two vertebraes in my back out of place.

My brother had a workhorse that he'd bring to rodeos. They'd give you fifteen dollars if you'd ride him; and if you couldn't ride him, why, the horse got the fifteen dollars. That was the meanest son of a gun I ever rode. By God, he got to rodeos three times, this workhorse did, and he never was rode barebacked. And that's the only way they'd ride them big horses.

The first automobile I ever saw was about 1908; a chain-drive car that a man I knowed'd made himself. Then about 1910 there was a Model T Ford that old Doc White bought. He got that damned car, and they told him how to work it. But he knowed more than they did, and he got in and stepped on it, you know. Well, when you pushed down on it, that was low, but when you'd take your foot off, that was high gear. So when he jerked his foot off, he just hit the door of a shed the car was in and took the door right out into the street with him.

Then old Doc Mosser had a Model T, and it couldn't pull a hill he was tryin' to make. So he got out to push it—but Hell, them cars'd run whether they went anyplace or not—and when he pushed the car over the hill, it took off. But he hung on to it and finally clumb into it and got it stopped before it went into a ditch.

In them days we never knowed what was goin' on in the rest of the country—heck, no. You got mail when you'd go to town sometime, or somebody'd bring it out to you. We got a telephone in 1915 or '16. Before that, when a doctor was needed, you'd just get on your horse and go. I've rode many a mile to get a doctor. Doctors'd come to look at you then, but they didn't know anything when they got there. Hell, they didn't know what appendicitis was then! And I had appendicitis when I was a kid—a pretty good-sized kid, big enough to cuss and raise the dickens around.

That pain'd hit me in the belly, and I'd double up and squawl, so they sent for old Doc Mosser. I'd cleaned the cistern—went down into it with a rope—and when he found I'd done that, he thought I'd hurt myself inside. He said he gave me enough morphine or chloroform to make ten men sleep; but every time the pain'd hit me, I'd come out of it and cuss.

I didn't feel just exactly right for two or three days, but I got over it [peritonitis]. Every now and then for years, though, pain'd double me up, and I had to crawl where I was goin'. So after I was married, they stretched me out on a table and cut my appendix out. And you could see by the scar on it where it'd busted when I was a kid.

Nobody knowed much about doctorin' animals in the old days, either. We used to have some trouble with blackleg; but before they had vaccination, there was nothin' you could do for cows, so I just let 'em die.

Once in a while you'd hear about somebody findin' some, but there wasn't much gold hereabouts. There was a fellow that worked across the river, pannin' and diggin' back in them hills. He was there a year or two—three or four maybe—and had quite a hole dug, and he never found nothin'.

But up Salt Crick somebody bought some chickens that was growed there, and by God, they had gold in their craws! They sure had a big crowd there for a while after that. They went up there and sanded and panned and sifted and everything, but they didn't find no gold. The crick ran right past where the chickens was growed, and they picked the gold out of the gravel. People never did find where, but, boy, there was quite a sweat about that for a while.

3

IN HIGH DESERT COUNTRY

"Some fellows stole a thousand head of weaned calves and got away with it."

J. SELBY BATT, Reno, Nevada

The son of a Nevada pioneer of the 1860's but born elsewhere in the West, Mr. Batt joined as a youngster the father and older brothers who had founded a mercantile and cattle empire fanning out from the upper reaches of the Humboldt. The town used by the family as headquarters was central to a range sprawling over the northeastern rim of the Great Basin. It was a region of extensive spreads and vast herds of cattle unschooled by fences to know where they belonged. Sometimes there were countless sheep as well, with mortal results.

Working first as a clerk but transferring to the role of cowpuncher, Mr. Batt was able to sketch a town and field enterprise as known to one who had been active in both phases of it. He was also able to tell of an aspect of pioneering of which sight has generally been lost today. Long before real-estate developers began seeing Florida morasses as the source of millions, there were opposite numbers who believed that fortunes could be reaped from remotely situated Western projects, remarkable for epic scope. As one such promotional scheme was built on acres sold to visionaries by his father, Mr. Batt here offers a brief on the blowing and bursting of a very expensive bubble.

Still in touch with stock-raising, he has interesting remarks about modern trends and practices. Included is what the Industrial Revolution has done to improve the ancient craft of rustling.

HIS CONTRIBUTION

I was born in San Francisco in 1881. On June 16, 1898, I came to Nevada. My father and brothers had a general-merchandise business in Wells, and I joined them there.

My father's name was M. Batt, and his store was known as M.

24

Batt's. His name was Morris Batt, but he always only used the "M."; just as I only use "J.," when it stands for James Abram Garfield [accounted for by the fact of that President's assassination in the year of the contributor's birth].

My father first came to Nevada the year before they drove the golden spike at Promontory [the Utah point where the eastward-pushing Central Pacific and the westward-thrusting Union Pacific railroads joined in 1869]. He came first to Elko in '68, and then came to Wells in '69 and established another store there.

It was a general-merchandise store. A lady would buy two yards of ribbon and then go down in the cellar and draw half a gallon of lac, or a gallon of whiskey. That's the way it went; they sold *everything*. There was harness hanging from the ceiling, you know, and saddles and reatas and bridles, and all the things the Indians used to make out of rawhide.

Wells was a central point for the stock men passing through from ranges in three states [the others being Utah and Idaho] and for the ranchers of three valleys. The Star Valley is west of Wells, the Clover Valley south, and Ruby Valley southwest. They were all stock ranges, and there were very few fences in that part of the country when I first came there. They raised cattle and some sheep. There were a couple of big sheep outfits, but it was mostly cattle range; and we had the sheep and cattle wars to keep it that way.

On that account there was the famous trial of Jack Davis and Jack Gleason. They were arrested for the murder of two sheep men and for burning up a sheep camp. The murder took place in the range north of Wells, over the Idaho line.

Officers found the remains of these two sheep men, and there was enough evidence to get Davis and Gleason indicted for murder. The trial was held in Albion, Idaho [since replaced by Burley as the seat of Cassia County], and my father went to Albion to testify in the case. They'd asked him to testify as to the character of Jack Gleason. He didn't know Davis personally, but he knew Gleason.

And they turned Jack Gleason loose and convicted Jack Davis—Diamondfield Jack Davis. He was afterwards famous for jumping claims in Tonopah and Goldfield and all that country. [For more about claim-jumping in the cited towns, see the contribution of Mrs. Miles, number 16.]

Gleason and Davis were both proved to have been together at the time of the murder, but the jury convicted one and turned the other loose. Gleason got out of it on account of the testimony as to his good character. Evidence proved that he was there at the same time as Jack Davis, though.

So every governor of Idaho from that time on was asked to turn Davis loose [Diamondfield Jack wasn't hanged, because as Dr. Catlett points out in contribution 15, Idaho didn't inflict capital punishment], but none of them did until Governor—I can't think of his name; but Jack Davis was pardoned. This governor had refused to pardon him all through his four years, but the last thing he did before he got out of office was to pardon Diamondfield Jack Davis.

As soon as he was turned loose, Diamondfield Jack went to Tonopah and Goldfield. I don't know which he went to first, but he did a lot of claim-jumping down there and got into a lot of hot scrapes, for he was still a gunman. I wasn't acquainted in that country at all, so I don't know the names of anybody he got in trouble with. But somebody finally got him. I don't know who killed Diamondfield Jack, but they found him shot full of holes along the tracks a few miles outside of Tonopah, I think it was.

In Wells I worked for my father's store there for two years. And I worked for a time out in the Metropolis country, when we started a store out there.

Then some Easterners that came in there after we'd ranched there for about five years bought out our interests, and they formed a desert-reclamation company—The Pacific Reclamation Company. They were going to colonize that whole country, and they did. That's what they built a dam, the Metropolis Dam, for. Then there was the townsite of the town of Metropolis; they surveyed that out in town lots and sold them all through the East. A Mr. Vandeveer did all the surveying; he was the chief surveyor for all that land—over a hundred thousand acres.

They advertised what a great place it was to be, and they put up

26

a hundred-thousand-dollar hotel right out in that desert. The opening of that hotel was quite an event. The Southern Pacific thought enough of it that they built a branch road, or sidetrack, from the station at Bishop, Nevada, out through this desert flat to Metropolis. And they put up such a good stationhouse there that it got first prize of any station of the Southern Pacific from San Francisco to Ogden. It was the best-looking one of them all, and this little town didn't have a hundred people in it.

But the hotel did good till the town kind of went to pieces, and the trouble was drought. When they started in we'd had an average rainfall of about fifteen inches. Then we had several dry seasons.

They were going to make it a dry wheat country, and that first crop of wheat they had there was something remarkable. Some fellows bought some land there and tested it and found it right and sowed it with wheat; and that one crop paid for the land and fencing it. They had stacks of wheat that first crop, but that was the last good one for most of the farmers on account of the drought. There was a couple of good farmers that only planted wheat one year and let the land lie idle the next year. And whenever they got any moisture, they harrowed the ground and tried to concentrate all the moisture; and they made several good crops where the other farmers failed.

When they got the dam built, there was irrigation, but because of the dry years there wasn't enough water for that, either. Instead of having irrigation for the twenty thousand acres they'd figured on, they had it for only about two thousand, so things fell apart.

The hotel was torn down and sold and taken to Wells. It was known as the Peacroft Hotel there and owned by the Supp Brothers. They tore down the prizewinning station, too, but I don't remember what happened to it or who got it. And the Southern Pacific, of course, tore up the tracks.

The dam was begun in 1909, and the town was started about 1911 or '12—along in there. If you don't think that was a sight to an old cowpuncher that was used to riding down in that country and seeing only wild horses and cattle—and then see that hotel and an engine come puffing toward him! It was some sight.

27

I punched cattle around there, you know. All the irrigated land there we'd owned, and we sold it to this Pacific Reclamation Company. That was the U-7 Ranch, when we had the spread. We bought it from Colonel E. P. Hardesty; he was a Texan that came up into that country.

I punched cattle for five years on that ranch before we sold it. That was in the days when there were no fences, and when we gathered beef in the fall we had a night guard. And the same thing went with the saddle horses; there was no place to hold them, either. When we worked with the Sparks-Howard Company—the two outfits worked together but with separate chuck wagons— there would be about twenty-two riders and about two hundred saddle horses.

Sparks was John Sparks, who was Governor of Nevada [from 1903 to 1908, dying in office]. After we sold out there, I went to Clover Valley. We had a ranch there called the Warm Creek Ranch. We used the U-7 brand there, and then after we bought another huge bunch of cattle, we used the 77-Bar there, and moved the U-7 herd to a separate spread. That brand is still being used by a Mr. Bruff in Clover Valley. We sold him that Clover Valley ranch.

And we had the KC Ranch in Clover Valley and the Warm Creek Ranch, which is really south of Clover Valley, at the same time that we had the U-7 outfit. So we had quite a holding there at one time. The U-7 ran about thirty-five hundred head, the KC Ranch twenty-five hundred, and the Warm Creek Ranch a thousand head—quite a bunch in all.

But when we were neighbors of the Sparks-Howard Company, they ran forty thousand head, and they branded twelve thousand calves a year. That's how we came to work with them, because our ranges met together, and there were bound to be cattle of theirs over on our side and cattle of ours over on their side. So we worked that range together about two weeks of every year.

We generally tied down, rather than dallied, when we caught anything. It was the boys from Wyoming that'd take a couple of turns around the saddle horn when they roped. And the Wyoming boys claimed they could never grow mustaches back there, because they said the wind blew so hard it used to snatch the whiskers off.

We had a few bad prairie fires that burned a lot of range; I remember one that started in one valley and swept clean over a mountain and through another valley before it burned itself out. But I don't remember one that we didn't see coming in time to get the cattle clear.

There were a few mountain lions, but they mostly hunted colts. They'd get on a rock or hide in brush and jump on the neck of a colt as it went by. The only thing that bothered the cattle—or the calves rather—was the coyotes. There were enough around to corner and kill a calf anytime they felt like it.

We were always losing cattle to rustlers, but there'd be not enough to amount to a great deal. It was a funny thing in that country: You could convict a man of horse-stealing, but you could never get a jury that would convict him of cattle-stealing. That's the way it was for years. I don't know why it was so, but that's the history of it. Come to think of it, there was one job of rustling in there that amounted to something. Some fellows stole a thousand head of weaned calves and got away with it, but I don't know who it was.

Actually there was more rustling after the trucks came in there than before there were trucks. They'd have their loading chutes with them and drive the cattle down into a corner and back the trucks up and load 'em on. The old-time rustlers might only take one or two at a time, but these fellows would take a whole truckload. Then, you see, they were right on the highway to go north to Twin Falls or go east to Ogden or west to Sacramento. Wells was sort of a crossroads.

In the early days Wells was a lively town with always a stud-poker game going on in any saloon you went in. What made it was the Central Pacific, and it picked up in later years when they built the Western Pacific through there. And that was just in the days of horses and mules and scrapers, when they built that Western Pacific. We didn't have any machines then. But it livened things

29

up, and there were fistfights every day. There were tent cities, you know, all along the right of way, and no law to speak of in any of them.

But we didn't use the railroad for cattle much, because we generally sold to the California market; and we didn't ship to any California point, as the California buyers used to come over to Nevada. It was different from the other markets, where the buyers waited for the cattle to be shipped there. We shipped cattle, when we sold to other markets, of course, but it wouldn't be once in ten years when one of the Eastern ones—Denver or Omaha—would be the better market.

In later years, when I was raising cattle under fence, I fed a bunch of three-year-old steers nothing but alfalfa of good quality, and they sold on the Omaha market for seven dollars and eighty cents a hundred. And the top corn-fed cattle sold for eight dollars and twenty cents—only forty cents more. The buyers wouldn't believe it when I told them that mine were hay-fed cattle. They were big steers; they weighed fifteen hundred and sixty-five pounds on an average.

They were a cross between Herefords and shorthorns. All the old-timers coming out to that part of Nevada, from Wisconsin or Ohio, say, always brought some shorthorn milk cows with them. And then, when in after years the Herefords came into prominence, you know, ranchers crossed them with the shorthorns and made the native range cattle.

And now the same thing is taking place. Instead of raising Herefords, they're turning to Aberdeen Angus steers because they don't have any pink eye, like the Herefords do. And they have no horns, which is a big advantage, too, because that's quite a chore to dehorn a thousand head of calves while you're branding them. And they're having enough done to 'em at that time without losing their horns and bleeding there as well as other places.

4

GOOD GRASS AND DEEP SNOW

"The whites and the Sioux had a little battle there at the beaver dam on Lightnin' Creek about 1904."

CHARLES A. BLAKE, Prescott, Arizona

As a boy, Mr. Blake knew William Barclay "Bat" Masterson, perhaps the most likable of all the West's famous peace officers and certainly an amiable figure as portrayed by this contributor. Slated to be an exponent, if not an enforcer, of law himself, he formed and stayed with far other plans.

Before becoming a rancher in Arizona's rugged north-central region, he roved a portion of Wyoming that epitomized the frontier of ballad and story. There and at that time the Wild Bunch—the scope of whose outlaw operations was only matched by the activities of the James gang—held forth when not on forays. Although the Dakotas have been generally thought of as pacific, following the collapse of the Ghost Dance uprising in 1891, they there took to the warpath much later. And there, too, with Mr. Blake as one of the warriors, a range war was staged.

Shifting his headquarters south, Mr. Blake found that it was hard to tell the difference between "neighbor" and "rustler" among people who hadn't been told that the frontier was passing. But as entertaining as his reminiscences are in other respects, some of the most interesting passages deal with his ideas about stock and methods of handling animals. Horses his abiding passion, he tells of tricks for getting along with them to win the admiration of one of George Borrow's Gipsies.

Mr. Blake preserves one grudge. He would like to try his knuckles out on the thieving collector who skipped with his copy of Mercer's The Banditti of the Plains *in the rare first edition.*

HIS CONTRIBUTION

I was born four miles north of Bedford, Iowa, in 1880. The folks went to western Kansas when I was about two and a half years old, and I stayed thereabouts until I was about nineteen.

The rest of the family was professional people; I was the only outlaw. I studied law for a couple of years, but I couldn't take that Blackstone stuff any longer. I was always crazy about horses and cattle, you know, and I didn't like it inside.

You see, I was raised on a frontier. I was born when western Iowa was a frontier, and I was raised when western Kansas—we went to King County, thirty miles from the Oklahoma line—was a frontier.

All the outlaws of Oklahoma would come over and rob banks and steal horses and get back across the line. The Kansas sheriffs couldn't cross the line. [As both Oklahoma proper and the Indian Territory were federally controlled, no reciprocal agreements between local authorities were possible.] Nothin' but a United States marshal could.

The Daltons was there. They went to rob the Coffeeville bank at that time. I seen a lot of outlaws there, but I was just a small kid then.

Bat Masterson's sister was married and lived right next door to us. He used to come and see her every so often, and he was a great hand amongst the kids. I think he'd rather play with us kids than to visit with the king angel.

In 1899 I went to Moorcroft, Wyoming, right up in the northeastern part, where I punched cows. I'd done that in Kansas, you know, and a little in northern Oklahoma. I hit Wyoming in a snowstorm. There was about two and a half feet of snow, and if I'd had money enough, I'd have went back. But I didn't have it, and I stayed there twenty years, working for quite a few different ranches before I had one of my own.

When I was a kid and'd just went up there, kids was let out in the wintertime—we didn't do much ridin' then—and the older men worked all winter. But after I was up there three years, I held a steady job the year around.

I was up along the Powder River, while I was in Wyoming, and that Hole-in-the-Wall bunch [the Wild Bunch, led by George Leroy Parker, alias Butch Cassidy] was there. They was the finest people in the world; they'd never bother nothin' but only a bank or a train. They could go to any of the little ranches around there for grub or fresh horses or anything they wanted.

The Sun Dance Kid [Harry Longbaugh] was raised right there in Sun Dance [the seat of Crook County, where Moorcroft was located]. He and some other kids stole some horses and headed for the Hole-in-the-Wall, and that was that. He was just a kid, nineteen or twenty years old. I never worked with him; I just seen him around. But they was all good cowpunchers in the Wild Bunch; and once in a while they'd help ranchers, though they didn't work regularly.

There was only two or three of 'em that was killers. That Oregon man [Harry Tracy] was a bad lot, and Curry [Kid Curry, the *nom de guerre* of Harvey Logan]. Curry was killed down in Glenwood Springs, Colorado [in 1903]. They crippled him, you know, and he shot himself, so they wouldn't take him and put him in jail. Jail couldn't hold that fellow they chased all over Oregon— I forget his name—and jail couldn't hold this Curry, either.

But most of the bunch was good fellows that wouldn't bother anybody. They'd go to dances, and women'd dance with 'em. They was gentlemen around any women. All them old cowpunchers was that way, and if one wasn't, he'd get educated by the other men. He'd get something pulled over his head that gentled him.

They'd lynch rustlers, too. I was never in on that, but they'd hang 'em. Well, they had to do somethin'; and if the government would start that now, maybe them college kids wouldn't be so rough.

We had lots of Sioux and Crows up there. You see, we was right on the railroad tracks of the Burlington line, and the Sioux and Crows'd go back and forth and visit. The whites and Sioux had a little battle there at the beaver dam on Lightnin' Creek about 1904. I wasn't in the battle, because I was with the T. Shannon outfit, and all us cowpunchers was workin' on the roundup, when the Indians killed Sheriff Miller of Weston County.

The Sioux had their wagons loaded up with game, you know, and they didn't object to takin' beef. They was from the Pine Ridge Agency, in South Dakota and Nebraska, but I don't remember the name of the chief that led 'em.

The Sioux'd come across there [the Wyoming line] huntin' for

34

beef and game, and the sheriff went out to arrest 'em. He picked up a wolfer [a professional trapper of wolves, paid by the bounties offered for carcasses] and talked him into goin' with him, but he didn't anticipate any trouble. But one Indian'd told Miller the year before, when he'd arrested him and took him into court, "I'll kill you some day."

The sheriff still didn't expect trouble, but they shot him and the wolfer, too. So the whites formed a posse and went out and had a little battle. They killed twenty-one Indians, but there wasn't no white man killed.

We used to have a lot of trouble with wolves, till finally they offered a hundred dollars for a she-wolf, seventy-five for a dog, and fifty dollars for the pups. I never trapped 'em myself, but I roped a couple of wolves.

When I got the first one, I'd never roped one before, so I didn't know too much about it. I caught him all right, but he bit my rope in two and got away. The next time I'd got wise. He was eatin' a beef, you know, and he was full, so I run him down; which you can do, if you've got a good horse. I caught him around the neck and didn't give him a chance to bite my rope. I never stopped that horse for a good lope of about a mile, and I choked the wolf to death.

They're pretty mean and vicious animals. The horse was afraid of wolves; but generally after I'd rode a horse awhile, he'd do anything I wanted. They all said I could ride a horse farther and bring him in in better shape than any man in the country. I don't know what it was about me, but I could take a horse that would buck with other fellows and get on and just ride him off. And in breakin' horses, I never had one that really bucked with me. I'd play with 'em a little before I got on, you know, and rub 'em, and not abuse 'em any.

My father told me, when I was a kid, "If you're goin' to break a horse, down below the knee there's a little wart. If you get a piece of that and rub it on your hands, and get your hands up to his nose and let him sniff it, he won't do nothin'." And by golly, I found that was so, after I happened to think of it, when I was in Wyoming.

35

Wild horses is the easiest broke there is. I'd rather break a dozen wild horses than an old barnyard-raised horse. You could ride a barnyard-raised horse two or three months, and all of a sudden something'd go wrong. But with a wild horse, you take him and pick up his front feet, you know, and throw him and tie him down and rub him around, and don't abuse him, and he's broke.

That takes the *ro*mance out of him, to pick up his front feet and tie him down. I've had my hands burnt with a rope, doin' that, so the skin'd just peel off. But it didn't hurt the horses. If a horse was poor, it might; but them horses in that country was always in good shape, because the grass was the finest in the world.

Up in Wyoming, in the winter, they'd put cows in a pasture that hadn't had any stock in it and just watch 'em. If any of 'em got down—and sometimes the cows did, when they had calves—they'd feed 'em. But when we had open range, the steers'd winter fat. Or take saddle horses that'd been rode all summer and had sore backs and cinch sores. You'd turn 'em out, and when you'd round 'em up in the spring, they'd be so fat and all healed up that you might think they was colts.

I was up there twenty years, and there was but one winter that a man needed to get excited about. That was the winter of '11 and '12, and it caused a big loss in cattle. It started snowin' there the twenty-third of October and never let up till the twentieth of May. We had about seventeen feet of snow in all, and it got down to sixty below.

It froze a steer to death, standin' up. I told fellows here in Arizona about that, and they said, "You're a liar." But a few years ago a picture come out in *Life* magazine—a picture of a steer froze to death, standin' up—and then they believed me.

I seen that myself, because I was feedin' seven hundred head of cattle that winter on a big ranch. I had a dog to round 'em up, so they'd come in for feed, and this steer didn't move. So I told a man that was with me, "Bill, go down there and kick that steer up here." So he went down there, and he just had German socks and overshoes on, you know, and he kicked it and like to've broke his foot.

Several years before that, I went into the saloon business at Moorcroft with another fellow. But I come near to gettin' killed, and I didn't want to kill a man myself, so I quit.

There was some pretty tough hombres from different places in and around that town, and one fellow in particular. He was a Texas cowpuncher named Hal Dodd, and his fun was cussin' a bartender. I didn't take that, and I put him to the rights.

And my brother-in-law—he was a banker up there—he said, "You damned fool! Don't you know that he'll kill you?"

I said, "Not as long as I'm lookin' at him, and I ain't turnin' my back."

Dodd never spoke to me after that, but he didn't bother me, either. He went up to Gillette and hung around about ten years; but he never spoke to me, nor I never spoke to him.

A little after that, I was in a range war between sheep and cattle men. For in 1908 I'd went to work for old man Guthrie, boss of the Empire, the biggest sheep outfit there.

I was layin' around town—I had a little money to carry me— and he said, "Come and work for me."

I said, "What do I know about sheep?"

He said, "You know more about sheep than you think you do."

"I'll let you know tomorrow mornin'," I said.

The next mornin' he was in town early and asked me, "Did you think it over?"

I said, "Yes; I've done everythin' else, so I might just as well be a sheepherder."

I started in as camptender, but one day the range boss come in, while the old man and I was at the bunkhouse. And he said, "Mr. Guthrie, you can take your choice: Blake or me. If he's in the outfit, I ain't."

The old man looked at me and him and said, "I'll keep Blake; go get your time."

When that fellow quit, I stepped in as foreman. I'd went to work for Guthrie the tenth of July, and this range war started on the thirty-first of August in 1908.

That was while I was still workin' as camptender, and cow men shot at the camp I was in. Nobody got killed, but a bullet creased one fellow's Adam's apple and another grazed the right corner of my mouth and slanted down across my chin.

I was milkin' a cow at the time, and the fellow that knicked me was shootin' with a rifle from a hill above us. I knowed who done it, and I went to see him about it. He lied and said it had to be somebody else; but I knowed it was him, because I'd tracked his horse to his place.

Later on the cow men killed some sheep and one thing and another, and burnt two or three ranches. They burnt up all my clothes, too.

I was in another camp, and I started over to the Empire, and a fellow said, "Where're you goin'?"

I said, "I'm goin' over to the Empire to get some clean clothes and take a bath."

He said, "You ain't got no clothes."

I said, "The heck I ain't; I got a whole trunkful over there." So I went over there, and there it was—ashes.

I went on into town to buy some more clothes, you know, and a fellow I met rode back to camp with me. Of course, we talked about what had happened, and he said, "What're you goin' to do? Goin' to quit?"

I said, "No, I ain't aquittin'. The fellows that burnt my clothes up're goin' to pay me for 'em."

So I went to the Empire and looked around. I was a pretty good tracker, naturally; every cowpuncher is. One of the fellows that burnt the ranch'd made a mistake. He'd rode a horse I'd caught out of a wild bunch and rode for five years. That horse stepped straight with one front foot and toed in with the other. So when I looked around, there was his tracks.

I'll get back to that horse; but anyhow I knowed who owned him then, and I told John La Forest, a Wool Growers' detective, the name of a fellow who was in on the burnin'. I remember his name, but I don't want to mention it.

Joe said, "Are you sure?" And I said I was.

I didn't know it at the time, but another fellow that was a detective for the Wool Growers was workin' on the case. He was supposed to be a gambler, but that was just a blind. We got discussin' the business after I'd talked to Joe, and I told him, "If this fellow comes to town, and you buy him all the whiskey he wants to drink, he'll tell you all about it."

The fellow come to town in a day or so, and the two detectives got him pretty full and said, "Let's go down to Newcastle and take in the town." And the fellow said that would be just fine; so they went down there, and before they got back, the detectives had the whole tale.

There was eight cow men—nine of 'em really, but one was just a little homesteader that didn't have much, so they let him go—in on the burnin'. The sheriff told one that another had talked, and then went to him and said the first had told, and so forth. And just before Christmas, he went out there and arrested the whole bunch.

Well, they throwed 'em all in jail, and between the lawyers and the Masonic Lodge that some of the fellows belonged to, they settled it and paid for what they'd done. It cost 'em a little over forty-eight thousand dollars; and I got paid for my trunkful of clothes and got part of the reward money on account of pickin' up that horse's tracks.

Now, before I went in the saloon business, I was workin' for the Bar-7-X outfit. There was a little bunch of wild horses runnin' out there, and we went out one day to round 'em up. We took a bunch of gentle mares, you know, and we run the wild horses in with a bunch of gentle ones and run 'em into a corral.

The boss roped at a horse and missed him, and he jumped the fence and took off. I liked the colt's looks, so I said, "What'll you take for him?"

And he says, "I'll take twenty-five dollars."

"All right," I said, "take it out of my wages; he's mine."

The boss said, "How're you goin' to get him?"

I said, "Just the way we got him this mornin'." So I took that gentle bunch of mares and drove 'em up there. The colt began to get a little nervous, so I dropped the mares and went around the hill and come up on the other side of him; and he was amongst 'em. So I just sauntered to the corral with 'em, and as he went in the gate, I roped him and pulled him around a bit.

The other fellows said, "What're you goin' to do with him, now you've got him?"

I said, "I'm goin' to ride him to the ranch."

And they says, "Huh?"

So I got up to him and petted him, you know. And finally I put my saddle and bridle on him and said, "If you fellows'll haze for me [see Mr. Payne's contribution, number 5, for explanation of term] I'll ride him to the ranch." I rode him over there, and he never did hump his back or buck.

And, you know, he was one of the best horses I ever rode in my life. I rode him for five years till he fell with me, when he caught a hind shoe on a front one. He didn't have as much confidence in himself as he'd had before, so I traded him off. But *that's* the horse that this fellow rode that I tracked when they burned Guthrie's ranch.

I left Wyoming because a horse fell with me up there and busted me all up. I was paralyzed from the hips down, and the doctor says, "I can give you all the medicine that's made, and it won't do no good. But if you can get to a masseur and take some electric treatments, you might get so you can walk, though you won't ride no more horses."

So I sold my horses and cattle and went down to Los Angeles, where my wife's folks lived. I found a masseur and took twenty-one treatments. Then I come here to Arizona to get back in the cow business.

The Verde Valley was frontier when I come in in 1920. I'd bought my outfit from a bank just as it set on the range, and they told me that other ranchers there'd been stealin' cattle from it for a long time. So I kind of laid back the first month or two. I let the neighbors lead out; and they thought I wasn't a cowboy and didn't know much.

Well, I went along with a couple of fellows one day and picked up a bunch of my calves with their brands on 'em. "What you fellows doin' with your brands on my calves?" I asked.

"Well," one said, "they run out of the brush and was followin' my cows."

I said, "You think I don't know the cow business? Listen, this

40

better not show up anymore. And you can either bar your brand out and put mine on these or give me some of yours that ain't branded."

They said, "We can't do that."

And I said, "It looks to me like you fellows're raisin' cattle to practice ropin'. Well, that's all right, but if you think I can't play that game, I'll show you."

I got along with 'em after that. I rode for over forty years in Arizona until another horse fell with me about four years ago [when Mr. Blake was about eighty-three] and busted me up again. I had my arms full of fence tools, and I went over the horse's head and hit on one of these boulders, right on my stomach; and it ruptured me on both sides. I didn't do anythin' for a couple of years, but then I went ridin' again.

5

A PARK IN THE ROCKIES

"I guess I was nine or ten years old, when I first took
my part as a cowboy."

STEPHEN PAYNE, Denver, Colorado

Although Mr. Payne was given John as a first name, it has not been
used here, for fear of confusing devoted fans who might not then
identify him. For if few would recognize John Payne, Stephen will
ring a bell with many, remembering him as an enjoyed novelist and
frequently anthologized short-story writer.

His chosen subject matter has always been the pioneer West, and
a secret of his success possessed by few competitors is that he began
his research when he opened his eyes in a "park." That is a geo-
graphical institution peculiar to Colorado, although in the case of
North Park, natural communications allied it rather with Wyoming.

Identical with a "hole" elsewhere in the Rockies—e.g., Jackson's
Hole, celebrated as the scene of fur-trade rendezvous, and the Hole-
in-the-Wall cited by Mr. Blake in contribution 4—a park is a lofty
grassland, well watered and with timber handy on encircling peaks.
The one in which Mr. Payne grew up was so fenced off from the
rest of the world by mountain barriers and only seasonably usable
trails that its denizens developed the outlook of islanders.

Of that peculiar phase of the frontier, Mr. Payne has written
an absorbing nonfiction account, authentic as only a native could
make it. Published by the late lamented Alan Swallow in 1966,
Where the Rockies Ride Herd *has been used as the takeoff point*
for Mr. Payne's reminiscences.

HIS CONTRIBUTION

Where the Rockies Ride Herd is the story of North Park written
from my viewpoint, so it's autobiographical as well as historical. It
tells of my experiences up to 1909, and general early-day ranching
experiences, with emphasis on my father, T. John Payne, and his
struggles as a cow man. He came over from England in 1884,

moved into North Park and took up a homestead, knowing nothing except his ability to work. Then he sent for the girl he'd left behind, who came over in 1885. My brother was born in North Park in 1886, and I in 1888.

In addition to telling of my father's career, and of my own up to the year mentioned, my book pretty well tells the settlement of the Park and gives sidelights on the old-timers. I had the privilege of knowing many of the real old-timers: the Cross boys, Montie Blevins and old man Pinkham [for whom Pinkham Mountain and Pinkham Creek were named]. I met him when I was a little bit of a boy, and remember him as a lean, spry gray-beard with keen eyes and sharp features. My father said that Pinkham was a French-Canadian hunter and trapper.

His full name was James O. Pinkham. He was the first settler, having moved into the Park from Laramie, Wyoming, to establish trade with the Indians in 1874. The Indians were Utes, but they were gone a few years later and before real settlement began.

The Utes had moved out of their own accord; I don't think they were actually driven out. Still they didn't want settlers in there, for when leaving the Park, they tried to set the country on fire to discourage the white men.

But I doubt if they'd ever lived there in the wintertime. [Eight thousand feet high, the Park was cold country for tepee dwellers.] I think they only used it as a hunting ground in the summer. It is said that they fought fierce battles with the Arapahoes and Cheyennes to hold the Park, way back in the '70's.

When I was a boy, anywhere beyond North Park boundaries was "Outside." The country was isolated, but, of course, being born there, I didn't know the difference. It was late in settlement, because of its isolation. You see, all around us other parts of the country were being settled, but North Park didn't get settled until 1879.

Pinkham, as I said, came in about '74. The Cross boys—Ben, Dillon, Will and Cal—and another outfit moved in about '76. Then, in '79, came the Teller boom—a silver-mining boom—and that really brought the people in.

Seventy-nine also saw the first big cattle men moving into the

Park. There'd been horse outfits first, but they moved out, because they could find no market for their horses thereabouts. But the cattle outfits moved in and stayed. The biggest cattle man who came in the early days was C. B. Mendenhall. He brought three thousand Texas cattle and six hundred horses into the Park; and Montie Blevins was his foreman. Montie stayed in the Park, but Mendenhall sold out; he sold to Haas and Evans.

I don't know when it took place, and I don't know where I could find out, but that country had been surveyed before the settlers arrived. There were cornerstones, so the people were able to get a pretty accurate idea of their boundaries when taking up their claims. They had put up a stone or something in the middle, with the number of the section on it and four corner-markers around it. Then the settlers had to get a county surveyor to mark out the homestead claim, which at that time was a quarter of a section, or a hundred and sixty acres.

We were supposed to take up only one claim, but some fellows made quite a business out of it. I don't know how he got away with it, but one fellow must have taken up twenty homesteads, all under his own name.

The bigger fellows, like Mendenhall, who was running twelve thousand head of cattle before he sold out, got possession of a lot of land by buying up the homesteaders quick as they could get a patent. In that area, at any rate, that was how they built up the big outfits—by buying up the homesteaders and buying out other ranchmen. But the homesteaders sold voluntarily; there were no range wars [between small landholders and big cattle men bent on clearing the vicinity of them, as in Wyoming's Johnson County War of 1892].

The cattle men actually helped the homesteaders in that area. They were glad to have them there to raise hay. The biggest cattle man in the Park—Montie Blevins eventually became that—helped my dad. He was a poor, ignorant Englishman who didn't know what it was all about and had to learn things the hard way.

The cattle men had good reason for helping hay-growers. We had our hard winters in '83 and '84. Eighty-four [the first North Park winter experienced by Payne senior] was the one they always

46

remembered. We and others saved our cattle by trailing them down out of the Park and onto the plains. But Haas and Evans were running twelve thousand head of cattle and lost six thousand of them because the snow was too deep for the steers to browse.

After that, hay became the great stuff in North Park; the end and aim of life was to put up hay. It was a natural wild grass, a very fine quality of mountain hay.

Some people grew hardy vegetables. Because of an altitude of eight thousand feet, a great many things wouldn't grow there. But some raised good potatoes and small garden stuff like radishes, onions, and spinach. No fruit grew there, but there were lots of wild berries—fine gooseberries, blackberries, and strawberries.

It was a wild-game paradise. There were no turkeys but lots of quail and sage hens. The antelope were in there by the thousands in the very early days; they'd come up from the plains in the spring and go back out in the fall. That was before my time, but we had plenty of deer, elk, bear, and some antelope. We never lacked for meat and never had to kill our own.

For the most part trouble with animal predators was minor. One winter, though, there was a band of wolves in the Park, and they really raised hell. We only had trouble with rustlers to a minor degree. Petty mavericking [beating an owner to branding his calf; see poem on subject in Mr. Higgins' contribution, number 8] was the only thing; that and a little butchery on the sly. I think it was too difficult for rustlers operating on any scale to get the cattle out of there. So the sheriff never had much to do.

My father had several brands. Let's see; there was the 1-7-1, then he changed to the U-Lazy 3. The cattle weren't really longhorns; I've never seen the real longhorn. They were Texas cattle with big horns, but they didn't have the magnificent curled ones.

Our first market was south Omaha; then Denver opened up as a market. The cattle drive in the early days was from North Park to Laramie, about sixty or seventy miles away. It took four days from our place, but ranchers from farther up the Park would take six or seven. We always made the drives in the fall, when the cattle were fattest.

The Park's main supply town was Laramie, too. Some people

would go to Fort Collins, but it never had the trade that Laramie did. That's where the freighters were sent by the Walden stores [those of the Park's metropolis] and that's where all the cattle were shipped. Most of the ranchers would go up there for supplies twice a year—in the spring and fall.

Vegetable-peddlers brought in stuff from Fort Collins sometimes. Then there was one dry-goods store on wheels; it was a wonderful thing. They had a three-horse wagon, fitted with drawers and cupboards, and the peddler'd open up these things and show his goods for men and women. The storekeepers in Walden, Laramie, and Fort Collins didn't like him; for he'd not only undersell them, he'd deliver.

The first school was established in Teller in 1883 or '84, and the next school was called the Canadian School, because of being located on Canadian Creek. It was to this Canadian School that I went, beginning in 1895. It was about three miles away, and my brother and I rode there, double on one horse.

The first school was a log building. I would say it was about sixteen feet wide by twenty or twenty-five long, with a dirt roof and four windows. They left that standing, to use as a stable, when they built a frame school—at a guess I'd say it was twenty feet by thirty—in 1895.

When I first started coming, there were about seventeen pupils, with one teacher for the first through the eighth grades. This was summer school; at that time it was almost impossible to have winter school. From 1895 to 1900 I went there. Summer school would start the first part of May and last into September, when the snow would start coming.

People would start in very bravely, sending their children; but in a little bit Dad needed his boys to help him with the work on the farm, and Mother the girls to help with the housekeeping. My own dad was very strict about attending school but not so strict that he didn't need my brother sometimes. He didn't need me, though. My brother could run a hay rake, and I wasn't big enough. I can remember times when I was the only pupil in the school.

Later I went to school where a man by the name of Charlie Cowdrey took a homestead and started a little town. Well, immediately, when he started a town, people would build cabins there and bring their children in to attend winter school.

I didn't go to high school. I went to the Fort Collins Agricultural College for a couple of winters, though—taking one short course in agriculture and another short course in horseshoeing.

But we kids read an awful lot. My brother and I were very fortunate in that respect. We had for neighbors the Scott boys— George and Charlie—who lived only half a mile away; and they were very well-educated men—graduates of Yale. They were on the order of remittance men; as they had run through a lot of other money that had been left them, their parents had tied up their estates, so the boys would only get a certain amount of cash every year. But they had plenty of books, and they took magazines, which we were welcome to read.

Residents of the Park got news of the rest of the country from Fort Collins and Laramie, when the trails in were usable. In the winter they often weren't, on account of snow, and spring thaws or heavy rains made quagmires of them. But anyway, for a while there was the Laramie *Boomerang* of Bill Nye. Bill once wrote, "There's only one thing to be said for tight boots: they make a man forget all his other sorrows."

The first riding I did was behind the saddle; my brother was in the saddle, and I hung on to the strings behind it. I guess I was nine or ten years old when I first took my part as a cowboy. And I worked at it from then until I left the Park, when I was thirty-five.

They weren't exactly wild horses, but we had plenty of stray horses in the Park. The big horse-raising outfits I mentioned had come in because of the grass and water, and some of them turned many of their brood mares loose when they moved out. Things changed later, but for years anybody could just help himself to horses, which were of so little value that nobody bothered to brand the colts. But they were excellent horses. Of course, after a while they got run down from being inbred, but until that happened, there were fine standard horses—trotting horses and a good deal of Morgans.

As it was part of the work, I broke a lot of horses. They're

49

pretty wild at the start, and the first thing to do is to get the colt in a corral by himself and catch him and halter-break him. Then you'd put a contrivance called the "Scotch hobble" on him—to draw one hind foot off the ground so he couldn't do much of anything. Next you'd saddle him up and move him around with that for a while. Then you'd finally take that hobble off and get on and ride him. First you'd corral ride him, and after a while you'd take him out in the open, with somebody to haze for you. The hazer would keep the wild horse from running into anything, and if necessary catch him with a halter rope and snub him up. A man riding a colt might have an awful time getting back to the corral, if he was all alone. We thought it lots of fun, though.

Where the Rockies Ride Herd carried me up to 1909, as I think I said earlier. I was twenty-one then, and as my father's venture was by then a success, it seemed a good place to stop. After that I worked for my father a little longer and then had a ranch of my own on Michigan Creek. I went busted at that in 1923 and came to Denver.

I'd always thought I could write—I'd done some while I was ranching, and though nothing came of it then, it was useful practice. So that's what I had in mind when going broke at ranching freed me to try. After I got to Denver, I worked as a laborer—at any job handy—while I was getting started. By 1925 I was selling regularly, and have been doing it ever since.

6

THE PERILS OF RANGE
MANAGEMENT

"It was the political leaders of the old mayordomo class that caused all the trouble."

ELLIOTT S. BARKER, Santa Fe, New Mexico

In the course of being interviewed, Mr. Barker remarked that he was looking forward to leading the annual field expedition of a group known as "Wilderness Trail Riders," with which he has been long connected. Another sphere in which he is still active is that of writing for Outdoor Life *and fellow periodicals concerned with adventures in the open.*

Of his books, the best known are Beatty's Cabin, *covering experiences in the Pecos headwaters country, and the self-explaining* When the Dogs Bark "Treed." *To qualify to write the second work, Mr. Barker was both a professional hunter himself and a guide to amateurs. And for twenty-two years he was State Game Warden of New Mexico.*

While so acting he became one of the best-known conservationists in the country not to mention achieving recognition abroad. He was on the board of directors of the National Wildlife Federation when it was first formed. He has served as President of the International Association of Game, Fish and Conservation Commissioners and has been given awards attesting to his renown in his chosen field.

But many years before he gained such laurels, he was a private in the ranks, and in a place where conservation was so far from earning honors that it was a dangerous trade to profess. In this connection he was called upon to buck the here described feudal system then surviving in parts of New Mexico.

HIS CONTRIBUTION

I was born at Moran, Shackleford County, Texas, on December 25, 1886. We started to move from Texas in 1889 [for details see contribution of Mr. Charles Barker, number 20] and finally settled north of Las Vegas, in Sapello Canyon.

We had a little bit of schooling out on the ranch for a few years—three months during the winters—but I didn't get to go to a regular school until I was thirteen years old. That was at Las Vegas; my mother moved in with us kids during the winter months so we could go to school. I started in the fifth grade. I made the fifth and sixth grade that year and the seventh and eighth the next. In three years I finished high school, and that's all the schooling I got.

For a year I went back to the ranch and helped with the cattle, and I also engaged in hunting. We had a bounty on predatory animals, and I hunted bears, mountain lions, bobcats, and coyotes for the bounties. I also packed in and guided hunters and fishermen into the interior of the mountain country.

The bears that I hunted were mostly black at first. We had grizzlies also, but I didn't do much grizzly-hunting right then, though I did a little bit later. The bears would kill cattle once in a while, the black bears would, but I think the mountain lion caused the most damage. And he wasn't so bad, except on horses. A mountain lion likes colts; you just can't raise colts in the mountains where there's lions.

Then I went to a school of photography in Effingham, Illinois for six months, because my brother-in-law had persuaded me that I wanted to become a photographer. I came back and worked with him at Texico, right on the line between Texas and New Mexico, just east of Clovis. It was a lively little pioneer town, but I just couldn't take the indoor work, so I threw up my hands and came back to my mountains, my horses, and my dogs.

I hunted the lions entirely with dogs. Some do it afoot, but we always had horses. But, of course, if the country got too rough, you had to leave your horses and go afoot. As for bobcats, they were no trouble to livestock, but if you had turkeys and other poultry, they were bad; so there was a bounty on them, too.

But when I got back to the ranch, I devoted myself almost entirely to packing in hunters for sport, and as a special guide to men hunting for bounties; and at that time I did hunt grizzlies. That was in the Sangre de Cristo Range—although they called it the Las Vegas Range, it was a spur of the Sangre de Cristos. We tried hunting grizzlies with dogs there but not with too much success, because a dog can't stop them for you.

Then after that—let's see, it was April 23 or 24 in 1908—I passed a Forest Service Ranger's examination, but I didn't get an appointment until December of 1908. Then I was given an appointment as Assistant Forest Ranger in the Jemez National Forest —which is now the Jemez Division of the Santa Fe—with headquarters in the little town of Cuba, on the west side of the Jemez Mountains.

I reached it in on January 1, 1909, and at that time it was the roughest—I'm not referring to topography; it was just about the roughest country that lay outdoors. The people resented the country being put into a national forest, and any control of the number of stock they grazed [for more on this subject, see the contributions of Messrs. Keleher and Bennett, numbers 10 and 11].

The common people were 98 percent Spanish-Americans, and very few of them spoke any English. They weren't naturally hostile but it was the political leaders of the old mayordomo class that caused all the trouble. Mayordomo could be translated as "the big boss." Usually they were merchants rather than ranchers. Some of them were very good people, but others were tyrannical and despotic in their dealings with the common run of natives.

Ninety percent of the Spanish-speaking natives were good people, but they lived way out in the country and had no advantages of schooling at all. And they were poor and easily led astray. They feared the Spanish mayordomos, did what their leaders wanted, and believed whatever was told them. So they were all against the Forest Service in Cuba, because the local mayordomo wanted us out-of-the-way.

Now the two rangers that were sent in there ahead of me got into serious trouble. They were beat up real, real badly. They'd made the mistake of going to a saloon and bawdy house about a mile below the town of Cuba, where they were not supposed to go. And the leader over there—I won't use his name, but we'll call him

Ortega—had a bodyguard, and really a killer, to do his dirty work. His name was John Clark, a former heavyweight pugilist. He'd once fought the world's champion [Jim Jeffries] and stayed with him for six rounds, so he was perfectly capable of handling three or four ordinary men at a time. And he'd beat those rangers up terribly. Then he threw them out, unsaddled their horses, and turned them loose. So they left the country; they'd had enough. And no prosecution was ever initiated even. There was no hope of getting a grand jury to indict anybody under that mayordomo's protection.

That's what I was sent up against as a young man just twenty-two years old. But I had a partner, almost twice my age, by the name of A. W. Sypher. He was a mountain man from the mountains of Kentucky who knew his way around in bad company. They assigned me to go with him over there, to take over that country and try to bring it under administration.

My partner didn't speak any Spanish, but I did—and still do—as well as I do English; and that solved some problems. When I got my orders I came through Santa Fe, en route from Las Vegas to Cuba. I had my saddle horse and my pack horse, with all the belongings I was going to use: a little camp outfit, a bed roll, and a few clothes. It took me a whole week to make that trip in midwinter.

But anyway I stopped by here in Santa Fe to get instructions from the forest supervisor, Ross Macmillan, who was killed during the first World War. When telling how to proceed with my work, this was the order he gave: "You and Sypher bach together." We had to rent our own quarters in those days; they didn't have any ranger stations. And he said, "Ride together; don't ever ride alone. Never be out after dark under any conditions; get home by then. And never step out of the door for any purpose at any time of the day or night without your sidearms on and without being alert."

Well, as I said a while ago, I spoke Spanish very well, and that was one of the first questions the supervisor asked me, "Do you speak Spanish?" Or "Mex," as he called it.

And I said, "Yes."

"Well," he said, "you and I are the only two people in the world that know that. You keep your mouth shut and your ears open, and we'll learn a lot of things."

Well, I was just a big, overgrown kid, you might say. I didn't have sense enough to be afraid of anything. But old Sypher, though he wasn't afraid of anything, either, he knew what situations to avoid and so on.

Well, we got along over there, although we had some difficulties. There was failure to comply with the rules and regulations of the Forest Service, before we got the situation under control. The leader over there—Ortega, as I said we'd call him—refused to take out a permit for his cattle and sheep in the forest. And we rounded them up and had a few little brushes when doing that.

The supervisor was in the process of having the United States Attorney file trespass proceedings against him; but finally, with all the pressure against him, he caved in and complied with the regulations. So by the fall of 1909 the thing was pretty well under control. We had some unpleasant experiences, though, and I'll tell a little bit about one of them.

This Ortega, who was a very shrewd man—known territory-wide as a politician—had a general store in Cuba, and he was the postmaster there. So he didn't want any trouble in the way of open personal brushes with us; he had more sense than that.

Anyway, one day I was left in his store by my partner, Sypher, contrary to the supervisor's orders. Sypher wanted me to stay in Ortega's place and learn what I could, while he did a little chore somewhere else. When he left, I was just lounging around the store, listening.

There were two fellows there about my age, though probably not as stout as I was. They got to talking in Spanish pretty rough about forest rangers in general, and about Sypher and me in particular. Well, I was just supposed to let that pass and pay no attention to it. But I was rather a hothead youngster—I've learned better now—and when they got around to discussing in rather uncomplimentary terms our ancestors, I hauled off and hit one of 'em. I knocked him winding and gave away my secret by cussing both out in Spanish as well as English.

Well, the other came after me, and I knocked him down, and

then the first undertook to do some boxing with me. But I'd had quite a bit of boxing at school. Oh, I wasn't any expert at all, but as I don't think they'd ever had the gloves on, I had an advantage that way. So I knocked him down again and took him by the scruff of the neck and threw him off the platform outside the store. It was where they used to load the wagons and was about five feet high.

When I went back in the store, the other one met me there, and he did land a pretty, dawggone good jolt. It didn't knock me down, though it staggered me. But I recovered and outboxed him and threw him from the platform, too.

By that time a crowd was building up. I had my gun on—a forty-five—but I sure didn't want to go after it or have to use it at all. And I made up my mind that I wouldn't except as a last resort. As I was outnumbered pretty badly, things were getting pretty tight. But about that time I saw Sypher coming on the lope, for he saw something was wrong.

Also about that time Ortega, back in his office, heard the big commotion out there, and he rushed out to see what was going on. Well, he stopped any fighting—he didn't want a fight there in the post office.

But he'd heard me talking in two languages and said, "You speak Spanish, do you?" I spoke to him back in Spanish, saying that I did a little bit. "I understand your game," he said. He was real smart and spoke English better than I did.

Well, anyway that was the worst brush that we had; and had Sypher not come, or Ortega not come out, I might have been in serious difficulty. I might have been able to work my way out of it, or I might have had to take serious measures that I didn't want to take.

One other ranger over there, on the district adjacent to ours, was a man by the name of Bletcher, who'd been there quite some time. The mountain country farther east had been under Forest Service administration longer than the part we were on, and that was pretty well under control. As a matter of fact, it was the resentment caused by the addition of our district that caused the trouble.

Well, one day Bletcher met this John Clark that I told about in the road, and they'd already had some difficulties. When they met this time, each of them was all alone. Bletcher said that Clark made a move to go for his gun—everybody carried a gun there. But Bletcher was pretty quick, and he covered the fellow; stopped him and made him put his hands on the saddle horn. He could hold the bridle rein while doing that.

Well, Bletcher told him how the cat ate the canary; told him that if they ever met again that Clark had better have his hands on the saddle horn; that if they were anywhere else, it'd be too bad for him. Well, he never had any more trouble with Clark after that.

What were then the Jemez National Forest and the Carson and the Pecos forests—now all divisions of the Santa Fe—were under one supervisor, this Ross Macmillan I mentioned. In October of 1909 they split the three up and gave each one of the forests a supervisor. So I asked to be transferred back to the Pecos country, where I used to hunt a lot. I knew Tom Stewart, the supervisor—we were good friends, in fact—and as he asked to have me, I got back to the Pecos in November.

I worked over on the Pecos until the fall of 1912. My district was north of the town of Pecos [not to be confused with the Texas one of the same name mentioned by Messrs. Higgins and Gray], most of it lying in what is now known as the Pecos Wilderness area—my favorite place.

In the fall of 1912 I was transferred to the Carson, where I worked first under Aldo Leopold [author of *Game Management, Sand County Almanac*, etc.], who later became the world's greatest authority on wildlife. He went through all the various positions in the Forest Service and then headed up the Wild Life Conservation Department at the University of Wisconsin.

We had no trouble to speak of in the Pecos Forest. But when I went up to the Carson, where I eventually became a supervisor myself and had to be in the middle of the thing, there was overgrazing. But this time it wasn't the Spanish-Americans, who were mostly small ranchers there, that were the troublemakers. There was an exceedingly large number of stock owned by the big ranchers, and for the most part the large owners were Anglos [not short for Anglo-Saxons; a localism, also used by Mr. Keleher in contribution 10, meaning English-speaking Americans of whatever extraction].

Just one outfit, McClure's, had twenty-three thousand head of sheep in the Carson Forest, and many more were out on what the Spanish called *partido*, or shares. The fellow that had them on shares would claim ownership, and it was very hard for us to tell whether he actually owned the sheep and was entitled to run them, or whether it was a subterfuge for other people. We did have a lot of trouble there in keeping the big owners from simply dominating the situation.

We had to make allotments according to the carrying capacity of the range; but that was done gradually so as not to cause too much hardship. And as we ferreted out these fraudulent cases where they had them out on shares, then the permit would be canceled if it was a case of overgrazing the range. Otherwise we didn't cancel any permits; it was a reduction proposition that we enforced.

The big owners brought all the political pressure they could on the Forest Service from the bottom to the top, clear on to the Washington headquarters and in Congress. They still do, in fact, but the forests have to be managed on a multiple-use basis.

Will C. Barnes [co-author with William McLeod Raine of *Cattle*] did more to work up proper grazing regulations than any other man, I think. He was quite a fellow; I never knew him intimately, but I used to meet him here and there.

But the grassland range, the range that wasn't a part of any forest, had no administration until the Taylor Grazing Act of 1934. That was the first time that range was put under any kind of control, and that's where they had the range wars. A sheep man who saw a patch of grass that he wanted could drive his flock right close to the headquarters of a cow man, and that's where the difficulties came from.

Anyway, as I said, I was eventually made supervisor of the Carson. I held that position until April of 1919 and then resigned to go back to ranching for some years.

7

WILD CATTLE IN THE WOODS

"They was so wild, you know, that when they was fenced in, they didn't like it and wouldn't graze."

CHARLES CHILSON, Payson, Arizona

A son of two early settlers, Mr. Chilson has spent most of his life in the rugged region below the sheer rise of what is known to map-makers as Mogollon Mesa. Because of the unparalleled stretch of rim rock that frames it, everybody else calls it Mogollon Rim, and the area at its foot the Rim country.

If it is now cattle range, it was by no means exclusively so when the twentieth century was teething. Mr. Chilson touches on such little-noticed phases of pioneer stock-growing as goat- and hog-ranching.

But cattle were abundant and raised under conditions which were suggested rather than described by Mr. Elliott Barker in contribution 6. Cows ranged among trees as well as in the open, and those who think of punching them only in connection with prairies, plains and mountain grasslands will get a new view of the cattle trade in reminiscences in which it is associated with pursuit of unreconstructed steers through heavy timber.

And because the Rim country was wooded, it was rife with stock predators, including an occasional dread visitor from Mexico. Telling of such matters, Mr. Chilson also shows himself versed in the lore of a region where all the bloodletting wasn't performed by wild fauna. It was the scene of that fiercest of struggles between cattle and sheep men, variously known as the Pleasant Valley and the Tonto Basin War. Then Apaches, Geronimo among them, were rampant there, too.

HIS CONTRIBUTION

I was born right here in Payson in 1894. My grandparents orig-inally migrated from Texas to California, but in 1870 they come back to Arizona, where they first landed in Globe. Then my grandfather ran a freight wagon from Miami to Willcox. They also had a little grocery store between Miami and Globe, where Midland is now. At that time there was nothing else there whatsoever.

When they migrated up here, there was nothing on the site of Payson. They called this Little Green Valley then. But people were afraid of Indians, so nobody lived in the valley; it was too much open.

My grandfather started a little grocery store down under the mountains in what they called Maryville [a fleeting ghost community]. There was a lot of chloride miners around here, mining gold and running arastras [water-turned wheels for crushing ore], and they was most of the trade the store had.

They got a little Apache scare in '77, I guess it was, and the family went to Globe again for a little while. But they come back and settled two miles west of here. They just squatted on the place, like all the old-timers did, and it was only proved up on by one of my uncles, after he'd growed up there.

They could have had any of this land in town here, but they was afraid of the Indians. There was an old fellow here that discovered the natural bridge [the Payson vicinity's great scenic attraction]. I forget what year it was, but he was an old Scotchman—Uncle Dave Gowan, we called him. He and his partner were up there prospecting, and he found the bridge then.

After he left the natural bridge, he went down to Gisela—about fifteen miles from here, but straight through it'd be about eight. It was all fertile land in that valley, and there was free water out of the Tonto. One would stand guard over the other while he worked on the irrigation ditch they dug. And Uncle Dave told me one time that he and his partner started to cross this valley on mules, and the Indians opened fire on them. He said he thought they was the slowest two mules he ever had anything to do with.

That all happened about the time my folks was settling here. Gradually my father, John Collins Chilson, and his brother worked into the cow business. They got cattle that had been driven from California to the East Verde.

We were there for years, and I walked about a mile to a little one-room school here. It wasn't a log cabin; it was made out of solid lumber, as they had several little sawmills around here by that time. I remember the first day I went to that school, which was in 1900. One teacher taught all the grades, and they had recitations up front, you know. He was a pretty bad old teacher for discipline, and he jerked a girl out of her seat in front of me and whipped her with a switch. I thought he was coming right down the row, so when they called recess, I just skidded for home.

I stayed in the school here till the seventh grade, and then my father bought the Diamond outfit down near Sunflower. At that time he moved the family down to a little place in the Salt River Valley—Tempe—and I went through high school there. But when I wasn't in school, I was working up here.

I followed my first roundup when I was nine years old. We only had about six months of school, and started work in the spring, over at Gisela. The cattle would drift down there, and I day-herded—picking up strays and driving them to the main bunch—with an old man. We had a big territory which took us thirty or forty days to cover. I was day-herding all that time, and I really got tired of it.

When I was fourteen years old, I started roping 'em, tieing 'em, and bringing 'em in. We had that Diamond outfit down by Sunflower, and those cattle hadn't been worked—hadn't been herded, that is—for years. Those steers was eight, ten, and fourteen years old, and they was pretty wild. They'd bunch up and run, ten or fifteen head in a bunch; and the only way you could get 'em was to rope 'em and tie 'em to trees, and lead 'em out of the woods one at a time. Of course, you'd saw off the tips of their horns, so they couldn't hurt your horse much.

The first year we gathered over a hundred of those old steers, tieing 'em up and leading 'em into pasture. There was Herefords, longhorns, Durhams, and in-betweens. They was all colors: white, spotted, liver-colored, buckskin, and every other shade. One of those steers'd punish your horse and punish your legs, before you got to leading him, but after that he'd follow along like a dog.

But it was rough going. When we'd start out in March, everybody was eager to catch something; but after they'd been at it three or four days, they didn't like it so much. And when you got the steers to pasture, some of 'em would just stand looking over the fence and starve themselves to death. They was so wild, you know, that when they was fenced in, they didn't like it and wouldn't graze.

Sometimes the bulls was pretty rough to handle; I saw one that had four horses down at once on a hillside. He was so big and stout, you know, and hadn't give to the rope yet. They had four on him, but it wasn't enough to keep him from grounding the riders.

Once in a while you'd get one that wouldn't lead at all; he'd just sull. I had one tied up, a big old fellow that was about twelve years old, I guess, that I never did get away from the tree where I'd tied him. He'd charge my horse three or four steps, then he'd just back up and drag that horse back under the tree and stay there.

I tied him up for six days. Every day I'd go back, I'd saw his horns a little more, thinking to make him lead; but I never did get him away from that tree.

Finally I put a big old bell on him, thinking that might tame him some. While I was working other cattle around there, I'd hear that bell ringing and abanging, and then pretty soon I wouldn't hear it anymore. When I come up, he'd be lying in the brush with his head down on that bell, so you couldn't hear it. There was only one way to get any good out of him, so I finally went up there and shot him and made jerky out of him.

And there was an old black stag that had horns straight out— they measured four and a half feet. When he was running in the timber, he'd swing his head that way and this, you know, to miss the trees. He was quite a steer. I run him I don't know how many times without doing any good, but I finally caught him in a trap.

He didn't belong to us; there were several outfits pitching in to work the cattle out of the woods, you know. Well, after I'd tied up that big black steer, I told the man that owned him where the stag was, and the fellow said, "Turn him loose!" He didn't want any part of him.

Then my father got a chance to buy an outfit near Rye Creek. We bought that place in 1912. On August the twenty-ninth we come up, and my father give me a checkbook and turned around and went back to Tempe. I was eighteen years old, and I was in charge.

What we bought there was a remnant [odds and ends of herds bearing a variety of brands] scattered all over Gila County. They was supposed to be Herefords, but they was mixed with longhorns and everything, you know.

My own brand was the H-Bar on the left ribs. When we bought this remnant, there was about ten different brands in it, and I had to remember them all and the different ear-marks, too.

We had to drive our cattle a long way to market 'em; anywhere we went, it was a hundred miles to a railroad. We'd drive 'em south to Phoenix sometimes, but mostly we went north to Flagstaff or Winslow. Anywhere we went, it was trouble. When we went to Phoenix, we had to go to Tonto Basin first and go over a pass into Sunflower and down an old wagon road. It would take us nine or ten days.

It took about that to go to Flagstaff, and I'll say driving cattle up on the Rim [two thousand feet above Payson's five thousand approx.] was rough. Part of the time we went up the old Strawberry grade. Other times, if we didn't have too big a herd, we'd go up the old Tonto trail—an old road off the Rim that a lot of the original settlers come in on.

They run a lot of goats and hogs here in the early days, but when the Forest Service took over in 1905, they put out the goats altogether and canceled about all the hog permits. They was too hard on the range. Wherever a goat grazed, he didn't leave anything, and the hogs was disturbing the water holes.

In 1904 there was a couple of sheepherders shot by goat-raisers in this vicinity, and I know all about that incident. It happened across the Tonto River beyond Gisela. The Booths—there was two families, but this was a pair of brothers—had goats at Gisela, and this fellow Barry brought sheep in there.

He and two boys—one was a Mexican, and one was young Barry—took 'em down the Tonto and was grazing 'em over in that basin across the Tonto from the Gisela settlement, which was the Booths' goat range. So the Booth brothers, Zach and John, went up there, and they had this shooting.

Well, Zach took all the blame, but Barry saw the two of 'em riding off on a big gray horse and a black. At that time my father was a deputy sheriff here, and he immediately knew who they had to be. He and Ben Pyle arrested the Booths and held 'em up here for a preliminary court in Payson. As Zach took all the blame, he was held for a couple of more weeks. That was a little before Christmas, as Zach was hung right at Christmastime in 1904.

We was living down in the ranger station then, and my father kept him there with us until his case was called in Globe. He'd known Zach all his life, or ever since the Booths come in from Texas, and he told him, "Zach, stand trial and tell the truth, and you'll come clear."

So he believed that. And he would have, I guess, because he told the court that he'd been protecting his mother's goat rights and that the boys had opened fire on him. And he had holes in the back of the cantle of his saddle and things like that.

But what convicted him was that he said that after he'd shot these boys in camp—old Barry wasn't there then; he was out with his sheep—one of them fell into the edge of the fire. And Zach said, "I just rode up and shot him again to put him out of his misery." Well, if it hadn't been for that, he'd have come clean.

My father had a race mare out in the barn, and she was fat, because he kept her grain-fed all the time. And after the trial Zach told my father, "I went out there several mornings while I was staying with you, thinking about how long it would take me to get to the line on that mare." At that time, if they got to old Mexico, they was pretty safe.

My father wasn't mixed up in it, but he knew all those people that was in the Pleasant Valley War. At that time [the feud began in 1886 and raged until 1892] he lived in the Little Green Valley between here and Kohl's [ranch resort]. He said that lots of those fellows would come by and stay all night.

He knew—and I knew of—Sheriff Commodore Perry Owens. And I knew the Blevins and some of the other fellows that was there at the time of that shooting in Holbrook [when the sheriff, single-handed, killed three defiers of his authority and wounded a fourth].

In the early days, before they got Geronimo—in 1886, I guess that was—he come through here and raided different ranches. He come to one ranch—I'm just telling this, because it's kind of a funny story—owned by a man called Christopher, a big, fat fellow. He'd gone out and killed a bear that was awfully fat, too, so Christopher just skinned down the hind quarters and the loin and brought that much in and hung it up under the little shed on the porch he had. Then he went out again, and while he was gone, Geronimo's Indians come along. They saw that bear hanging up there and thought it was a man skinned, so they took off.

That was the same time the Apaches attacked the Hendershots. They killed the old man and crippled one of the boys. But the women got 'em inside, and they buried the old man in the dirt floor of the cabin. He was buried there for years, but they finally moved him to a cemetery.

The Indians made several raids about then, which was when my folks moved back to Globe for a while. But some stayed, and at one time there was a rock fort out here on this little, flat hill. It was built by settlers and called Fort MacDonald. We kids used to play around it, when I was ten or twelve years old. It was built out of limestone, and it was as high as your head. The door was a kind of dodge-lane door, you know—you'd come down a lane and back into the place.

That was before my time; of course, but we had lots of trouble with animal predators—lions mostly. They put a bounty of twenty-five dollars on 'em in 1900, and the bounty finally went to seventy-five dollars, paid by the state. Then lots of times ranchers got together and made that bounty a hundred and fifty dollars, so professionals using dogs hunted them pretty regularly. Hunters knew that the old toms around here'd make their rounds about every two weeks, covering the same country and pretty much on the same trail they'd used before. So when we had trouble, we'd call in hunters that knew the layout here.

We used to have silvertips, and they was bad, but most of the bears was black. All bears aren't stock-killers. But there'll be one that lives on nothing but meat. He kills, and when the rest help eat what he kills, that gets them started, too.

68

We had wolves drifting up from old Mexico now and then, and once in a while a leopard [jaguar]. They're bad, and they're hard to catch, too. They're so darned smart that they back-track their-selves to put the dogs off the trail. And if dogs overtake one, he's likely to kill half of 'em, before you can get up to 'em and shoot the tiger.

8

RIDING ALL SORTS OF TRAILS

"I went years and never slept in a house—wouldn't sleep in one."

EUGENE HIGGINS, Prescott, Arizona

Perhaps the most legendary of all the surviving Western old-timers, Mr. Higgins has a renown that wasn't earned on a local basis. Not many Americans of any vintage, or native to any region, can claim to have had experiences on both sides of the Atlantic as diverse as his. Not many, that is to say, have both been on the dodge below the Mexican border and rubbed shoulders with a British monarch.

At least as interesting as these recollections, however, are those in which Mr. Higgins recalls the feelings and attitudes which emerged from the frontier mode of living. Briefly but poignantly he expounds a breed of people who were at once matter-of-factly hospitable and as carefully incurious about the affairs of others as they were personally reserved. Or perhaps those are not apt enough words to apply to a social order in which idle questions might bring permanent idleness to the questioner.

As was remarked by Mr. Gray—an old friend of Mr. Higgins—in contribution 1, a privacy often insisted on was one's official name. Because of early association with a river shared between Texas and New Mexico, this contributor was known as "Pecos," with or without Higgins attached. And he also had other aliases, sometimes used on the general principle that how he was christened was nobody's concern and sometimes for a specific reason.

But whatever his standing with the law at any given time, Mr. Higgins wrote poetry. Interesting examples of his work form, indeed, a part of his reminiscences.'

HIS CONTRIBUTION

I've been called Pecos for nearly seventy years, but at different times I went by two or three different names. I went by one in old

Mexico: Rush—Eugene Rush. And they used to call me Ox-Bar. The reason I went by that name was that my daddy's brand was Ox-Bar, and that was on my horses.

Men didn't know my name, so I went by that; but lots of fellows did then. People didn't inquire into your business in them days like they do now. Hell, they'll ask you anything now! But in them days, if they didn't know your name, they didn't ask it.

I was born in Matagorda County, Texas, in 1883. I remember when I was a kid, an awful little kid, in Matagorda County. There was grass up to your knees and worlds of cattle—worlds of 'em, and no fences. The whole country was wide open, but that was a long time ago. The world then was altogether different, and the people was altogether different.

People now don't realize the things I seen, when I was kid six or eight years old. We used to build cow-chip fires at night to smoke them mosquitoes—awful mosquitoes. They'd haul them cow chips in wagons, and they'd have big piles of cow chips right at the house.

Cattle wasn't worth nothin'—two and a half or five dollars a head; and the hides was worth more than the cattle was. There was good grass and good cow country part of the year; but winters, when the grass got wet, it lost its strength, you know.

So the hides was worth more than the cows was, and men'd get out and skin 'em. That's when they caught them mavericks. I've seen 'em catch four- or five-year old bulls that didn't have a scratch [neither a brand nor an ear-mark] on 'em.

Them old, wild longhorn cows—they'd go to fightin' you. But men'd saddle up and club 'em. If they wasn't dead when they was knocked down, their throats'd be cut, of course. And they'd have tags, showin' who'd knocked down which ones. Men'd go out and tag cattle all one day and skin 'em the next. That was when I was a *little* kid, before we left Matagorda County.

There was worlds of cattle and no people hardly. There was just towns a ways apart, like Wharton and Bay City. That was just a little town then.

My mother went to school there, I think—just a little. I never went to school. Most of the fellows didn't go to school, and I've seen many old men that couldn't read or write. But my dad could read and write, and Mother, too; and she taught me.

The world was altogether different, and the people was different. You'd never ask a man his name. That was one thing they'd actually beat us kids for. If fellows come along the road by our house and us kids talked to 'em, as soon as they left, Mama'd call us in. And the first thing she'd ask was, "You didn't ask any of 'em their names, did you?" Even yet I sure hate for a fellow to ask me my name. It was just ground in me.

Back then a lot of people was on their guard, you know. There was old gray-haired fellows with beards halfway down to their belts, with six-shooters buckled on. And they'd kill you, too, if you messed with 'em. You didn't have to mess with 'em much, either; just ask 'em a little question. So you never asked 'em nothin', and they learned us kids to keep our mouths shut.

But they was good people. You could get anything they had; they didn't care nothin' about that almighty dollar. They didn't want it. Nowadays if you want anything and ain't got that dollar, you don't git it.

We never had the industries then that we got now. I was six years old before I ever saw a train. That's when we left southern Texas and come northwest to Breckenridge, in Stephens County. Dad drove trail herds out of there to a market in the Indian Territory.

One time the soldiers arrested him and some others, because one of 'em hit a chief over the head that was askin' for more beef than it was usual to give 'em, when you went through their country. But I wasn't ten years old, and I don't know what kind of Indians they was now. It was a long time ago, and a fellow forgets things.

Then we come to New Mexico and spent a few years in Lovington. And after that we went down to Pecos City, in Texas, where I punched cows as a kid on the old OW Ranch.

When my mother got sick quite a few years ago, I went back home to be with her and got me a job on the same ranch. But when she died, I come on back to Arizona. I didn't want to live there, because it's all oil country; nothin' like it was when I left.

It was more like a town, you know, and when I left, she was

wide-open spaces. And you could do anything you was big enough to do. Now it's all civilized, with roads and fences and everything. There wasn't no fences then. The line of old Mexico was fenced, and between Texas and New Mexico was fenced, but that was all.

I was all over that country, when it was open. And I went years and never slept in a house—wouldn't sleep in one. If I was visitin' one, I'd haul my bed off my horse out in the yard.

I've been in Arizona since about 1904 or '05. At first I was around Tombstone; in fact our range, when I worked down there, run right into Tombstone. I worked for old Robinson there and down the San Pedro Valley for the old O-Bar Ranch, and I worked for the Harkins-Neal Cattle Company. A fellow named George Storms ran the outfit. He was a kid around Tombstone but went north and run an outfit there for a long time. But Bill Neal brought him back there, and I worked under him for four or five years. But he's been dead for a long time now. There's a few fellows down there yet that I know, but most of the ones that was there when I come to the territory are gone.

I knew Burt Alvord that used to be an outlaw around Tombstone. Billy Stiles and Burt Alvord held that train up one time [for more about this robbery see the contribution of Mr. Powell, number 24]. But that was before I come to the territory. But I heard George and Leonard Alverton and all them old-timers talkin' about it.

Well, I was in jail around here myself for sellin' liquor to the Indians; and I was in Florence [the seat of Arizona's penitentiary] for stealing beef.

But there was another time that I might have been caught at it that I wasn't; and I wrote about it. I can write poems; make anything rhyme. I've been writing poems all my life, and when this thing happened, I wrote this piece I'll read called *My Little Blue Roan* [here reproduced as Mr. Higgins spelled and punctuated it in a later referred-to pamphlet].

You Boys have all Rode Horses Like that.
He Was'ent to thin and he Was'ant to fat.

75

Ears always up, Black Wicked eyes
But don't forget Boys He Was Plenty Cow Wise.
For an afternoon Horse, or Working a Herd
He could turn anything but a Lizzard or Bird.
Cold mornings He'd Buck and All Ways Would Kick.
No Horse for a Kid or a man that Was sick.

But oh What a Pile of Mussel and Bone
A Horse for a cowboy was my little Blue Roan.
One day in the foot Hills he Give me a Break
And Kept me from making an Auful Mistake.
I was Just Rideing along At a slow easy Pace
Takeing stock of the Cattle that was Raised in that Place,
When I Spies a Big Heifer Without any Brand
How the Boys ever missed Her I can't understand.

For none of the Cattle in that Country Was Wild
It Was Just like takeing candy away from a Child
She did'ent know What I had on my mind
Till I Bedded her down at the end of my line
Wrapped up her feet with my old Hogging string,
And Was Building a fire to Heat up my Ring.
You see I thought I was there all alone
Till I happened to look at my little Blue Roan.

My Pony Was Watching a Bunch of Pinion
And I sure took a Hint from that little Blue Roan
Instead of my Brand I wrote on another
By useing the one that was on the calf's mother.
Untied her feet Yanked her up by the Tail
With a Kick in the rear to make the Calf sail
I had branded her Proper and marked Both her ears
When out of them Pinions two cow men apears.

They turned her around Both took a good look,
While I Wrote her down in my old Tally Book.

Thare Was Nothing they could do so they rode up and
    spoke
And We all set down for a soceable smoke.
One owned the Heifer I Happened to Brand
He told me his Name We Grinned and shook hands.
Which We might Not have done If he had of Known
The Hint that I got from that little Blue Roan.

I wish I'd had that pony to warn me the day I did get caught.
But I paid with my time, and I'm all right with the law now.

Well, before them things happened, I'd been across the Mexican
line lots of times in different places. But I didn't want people to
know just where I was across there and what I was doin'; and I
don't yet. I know an awful lot of things I don't tell.

But I was in jail one time in old Mexico. I had a little trouble
down there with some Mexicans. I've been in every kind of fight
there is in the world, but I don't talk about 'em.

The time I was in jail in Mexico must've been the winter of
1909, I guess. It was in Cananea, where Bill Greene [for more
about Greene, see Mr. Powell's contribution, number 24] had him
a minin' company.

There was gold, silver, and copper, too—it was a big outfit.
Four, five, or six hundred men'd go on shift at a time—three shifts
a day. They paid good wages, too. They paid me four dollars in
gold for eight hours, and at that time that was eight dollars in
Mexican money. But I didn't like that minin' business.

I worked twenty-two shifts. And all I was doin' was sittin' on a
block of wood, seein' some Mexicans put the ore in the chute. It
was the best job I ever had in my life; but I didn't know nothin'
about mines, and I didn't like it.

But the boss wouldn't bring me my slip so I could get my money
and quit. Usually when you ask for your time, you can git it, but
he was three nights abringin' it. And he told me—this was a long
while ago, when I was a young fellow, "If you'll stay with me, I'll
put you to the top of this mine."

I said, "I wouldn't stay here for nothin'. I want my slip."

77

I had my saddle and my whole outfit at Naco, right on the line, and I wanted to get over there and ride some of them Arizona ponies.

But the boss wouldn't bring me my slip for them three nights, and the last one he sat on a bench with me and talked to me for a long time. And he said again, "If you'll stay with me, I'll put you to the top of this damned mine."

And I said, "No, I want to get over where my saddle is. They've got some jumpin' ponies, and I want to ride 'em."

When he finally brought me my slip, he shook hands with me and said, "I hope the first damned horse you ride kills you." He was gettin' a little worked up then.

I've been everywhere with different Wild West shows. I've been in New York a lot, and I knowed that rope-spinner [Will Rogers]. He'd spin the rope at the Manhattan Theater, and then he'd come up to our show [at the old Madison Square Garden] every Sunday and bring a couple of girls with him. He'd never take a drink himself, but he'd buy us all we wanted. He was makin' good money, you know.

That was in 1907, and I was with the 101 Wild West Show [for more about this troupe see the contribution of Mr. Bibbs, number 23]. I went to England with another show in 1908. I got my hip broke now, but I had it broke in 1908, ridin' a pitchin' horse for old King Edward [the seventh of that name].

Me and him got drunk, and I told him to come around to the show that evenin', as I was ridin' a pitchin' horse. I never saw this horse jump and fall before. But he was gettin' awful high and that old king was settin' in that audience, and I got to seein' if he was takin' a look. And that old pony got too high and missed the ground and fell right on top of me and broke that hip.

We stayed over there about nine months, and I got to be a citizen, I guess. I knew everybody, and I write letters there yet—to England and Ireland, too. I was in Queenstown, The boat don't stop there, but it kind of slows up at Queenstown, and they come out in other boats and bring stuff and take stuff back, and people, too.

After I come back from England, I was in the country around

78

Tombstone again, but in 1910 I left there and lived in the White Mountains, both in Navajo and Apache counties. For a long time I ranched near Alpine and got my mail at Nutrioso, where I had a place called Wild Cat Camp.

But I've got a brother that lives in California now—he's two years and two months younger'n me—that used to ranch right around here. He knowed Prescott pretty good and used to play the fiddle on Whiskey Row [a famous frontier strip on the west side of the town's courthouse square].

I never thought I'd be livin' in Prescott then, but this here Pioneers' Home is the best place I ever struck. I've only been here seven years, though if I'd knowed about it, I was eligible for a good many years before I come.

When I first come, there was a lot of old-timers stayin' in the home that was right here in Prescott when she was a tough town, but they've died since then. One of 'em was old Yaqui [Espisano S. Ordunez], who rode the kickin' horse in the old pioneers' rodeo [Prescott seems justified in claiming to be the place where this sport originated] in 1888. I was pretty small then; I was five years old. But I talked to him many times before he died. Of course, old Yaqui couldn't talk much—well he could talk, but you couldn't understand him a lot of the time.

Lots of fellows here told me lots of things that happened in Prescott, but there was other old-timers that didn't talk. They'd done it, you see, and they was through with it. They didn't care about interestin' anybody no ways; they was just like an old bull that's already sulled. But if I know anythin' that wouldn't hurt anybody, I don't mind tellin' it.

But mostly I stay in my room and write. I got lots of stories here. I write one, and when the pain hits me—I'm broke up all over; had my neck broke once—I stick it in an envelope and put it away somewhere, thinkin' that some day I might have it printed. It takes money, though, and you don't know nothin' about gettin' a book printed till you've tried. That was one of the hardest jobs I ever had.

A few years ago Joe Evans and me had that book I was readin' from printed [*Pecos' Poems*, El Paso, Texas, 1956; second edition, 1957] and sold copies for a dollar apiece, and we made nine cents on 'em. You can't monkey with a thing like that. We sold six thousand of 'em just as fast, by golly, as we could hand 'em out. But we didn't make no money on 'em, so they was more trouble than it paid off.

Joe's the man that promoted the outfit. I just told the stories and wrote the poems in it. It's a funny thing about Joe: he couldn't write a cowpuncher poem, and he was a cowpuncher, too. But I always could, and I'll read the one I wrote when I come back to Texas and found what'd happened to the country I'd punched cows in as a kid. I just called it *The Pecos.*

I've wandered back to the Texas Plains
Where the wind blows hard and it seldom rains
That once was the home of the old Longhorns
And the best cowboys on earth was borned.
But the longhorn steer and the bronco steed
Are replaced now by a different breed,
And the old cowboys that shot up the town
Are plenty few, and thin on the ground.

And the old Pecos River that mothered the spread
Looks very sick—she's almost dead.
I knew her when she was in her prime
And her banks run full 'most all the time.
Her waters flowed both far and near
For the bronco ponies and the longhorn steers;
Made plenty coffee for the cowboys, too,
Tempered the beans and made the stew.

Her salt grass valleys—rich and green,
Her quicksand deep and her waters mean;
She raised mosquitoes the size of a lark
They could bite right through a cowboy's tarp.
She wuz feared by men that wuz wild and rough
For the Pecos herself was plenty tough.

80

Her mesquite thickets for brush and thorns
Made "getaway places" for wild longhorns.

Men could not touch her with the tools they had
When they "riled her up"—it made her mad!
She'd wash 'em away with her strong tide.
And bogged 'em down on either side.
But the years of time have made a change
She's no more needed to water the range
The Pecos River, the Longhorns too,
Cowboys and broncos—have done their due.

MOSTLY ABOUT FRONTIER TOWNS

9
ON THE SALESMAN'S ROAD

*"A man that ever made a move at a woman got hung—
and that was all there was to it."*

WILLIAM S. WATSON, Denver, Colorado

*A man that saw the Stars and Stripes hoisted to fly above historic
Wake Island for the first time, Mr. Watson was a native of the
plains falling away eastward from Colorado's Rockies. He and his
family were not the sole occupants of that grassland, which was
ranged by as yet unconfined bands of Sioux.*

*His birthplace a house of turf—a "soddy," as the pioneers
termed such residences—he experienced in boyhood the life of a
frontier farmer. His destiny, though, was to be a commercial
traveler working out of Denver, the capital city of the inland West
and the main* entrepôt *for all the Mountain states and territories
and some besides. In a day of few and generally wretched roads,
trains were the means by which salesmen fanned out to take orders
in the satellite cities dotting something like a million square miles.*

*Mr. Watson's own territory, concerning which he has much of
interest to relate, was at first suburban and at length so vast that all
Colorado would have rattled around in it. But first came service in
the Philippine Islands, where he and fellow Westerners were engaged both with the Spanish and native insurrectionists.*

*Returning from that stint, Mr. Watson traveled in Arizona,
New Mexico, and western Texas. Among his experiences at this
period was being on the Mexican border while guerillas led by the
celebrated Francisco, or "Pancho," Villa were menacing a series of
American towns.*

HIS CONTRIBUTION

This happened about three months before I was born. Where my
parents were living was a two-room soddy. There was no timber;
everything was dirt. And there was a fence of sod in front of the
house, so you could keep the cattle away from the door. It was just

high enough to kneel behind, if you wanted to shoot, but not at cattle, of course.

There was a rule that you must never let an Indian in the house unless there was a man around. My father was back in the fields somewhere, and my sister—she was about three years older than I—saw Indians coming. My mother ran out and got the back door shut, but by the time she got to the front door, the Indians—they were Sioux—were at the gate.

The chief was named Calorom. He said, "We want something to eat; you cook for us."

She said, "No, get out." He rode his horse up and started for the gate. She picked my sister up and reached up for a forty-five, took it from its holster, walked down to the gate and said, "You're not coming in."

He looked at her and said, "The white squaw won't shoot; she's scared."

She said, "You put a foot on the fence, and see if I'm scared."

He looked at her a minute and then turned away and rode off.

My father saw them, and he was rushing up as fast as he could. He came in the back door as they were leaving, and when she saw him, she went over in a faint. And when I was born, I was just as red as an Indian.

I was born in 1875 in the town of Sterling, Colorado, in the northeast corner of the state. My father was a farmer who came from England in '72 and homesteaded in Sterling in '73. It was all cattle country down there, and as there wasn't any barbed wire then, it was almost impossible to keep the cattle off the fields.

The people from the south side of the river [the South Platte] went to a town in Nebraska [of which the nearest point was about sixty miles due east of Sterling] for supplies. But the people where we lived were cut off, because there was no bridge or ferry, and went over a hundred miles to Evans, Colorado. I can remember riding a hundred miles in a wagon to get groceries. It took us three weeks—a week to come, a week to go back, and one there. We were supposed to make the trip twice a year, though we'd go oftener, if necessary.

In spite of the trouble with cattle, my father did pretty well at

Sterling for a while, and then we came to Evans and farmed there a year or two. And my father kept a hotel there.

Evans was started on account of Greeley, Colorado. Greeley is the only town—well, maybe they've broken it now, but there was a clause in the original charter of Greeley that if a man was caught selling or harboring liquor, they could take all his property and sell it and give the money to the school board. There was no question about it. If he was selling liquor—boom!—he was done. So Evans was started over the hill to take care of the drought.

I went to school at Sterling—we went back there from Evans. I went to three years of high school there, and I went one year to the agricultural college at Fort Collins [also attended by Mr. Payne; see contribution 5]. Then my father died, and from then on it was the college of hard knocks and experience for me.

Before that my father went into business and came up to Denver in 1890. I remember there was no paving on the streets, and we had gas lights. They were just beginning to build the Brown Palace Hotel, and the hill where the capitol now stands was developing as the residential part of town. Larimer [which now serves as the Denver branch of Bohemia] was the main street, the honky tonks were in full blast, and they had plenty of palaces of sin. Denver wasn't a very big town then, but it was a very lively one.

My father had a hardware store when we came, but he hurt himself and died soon after we got here. He'd married again—my mother died in 1883, when I was eight—so my brother and I took care of our stepmother and half-sister until they both got married.

I stayed in the hardware business for a while, and then I got on with the Goodrich Rubber Company, selling footwear. I traveled what we called "the Horn." It was made up of eight towns right around Denver—Fort Collins, Boulder, Longmont, Loveland, Greeley, and the little towns in-between.

When I was going down to Arizona and other border states, I was selling hardware, newspaper metal, and plumbing supplies. But that was later. First I was in the Spanish-American War, though in the Philippines, not Cuba. I was with the regiment that raised the first American flag at Manila in August of 1898. That was the First Colorado. We weren't the only regiment in the action [the land

Battle of Manila as opposed to the sea Battle of Manila Bay]. But our regiment was on the beach, and we made the attack on San Antonio de Bahia, and that was the key to the fortification of Manila.

You see, each state was called on to supply so many men. It wasn't like World Wars I and II, when they drafted men who had no assignments. We were a Colorado regiment, and we held our identity. Some states wouldn't let their guard go and organized separate regiments for war service, but we were a National Guard unit. We trained and organized right up here at Twenty-sixth Street and Colorado, on the northeast corner of City Park. Then we went to San Francisco—we were in what they called the Hawthorn Section—and trained there a little while, too, before we went over.

Our whole brigade was there: units from Kansas, Nebraska, and Wyoming, as well as our outfit. When we went over our brigade commander was General Greene—Francis Greene, from New York. When we went home our brigade commander was Arthur MacArthur, father of Douglas MacArthur.

We left San Francisco on June 5, 1898, and Honolulu on the twenty-sixth. On July 4 we raised the first flag on Wake Island [previously unclaimed by any country, it was officially taken over by the United States, on General Greene's recommendation, the following year] and we dropped anchor in Manila Bay July 16.

The whole world knew where we were going, but after we left Honolulu, we disappeared. By sailing off the beaten track [the precaution was taken because it was rumored that another Spanish fleet, replacing the one Dewey had destroyed on May 1, was en route to Asiatic waters] we were lost to the world until we got to Hong Kong, where Dewey sent a dispatch boat with orders for us to go to Manila. They had to send a dispatch boat, because there was no cable connection between Manila and Hong Kong at that time. All the cables had been cut by Dewey. He said he wasn't going to have any goddamned people at Washington telling him what to do.

We were in the Philippines a year; got there in July of 1898 and left in August of 1899. We went there just for the war with Spain, but [Emilio] Aguinaldo was kicking up a fuss, and the government had taken over the obligation to maintain peace over there, so we had to stay until they organized another army to take our place.

We took part in suppressing Aguinaldo's insurrection from February, 1899, until we were ordered to leave. Then the action was taken over by the replacing regiments. We came back to Colorado by way of San Francisco then and mustered out here.

Then I went back to selling. I started going on the road in 1907, and in 1910 I took a full-time traveling job. Although I took a couple of stagecoach trips, we almost always traveled by train. It was very different than it is now; and it was as different then from what it was when I was a boy. Because when I was a boy, that was when they used to travel by stage and horseback and everything else to get around.

When I traveled, the trains didn't have air brakes; they just had the hand brakes, the ones clamped by the wheels you still see atop of freight cars. There were lots of wrecks, because the trains would get out of control. Of course, the road beds weren't anything like they are now, and if trains made thirty miles an hour they were doing well.

But they had sleeping accommodations, and by that time most of the towns had hotels. Some were hotels, and some were "oh hells." But after we'd been on the road three or four months, we knew how to time ourselves so that we could hit the good hotels whenever possible.

I'll tell a story about the first time I went to Phoenix, Arizona. It was summer, and we went down [south from the main Santa Fe line and dropping from an elevation of about seven thousand to not much more than a thousand feet] on a train with little dinky coaches. It was all right from Ash Fork to Prescott [a mile high] but then we started going into that hole [the Salt River Valley, about which even boosters can't carol when summer comes to linger]. We'd drink water, you know, and it just run off us.

There was one overweight fellow who looked like he'd never done a day's work in his life. They were dumping consumptives in Phoenix by the carload then, and this fellow knew somebody who'd had to go out there for his health—a real estate man from back East in Kansas City—and he'd talked this fellow into coming out and said he'd set him up in business.

The fellow'd get up and wipe his face off every few minutes in the washroom, where they brought in ice from the baggage car, and he'd say, "God damn this country! I don't see why anyone wants to live here." That's about all we could get out of him.

Well, we got down there, and the man he was coming to see met him in a new car—cars were just coming in then—and took him around. We got there in the melon season. The whole country was covered with fine ones, everything looked prosperous, and his friend showed him some attractive properties that he was handling.

Then when we got back to the hotel—the Adams Hotel—we said, "Get that coat off. We don't wear coats in the summertime."

"Go into the *dining room* without a coat?"

"Oh, yes. Take that coat off and roll up your sleeves."

So we went in, and they had punkas—fans to make it comfortable [see Mr. Stauffer's contribution, number 13, for description of these]. Then he said, "I saw some beautiful melons today, and the first thing I want is half a cantaloupe." So they brought him a fine cantaloupe in a bowl of cracked ice and he said, "This is a wonderful country they've got here, ain't it?"

They had no coolers then, so you'd take a bath and stretch out in bed wringing wet, and as long as you were wet, you could sleep. When you got too damned hot, you'd get up and take a dip in the tub again.

I was in El Paso [in 1916] on the night that Villa was supposed to make an attack there. One of the things I was selling was newspaper metal [for linotypes, stereotype plates, etc.], so I was around newspapers a good deal and would catch the morning papers at night. I was in a press room, and they were holding up the press for something definite from Washington about Villa.

I told the head of the press room I was going out for coffee, and while I was having it he came tearing in and said, "Didn't you tell me you were a sergeant in the Philippines?"

I said, "Yes, what's the matter?"

"Never mind, but come on," he said.

So I went with him, and there was a burly man in uniform who asked me if I'd seen service as a sergeant. When I told him yes, he said, "You go to your hotel room. If I want you, I'll call you; and there'll be twenty men downstairs that you and another fellow will have charge of. You'll be a part of a group protecting that part of town." They thought Pancho Villa was coming into Juarez [directly across the Rio Grande from El Paso], but he didn't come. [Contrary to expectations, Villa struck Columbus, New Mexico, sixty miles west of El Paso, on March 9, 1916, killing seventeen Americans.]

Douglas, Arizona, is down on the border. A week later I was woke up in Douglas by gunfire. *Bar-r-r-r!* It sounds funny now, but I was in the middle of the floor before I got my eyes open. It lasted about a half an hour, but it didn't amount to anything. Villa's Mexicans had been making a raid, but the Americans got reinforcements that stopped them at the border and turned them back.

I don't know how it was back East, because I was never there, but such things as a long-distance phone call was something to talk about in those days. It used to cost me a dollar to phone my outfit in Denver from Pueblo—one hundred miles. I was dealing down there once, and I had to have a price right away. I held the line for five minutes and that cost me a dollar, too.

And a dollar was something then. If you made a hundred dollars a month, you had a good job. You could get whiskey at five dollars a gallon. You could get a hotel room for a dollar, a room with a bath for a dollar and a half, and your meals would be a dollar and a half or sometimes only a dollar. If you paid two dollars for a dinner, that was for a banquet.

I've eaten many a meal at a free-lunch counter. You could get a glass of beer for a nickel and get a sandwich and some pretzels and go and sit down and eat 'em. If you got a stein for ten cents, you could have two sandwiches.

Loafers were always trying to mooch free lunches. I've seen more than one customer thrown out when he tried to sneak into the lunch counter without buying. Or they'd stand outside and say, "Buy me a glass of beer, mister, so I can get a sandwich. Jesus! I haven't had anything to eat for a week."

"Oh, you don't look that bad."

"I'm really hungry."

"Well, go to work."

"I don't work."

And we had the union I Won't Works out here. The I. W. W. was more or less a Western proposition [see the contributions of Judge Guild, Dr. Catlett, Mrs. Miles, and Mr. Powell, numbers 14, 15, 16, and 24, for more about this organization]. They started in Idaho, but though I don't remember where, we had them in Colorado, too. But when we had a bunch of instigators here, officers'd generally herd them up and put 'em in a boxcar and tell them to get the hell out.

There was a lot more respect for the law than there is now. When I was a boy, a woman that had the reputation of being a good woman could go anywhere in the country, and nobody would touch her. A man that ever made a move at a woman got hung—and that was all there was to it. There was no foolishness. On the other hand, if a woman was promiscuous, why God help her if the boys took a notion to get heavy.

If a man fooled around in other ways back in those days, if he wasn't careful, he'd get shot. They'd hang a man for stealing a horse, too. Or not minding your own business could get you killed or beaten up. If you kept your mouth shut in those Texas, New Mexico, and Arizona towns, you wouldn't have any trouble, but if you went looking for it, there was always somebody to accommodate you. If a man got a snootful and declared he was a bad boy, there was always somebody willing to find out just how bad he was.

I heard and saw a lot of things while I was on the road, but this true one that I picked up in Amarillo is the best Western story I can think of. There was a case along about 1912, when there was a triangle—one woman and two men. Two pioneer families had come out to the country around Amarillo together, they'd started ranches together, and the children had grown up together. But when a son of one of the families married, a boy belonging to the other family took up with the other fellow's wife.

There was a good deal of feeling over it; but they got together

93

and settled it up, and he [the claim-jumper] agreed to go away and *stay* away. But instead of staying away, he came back to Amarillo.

There was an irrigation ditch alongside the courthouse there in those days; they'd dam it up and run water for the trees around it. But once when it was dry, the married man got a sawed-off shotgun and laid down in that ditch. He waited for the other fellow—his wife had told him that she was going to meet the man there—and when he was coming past, the husband gave him both barrels.

People took sides, and you could get an argument or a fight on any streetcorner in Amarillo over what had happened. Well, one of my customers was a plumber. His father was a cow man who'd set the boy up in business, and the old man would hang around there. And when I came along, he asked me what I thought about the shooting.

"The reason I feel so bad about it myself," he said, "is that here was two families that went through all the hardships of pioneering together—and they was some hardships; I know, for I went through 'em myself—and something like this had to happen." Then old man Bisbee went over and hunkered down in a corner and took out his smoke makings. "The darned so and so didn't do right," he said.

His kid said, "Shut up! Don't express any opinion. You know you got in a fight about that the other day."

"I don't care," the old man said. "He didn't do right. If he'd told young Joe Hardy that if he didn't quit pesterkating around his wife he'd fill him full of bullets, why they could've stepped out into Main Street here, to shoot it out with a couple of forty-fives. But he don't do that. Instead he gets him a tenderfoot weapon—he gets him a *shotgun*. That ain't no way to act!"

10

FRONTIER REAL ESTATE PROBLEMS

*"From a legal standpoint trying to recover those grants
is barking up the wrong tree."*

WILLIAM A. KELEHER, Albuquerque, New Mexico

*Attorney and author in his maturity, Mr. Keleher followed a wide
variety of other careers in his earlier days. Although not necessarily in this order, he was by turns a railroad hand, a Board of
Education clerk, a construction worker, a newspaperman, and a
telegraph operator. He thus came to view territorial New Mexico
from a gamut of angles, adding up to an authoritative understanding of his section of the frontier.*

*When he came to write of the old West, he was able to add
personal knowledge of pioneer problems to the fruits of research
common to historians. And as a lawyer, he was able to bring to
political aspects of his state's early history, the understanding
peculiar to his profession.*

*Resulting have been such valuable items of Western Americana
as* The Maxwell Land Grant *and* Violence in Lincoln County. *The
first is a case history of a grant also referred to in Charles Barker's
contribution, number 20. The second is a study of the range war
involving Billy the Kid, together with its array of causes and
aftermaths.*

*An advantage enjoyed by Mr. Keleher, considered as a historian
is that he had met persons who could give him firsthand descriptions of many of the figures who people his books. And for
lagniappe, as he here makes clear, he even encountered the prosecutor who finally succeeded in besting that most artful of American dodgers, the Baron of Arizona.*

HIS CONTRIBUTION

I was born in Lawrence, Kansas, in 1886. When I was two years
old, or in 1888, my parents brought me to New Mexico, making
their home here in Albuquerque.

When I was a boy and young man, the city had a population of from six to eight thousand, but that embraced what we thought of as two communities. At that time most of the people in Albuquerque proper were of Anglo extraction [see contribution of Elliott Barker, number 6, for comment on that term]. The so-called Spanish-Americans—we never refer to them as Mexicans, because that would imply they were citizens of another country—lived in Old Albuquerque, or Old Town, as it's now usually called.

I went to school in Albuquerque from 1893 to 1900, attending the St. Mary's grammar school, a parochial school. But I had a funny educational scheme. I left school in May of 1900 and never went back to classes for thirteen years.

Then I got my legal education at Washington and Lee University at Lexington, Virginia. Entering in 1913, I graduated on June 15, 1915, with the degree of L.L.B. But I completed my law course almost entirely in one year. The rest of the time I went over to the academic department, studying poetry, English history, and American history.

When I got out of grammar school in 1900, I went to work for the Western Union Telegraph Company as a messenger boy. I became a clerk there when I was through being a messenger boy, and then I was a telegraph operator for four years. I was with Western Union six years in all, leaving the company in 1906.

Albuquerque, when I was a boy and young man, was a wide-open town. There was a great deal of gambling. Roulette, chucka-luck, blackjack—any kind of gambling you can name, they had it here. There were about forty combination saloons and gambling houses, all running legally, for gambling wasn't outlawed until 1907.

At that time the town was quite a livestock center. The banks of Albuquerque financed cattle men and wool growers or sheep men, too. They used to bring wool into Albuquerque from the Estancia Valley by ox teams. But the town wasn't the lumber center that it became and is today. The automobile and the truck were not yet in existence as commercial factors, so that all the forests in the vicinity were locked up, as you might say.

Until the development of the truck and the tractor they couldn't

97

get the timber out, because it grows high up in rugged mountains; but then Albuquerque became an important center for timber. There's no timber to speak of in the Sandias, though. They got it from the Jemez Mountains and the Zuni Mountains. It was a haul of about a hundred miles from the Zunis, and for a long time they hauled the timber from a place called Thoreau, New Mexico, east of Gallup, bringing in thirty carloads every day.

But I didn't spend all my time in Albuquerque. After I left Western Union, I worked for a year at several different jobs. I worked for the Blue Water Development Company at Blue Water, New Mexico. I worked for the Eastern Railway Company, a wholly owned subsidiary of the Santa Fe Railroad, at Vaughn, New Mexico, building what they called the Belen cut-off. The Eastern ran from Vaughn to Clovis, New Mexico, and east over the Panhandle of Texas. And I worked down in Belen, New Mexico, as a railroad yard man.

I worked wherever I could get a job, before I got to be a clerk of the Board of Education and secretary to the Superintendent of Schools of the City of Albuquerque in 1907. Then from 1908 to 1913 I was a newspaperman. I worked for the Albuquerque *Morning Journal* for four years, and for the *Herald* two, before I decided to turn to law.

I don't recall any particularly important story that I covered while working for newspapers, but learned a lot about the territory; New Mexico wasn't a state [it became one in 1912] most of those years. For instance, the whole country between the Rio Grande here and the Pecos River was a vast grazing ground without a fence in it. They had no public-domain laws, no Taylor Grazing Act, no Forest Service—no nothing. The man with the shotgun at the waterhole was the king-of-the-range.

Before the Forest Service came in, they used to have a good many killings over the range. It used to be that sheep men and cattle men couldn't use the same range. Although it's different today, that was the understanding then.

The trouble between the cattle and sheep men was over grazing rights, for it was believed that cattle couldn't live where sheep grazed, too. But that was all changed by the United States Forest

Service, which was established by Colonel Theodore Roosevelt in 1903.

The Forest Service was fathered by Gifford Pinchot—a wealthy man with a hobby, and a very dear friend of Theodore Roosevelt. He got men from Yale University—from the Sheffield Scientific School there—to run the service, and that's why it became a success. Pinchot started with the rule of no politics in the Forest Service. A politician might have been a very important man on a national committee in Washington, but to Gifford Pinchot that didn't make any difference. Nobody got any more privileges than anybody else.

The thing simmered along for some years in New Mexico, but in 1908 the Forest Service [for more about the workings of this government arm in the West, see the contributions of Mr. Elliott Barker, number 6, and Mr. Bennett, number 11] established headquarters in Albuquerque; and from that time on things were run by rules and regulations. The Forest Service did a good job of educating the cattle and sheep men; that was their primary objective. They hired a man by the name of Will C. Barnes of Arizona, and Will Barnes was what they would call today a public-relations man. He had been a cattle man himself and knew the problems of the range.

He was the go-between for the hostile livestock men and the Forest Service. His job was to prove to cattle and sheep men that range management, as they called it, was ultimately for the benefit of the livestock men. But it really took a whole generation to educate them. The old-timers couldn't be reconciled to the fact that Washington directed where they should graze their stock, and asked them to pay for the privilege; or for the lease of land, or how many head of sheep or cattle they should graze on a certain area. Most of them never became reconciled—they were diehards. They were accustomed to their own ways, and they refused to bow to the inevitable.

There were never many goats in New Mexico, and anyhow the Forest Service didn't want goats on the range, as they eat the grass too low—they eat the roots and all. But I think goats were commercially unprofitable in a country where there wasn't much demand for their milk. They were no good for meat, the hide wasn't worth much, and there was a heavy mortality.

The Forest Service took over all the country they could possibly call timber country, but they couldn't claim the great grassland between the Rio Grande and the Pecos and had no jurisdiction there. Neither did anybody else until the Taylor Grazing Act was passed in 1934.

There was a great deal of mining going on in New Mexico at the turn of the century. There was a great gold-mining camp at Bland, up in Sandoval County, and at San Pedro and Golden. Other metals were mined, too, and some of the oldest streets in Albuquerque were named for the territory's mineral wealth: Gold, Silver, and Copper streets, for example. And it was New Mexico's coal that kept the mines of Arizona going, too, such as the great Copper Queen mine at Bisbee.

Then there were minerals which weren't known about in territorial days. In 1868 there was a treaty between the Navajo Indians and the United States Government, negotiated by General William Tecumseh Sherman, and the United States gave the Navajos the worst land possible. Unfortunately it turned out that there's oil and gas there, as well as uranium.

I mentioned coal. Most of the miners of it were Slavs. There were not many miners belonging to other foreign nationalities, as there were in some of the Western states and territories. But there were a good many Chinamen brought into New Mexico from the Texas side; they came in through Juarez, Mexico, and fanned out into the Southwest from El Paso.

Undoubtedly there was an underground railroad operating here, for the United States Marshal's office was busy all the time, chasing information about it. They tried to keep Chinamen out of the country by the Chinese Exclusion Act [passed in 1882 and supplemented by the Geary Act ten years later]. But they got here, and I have no doubt they were brought in with the previous understanding that there'd be a pay-off someplace.

I know they were smuggled into Albuquerque, for every now and then I'd see strange Chinese, and if they were asked for their papers, they'd get nervous. There must have been a conspiracy of

100

some sort; but anything I'd say would be mere suspicion on my part, although I knew some that I thought were involved.

Before Villa's time they had very little trouble along our part of the Mexican border, because of a stability of a kind provided by Porfirio Diaz—President of Mexico for many, many years [from 1877 to 1880 and from 1884 to 1911]. He maintained discipline and law and order along the border; and anybody who didn't obey what he said was shot and killed right now. He didn't have to wait for the United States Supreme Court to discuss the case.

But now there's trouble being raised right in New Mexico by a man who's stirring up Spanish-Americans and reopening a long-healed breach. He's basing his case on the Forest Service's preemption of the land that formed the Carson National Forest around Taos. He claims that the government took that land away from Spanish-Americans who'd received grants to it. But as a lawyer I'd have to say that the government did not.

The Forest Service has made some mistakes, but this wasn't one of them. In 1846, by virtue of the American occupation of New Mexico, and confirmed by the Treaty of Guadalupe-Hidalgo in 1848, it became American territory. When the American troops came in and conquered New Mexico, it seemed to me that the United States had a right to *all* the land, in plain English; but actually at the close of the war Spanish and Mexican land grants were recognized. The Spanish grants were made up to the time of the Mexican Revolution of 1821. The Mexican grants were made between 1821, the year of the revolution, and 1846, the year of the American occupation. [For more about such grants see contribution of Mrs. Gilbert, number 17].

These grants were all recognized by the Treaty of Guadalupe-Hidalgo. But the people who owned them failed to live up to the terms of that treaty, which specified that they could keep them as long as they maintained a property-holder's normal responsibility to the Government of the United States. They didn't, though. What broke down the grants and laid them open to preemption was the failure of the owners to pay the necessary taxes.

That was inevitable, because of the cloudy ownership that developed. For example, a grant would be originally in the name of

101

one man. He'd die and leave it to several children, who in turn would all leave it to children of theirs. The ownership would be so diluted, and the land would be disputed by so many factional interests, that it would be impossible to get them together. So the land would be sold for taxes.

Of course, I contend that the policy of the United States was otherwise unsound with respect to the conquered citizens of New Mexico. The government refused to do anything for a people handicapped by being non-English-speaking. It is true that their rights as American citizens were recognized and protected, but to the best of my belief the United States never spent one dollar to educate the Mexican people after the American occupation.

That's not true of the Indians; they took the civilized Indians of New Mexico [the Pueblo natives as opposed to the Apaches and Navajos] and established schools for them, or at least maintained classes for them. It was also possible for Indians to get a free education in the East, but not for the Spanish-Americans.

To that extent the claims of injustice are true. But from a legal standpoint, trying to recover those grants is barking up the wrong tree. They were nullified long ago by decisions of the United States Court of Private Land Claims, which was established in 1893 under the second Cleveland administration.

I investigated some of the grants, a subject in which I became interested when the Texas Bar Association asked me to read a paper on the New Mexico laws bearing on them, which differed from the Texas ones. Eventually I published a book about the Maxwell Land Grant, which I found the most interesting of them.

I also made a study of the grant in the famous James Addison Reavis case [the fraudulent and for long successful try of the so-called Baron of Arizona to claim the Peralta Grant, eventually stretched until its dimensions equaled the combined areas of New Hampshire and New Jersey]. I was going to publish a book about it from a legal point of view, but I decided that he was a conniving, scheming old devil. His capacity for hard work was beyond belief, and in attempts to prove his case [which included forging imperial and colonial documents in archaic Spanish] he was the most industrious guy you ever heard of.

102

It's a funny thing, but some years ago I met in New York City the man who prosecuted Reavis. His name was Severo Mallet-Prevost. He told me that he was a lawyer in New York City when Grover Cleveland sent for him and asked him to represent the United States in the case. He had been recommended to the President because of his background. His father, who'd been a surgeon in the American army in the war of 1846, had settled in Zacatecas, Mexico, and married a Mexican woman. So this Mallet-Prevost was half Mexican.

He was ninety-three years old when I talked to him, and he told me how he went to Madrid and Mexico City, and how he finally discovered the fraud, as he said, and won the case in 1896. At the conclusion of his talk I said, "Mr. Mallet-Prevost, what you've told me is so interesting that I wonder if you'd mind writing it out for me."

He said, "Not at all, not at all; I'll write you a letter about it." Which he did, and I've still got it.

Reavis was fighting for a strip of land fifty miles in depth from Phoenix, Arizona, to Lordsburg, New Mexico. But he would have been bogged down, too, because he couldn't have paid the taxes.

II

IN AND ABOUT A BOOM TOWN

"I wasn't tempted very badly to shoot this sheepherder;
I just kind of wanted to."

EDWIN BENNETT, Mesa, Arizona

To all intents and purposes a native of Creede, Mr. Bennett grew up in and around that silver camp. One of the capital cities of the treasure stampeders' circuit, it counted among its citizens many whose names have since been fixtures of Western literature.

A fine place for a youngster to store memories, it wouldn't have been chosen as the best place to rear a lad by the more conservative educational counselors of today. Creede, to be frank about it, failed of being a family man's town. Children were in such short supply among its hustling thousands that Mr. Bennett reached a certain grade as a solitaire. Schooling stopped for him then, because a community not then celebrated for its interest in matters cultural refused to provide another class for just one pupil.

Undisturbed, Mr. Bennett equipped himself with an excellent education, some of it gained as a hard-rock miner, a horseback mailman, a cowhand, a Forest Service ranger, and a soldier in World War I. Retired from other professions, he now makes a business of frontier history, a field to which he has contributed the first of several planned books. Published in 1968, Boom Town Boy *is more than the personal memoir implied in the title. Mr. Bennett's own lively recollections have been supplemented by consultations and correspondence with other old-timers, as well as research in various historical libraries. Emerging from these multiple sources was a perceptive review of a locality and a period.*

HIS CONTRIBUTION

I was born in Cambria, Michigan, in '89. I was brought out West, direct to Colorado, in '92. We went there because my father had itching feet.

He and another fellow owned a store in Michigan, but he came home one day and told his wife, "We're going to Creede."

106

And she asked, "Where's that?"

Then he said, "I don't know what state it's in, but we'll go as soon as I find out."

We lived in Weaver before going to Creede proper. It's a dead burg now and has been for years. I don't know what the population was then, probably about two hundred and fifty. It was three or four miles from Creede—not a mining camp itself, but just a handy place to live for the fellows who worked in the mines: the Amethyst, the Last Chance, the Partridge, the Happy Thought, and others.

In those early days everybody was a boss. You never hear people tell of any of their ancestors being buck privates; they were all bosses. Well, my father was the *boss* of the ore house at the Amethyst Mine; a post of very limited dignity. But the top workings of the mine burned in '94. He thought he was going to lose his job, but he didn't. They put him in charge—in *charge*, you understand—of one of the crews.

He could make his living anyplace, but his curse was the itching foot that wouldn't let him stay in any place. He quit his job and left for Cripple Creek, where he was a hoist man on the Portland. Then he went to Grand Encampment, Wyoming—it's just Encampment now. And from then on I don't know. He might have written occasionally, but I'm not sure whether he did or not. My mother and I stayed in Creede, you see. She told him that if he wanted to wander, he could do it by himself.

We were in Weaver only a year or so. I wasn't four when we went to Creede; that was in March of '93. I was a three-year-old, and I went to school at that age. They wanted a school up there, and in order to get it they had to have—I think it was twenty-two pupils. And in order to get twenty-two they had to rob the cradle. It didn't last very long, but I do remember being in that schoolhouse.

I went to school in Creede for as many grades as they had, but that's what stopped me; there were only nine. Except for three or four kids who were sent away to school, I was the only one that got that far; and they told me they weren't going to start a tenth grade for just one pupil.

But I was three or four years getting through the ninth grade. I was in and out of school like using a revolving door, because I'd get a job someplace and go to work. When I was thirteen—I remember that, because it crippled me up some—I was flipping a number-two scraper on a damn construction project. At different times I worked on our ranch, nine miles up the Rio Grande from Creede, where my stepfather took up a homestead. And I remember working in the mines.

I finished the ninth grade sometime after 1902, but I didn't care whether I got an education or not. One of the professors tried to get me to do as he had done—go down to Colorado College at the Springs and work my way through prep and then college. But I told him I didn't want an education that badly; I had other ways to spend my life.

After I got out of school, I carried mail a short while to Bachelor by horseback. It was about two and a half miles away, all uphill. Gone now, the town of Bachelor was about ten thousand feet high, and Creede is eighty-eight hundred and four. But mostly I worked in the mines or on ranches for the next eight years.

I wrote a book about my Creede experiences: *Boom Town Boy*. I'm told that it has been printed and has been sent East for binding; but I don't know when it'll be published. It has been advertised, and apparently quite extensively in Colorado; for friends in Creede have heard about it. But I haven't seen any notices myself. Everybody seems to know more about that book than I do. [*Boom Town Boy* was published in Chicago in May of 1968.]

My book about Creede covers the period from '93 to 1910. There's nothing dramatic about it; just what a fellow does. There's nothing to recommend it as literature, *I* would think.

But there were some lively doings in Creede while I was there. There were what you might call notorious characters there, and some rather famous ones. Bob Ford [for more about him see the contribution of Mr. Rhodes, number 22] had already been killed. But Bat Masterson [see Mr. Blake's contribution, number 4] was still there, running a saloon and gambling house.

And Dave Sponsalier was there. He ran a dance hall and theater, and that sort of thing. This theater was—I don't know exactly what you'd call it, but the girls' nightlife wasn't over when they

108

finished on the stage. They still had work to do between then and morning.

But Dave was rather well-liked and was one of the influential characters there, regardless of the fact that his activities were all in the theater and dance-hall line. And I believe he was one of the city officials for a while.

One thing that amuses me is the status they give Soapy Smith [the best known of all Western bunco artists] in books about the frontier today. So far as I ever heard around there, nobody took Soapy Smith seriously. Of course, he ran his part of town; but that was because the businessmen and everybody of that class were too busy running *their* end of the town. So he was king of the crooks.

Creede was hit hard by the silver panic of '93, when the price dropped from a dollar to about fifty-seven cents. But the lead and zinc evidently kept the mines going, because the production record didn't show a big drop. Of course, there weren't ten thousand anymore, but a lot of people stayed. There must have been a dozen outfits hauling ore, so it wasn't dead by any means.

But most of the famous characters had left by the time I was grown or about that. The only gambler I knew well was Jim Dunn. There were lots of tinhorns around but not what you'd call real gamblers, except for him.

Boom Town Boy covers my life outside of town, too. I had a few ranch experiences that I told of in my book—and a few I didn't tell. Those, you see, that were fit to print, I wrote up, and I left out the others. But the trouble is that the ones that are fit to print are so deadly dull.

There was no trouble between cattle-ranchers where we lived; that was very peaceable country. But—well—I was tempted to shoot a sheepherder one time. It was the first time they brought sheep on our side of the river, you see, and I didn't like it. I wasn't tempted very badly to shoot this sheepherder; I just kind of wanted to. I covered the story in my book, except for that impulse.

After that I picked up a bunch of bum lambs and raised them on cow's milk, you know, and we had lamb all fall. The sheepherders were *very* glad for us to pick up those lambs and look out for 'em. They didn't mind losing 'em so much, but they hated for the little things to lay out there and starve to death. We saved 'em from that, so it wasn't a complete curse having the sheep go through our country.

Years later when I was a ranger in the Forest Service, a sheep-herder gave my wife a lamb. Well, we took it to the ranger station and raised it on canned milk; and, you know, by the time we got through raising it on canned milk, it was damned expensive lamb.

Then we turned it out with the sheep of a man who had a bunch of 'em up on the hillside of the San Juan range. Well, when we wanted it, my brother-in-law and I just went down and shot the lamb; and we butchered it up on the mountainside. The kids that were herding phoned the sheriff's office that a ranger was there killing their sheep. The man who got the call—I knew him, and he was a good officer—guessed at once what was going on, but the kids were all worked up about it.

To return to the ranch, the only time we had any rustler trouble, we lost a stallion and a whole bunch of his mares up above Creede. I don't know whether there were eight or nine mares, and their colts; but they just disappeared and nobody ever saw them again—evidently. The only place they could have gone was over in the Saguache country, out through Half Moon Pass. But nobody ever found out about 'em, so whoever got away with 'em—they didn't all lie down and die—did a very slick job.

We didn't have any trouble with animal predators, especially; but one of 'em helped us one time—a mountain lion. We had an orphan colt, and we raised him at the house in town. Of course, you know, it was a lot of fun for a kid to tease him; but he took it hard and got mean. Well, finally it reached the point that you couldn't walk out our back door and go to the—corral—without a club to fight him off.

Something had to be done, so I took him down to a fellow named Goocher at Wagon Wheel Gap and turned him out with a bunch of horses running down there—a bunch of geldings. And that's the last we ever saw of him; mountain lions were numerous down there, and mountain lions like horse. So I didn't have to bring him back, and it stayed safe to go out the back door. But if you ever raise an orphan colt, don't tease him.

Outside of him, though, animals didn't bother us much. All we had in our country was an occasional bear or occasional lion, and coyotes. The bears were black or brown—all full-grown ones drifted in from some other range, because it wasn't natural bear country.

There was a rancher named George Bernouth above us who killed a bear every now and then. He had a. couple of cow dogs, and the dogs would get on each side of the bear. When the bear would swipe at one of 'em, the other would heel him. And by the time the bear'd turn to swipe at that one, the first would heel him. They'd keep the bear so busy that Bernouth could just walk up close and get him with one shot.

After the period covered by *Boom Town Boy*, I was a Forest Service ranger until I served in World War I, and for a few years after that. For a while I was assigned to the national forest at the headwaters of the Rio Grande. There were five hundred and fifty square miles of it, and I covered it as well as I could all by myself.

When I started in, it was the early days of forestry, and we had the job of breaking in cattle and sheep-raisers that weren't used to being told how to do anything and didn't like it. [See contributions of Mr. Elliott Barker, number 6, and Mr. Keleher, number 10, for more on this subject.] Of course, if we'd tried to make 'em do everything in the government's book, we wouldn't have gotten anywhere with 'em. We only tried to make 'em do what we thought was reasonable and what would help 'em, you know.

On account of predators the sheepherders had always practiced bunch feeding, and they fought us when we ordered scattered feeding. Well, they lost some sheep to coyotes that way, but the rest got so much fatter that the owners more than made up the loss.

Then the sheep-growers hated the idea of shed lambing [the yeaning season attended to under cover] because they'd always done it in the open. When we finally talked one man into trying it our way, the rest wouldn't speak to him—until they saw the results he got.

There were wild sheep up in the Rockies, too—bighorns. One day I saw a bighorn ewe leading a lamb along a cliff, and when she

111

came to a break in it about four or five feet wide, she hopped over to a ledge just barely wide enough for her to stand on. But the lamb didn't follow; he just stood there, looking at the ewe.

I don't know what signals she used, but in some way she coached him. For all of a sudden that lamb backed away, got a running start for his jump, hit the ledge on the other side and trotted along it after his mother. Neither of 'em seemed to think anything bout it. I was the only one that was scared.

We had a superintendent, when I was first in the Forest Service, that was a wonderful rider. A big fellow, he was a good all-around man; but when he'd been working hard, he had a trick of falling asleep in the saddle.

Well, when his horse raised its tail to switch flies, one of the fellows'd shove a little stick under it. Until it was pulled out, the horse'd go just about crazy, you know. Almost any other rider, taken by surprise that way, would have been thrown when the circus started. But it never bothered that superintendent, or made him mad, either. He expected it.

112

12
THE WORKINGS OF A MARKET CENTER

"Whitney was taken to a hospital in Santa Fe, and they stole him out of the hospital."

MANUEL O. HENRIQUEZ, Las Vegas, New Mexico

Very few sources present a clear picture of how the West did business and fitted into the national scheme of trade, but Mr. Henriquez is successful in making this dramatically understandable. In the employ of a great wholesaling house in pioneer times, he tells of the complex of operations through which retailers of the frontier were supplied, and by which Western farmers as well as stock men disposed of their products.

The firm for which Mr. Henriquez worked was a two-way clearing house. Incoming from the Missouri cities which had served as supply points for the West, ever since pack animals first slogged along the Santa Fe Trail, were carloads of whatever settlers found usable. Outgoing, and often bound for points as distant as New England, were shipments of everything they had to offer the market. All this, together with the wagons plying back and forth from numberless outlets and supply points are here vividly set in motion.

But the commerce of the Old West constitutes but one aspect of Mr. Henriquez's contribution. His memories are conditioned by the fact that for many years Las Vegas was a very tough town, as well as an industrially active one. Traveling about a territory liberally peopled with kinsmen, besides, he picked up a great deal of lore, plus a wide acquaintance. He knew, for example, the man suspected of having somehow committed what remains the most mysterious crime in the annals of the frontier, in view of the prominence of the chief victim.

HIS CONTRIBUTION

I'll begin by telling something that happened when I wasn't yet a year old. I was born here in '82, and this fight must have been in '83.

114

The railroad was through here then. [Transcontinental service through the Southwest was effected when the Santa Fe connected with the Southern Pacific in New Mexico in 1881.] The Whitneys were a railroad family from Boston, and they came and squatted on the place that my grandfather had down there below Lamy.

So this uncle of mine, my mother's brother, who was running the ranch there, he phoned up to my father to meet him at Lamy. And he also phoned Charlie Armijo, who married my mother's sister, to meet him there; and the three of them went down to this ranch. Well, Charlie Armijo went down there and never had a gun in his pocket. My father had four shells in his gun; and of course my uncle, Manuel Otero, was pretty well armed, you see.

I don't remember which Whitney it was, but they got in a little old ten-by-ten room with him and another man and asked 'em what right they had to take possession of the place. And old Whitney pulled out his gun, and he shot my mother's brother right in the neck. Well, that started the fight, and Whitney was shot eight times; but it never killed him. But his brother-in-law was killed; his brother-in-law was named Fernandez. He was shot and crawled under a bed, but when they went to pull him out, he was dead, you see.

My father was shot in the shoulder, but Charlie Armijo didn't have a gun, so he walked out of the place—he wasn't going to stay there. My Uncle Manuel Otero, who had charge of the ranch, was shot in the neck; the shot severed the jugular artery, and he died two weeks before my cousin Manuel was born.

They were sixty-five miles from Santa Fe, and going overland would take 'em a good day and a half, if they tried their best. Whitney was taken to a hospital in Santa Fe, and they stole him out of the hospital. The Whitneys got him out; he had a brother that came from California in his private car. They were railroad people, you see, back East as well as here.

The Governor of New Mexico, he appointed Miguel Otero [later Governor of New Mexico himself and author of *My Life on the Frontier*], who was then just a lad about twenty years old, a deputy sheriff. And he stopped the Whitney's private car down in Glorieta. Well, Whitney's brother said they had better medical facilities in California than they had here. [The fugitives had been

115

heading East when stopped, though, witness the relative positions of Glorieta and Santa Fe.] And they promised to be back for the trial, if they were allowed to go to California.

Well, they held the hearing out of Santa Fe. As that was a Mexican district, they held it instead at Raton in Colfax County, because that was American, right in newly settled territory. Well, the judge told 'em that neither one of 'em had any right to the land and dismissed the case, you see.

None of 'em went to prison or anything on account of the shooting—that was settled out of court. And my folks got—oh, I guess a couple of hundred thousand acres, and they could live on that. The land was down at Constancia—later they changed the name to Estancia—down in Torrance County.

There are two towns called Las Vegas [for more about the history of this community, see Mrs. Gilbert's contribution, number 17], and I was born in what they called New Town. I went to school there, the public school.

Then I went to the Territorial Normal; I was in the first freshman class in 1898. They had only one building, and they'd only finished one story of that [for amplification see Mr. Charles Barker's contribution, number 20].

Frank Springer was the first president of the Normal School's board of directors. He was a rancher; he owned the C. S. Ranch, which is one of the big spreads of northern New Mexico. It runs from Cimarron pretty near to Springer and takes in about 150,000 acres. That's where Will James got his start as a writer and an artist. A friend of Springer's from New York was visiting the ranch, and he took an interest in Will James.

But I didn't graduate from the Normal School; I just went one year, because my father died and my mother had to go to California. So I stayed with my brother, who was working for Gross-Kelly, one of the two big wholesaling outfits in Las Vegas. And I started in working for them myself.

Gross-Kelly dealt mainly in groceries, but they ran sheep and cattle, too; and they sold supplies to the government. There was an overlap of the Beck and Anton Chico grants, and Gross-Kelly got that overlap, besides twenty-four thousand acres that they bought

116

down there. And they used to raise a lot of oats up in Sapello Canyon and the Mora Valley and all over. They'd raise five million pounds of oats up there, besides wheat and corn.

They had three flour mills up in Mora, and we had one here, and they had one in Sapello. Those people up in Mora all farmed, and they used wagons. We used to sell a carload of wagons every month. They didn't have fences down on the plains at first, and we sold a lot of wire; we used to get in a couple of carloads of wire every month.

And we used to furnish groceries to stores down below and up in Mora and Springer and clear down to Liberty, pretty near the Texas line, down on the Canadian. Everything in those places came from Gross-Kelly and Company, you might say. We did the storaging and forwarding, too. Whiskey, for instance. We'd get in five or six barrels of whiskey for somebody clear down at Liberty. Then he'd send after it with a wagon. Well, by the time it got down there in a wagon it was pretty well aged. For they didn't have any roads then, just wagon trails.

We used to get all the wool from the plains and from up there in Mora County. We shipped to Boston. I know one car of wool we shipped, and a Negro got in there between the sacks and suffocated. I don't know where he got in—Kansas City or Chicago likely—but he got a ride clear to Boston. And they wrote back, wanting to know how much we were going to charge them for the black wool.

We got our supplies mostly from Kansas City and St. Louis. And we used to have up to fifty wagons camped in our yard every morning, especially on a Tuesday. They'd come from Mora on Monday, and you couldn't travel much faster than fifteen miles a day. So they'd camp at the Sapello River and get in here Tuesday morning early.

The Santa Fe might have a contractor around here, straightening out a little curve—a quarter of a mile long or something like that. But it'd take 'em six months, and they'd order a thousand pounds of oats. So we'd send the sacks up to the different merchants and tell 'em that we wanted the oats down by Tuesday morning. And we'd have a railroad car setting there, and all we'd have to do was to unload it from the wagons and weigh the oats and put 'em in the car. Then the railroad would ship it up to Azul, Onava, or maybe up to Springer and them places. So the merchants did a good business up there, and a lot of 'em got rich.

Gross-Kelly was in the lumber business, too, selling railroad ties and mining props. And there were all kinds of sheep around Las Vegas, and we had four scouring mills here. They brought wool up from Roswell and clear from Texas up here to scour and ship to the East, but sometimes they shipped the wool with the grease [the wool fat and suint which form sizable components of wool before scouring]. If it was light, they'd ship it that way, but heavy wool as a rule they'd scour. Oh, we used to ship five million pounds of wool here, and I'm just talking about Gross-Kelly's figures, for there were other shippers.

Las Vegas was a lively town then. I remember one day—it was my birthday, and I'd gone down to the drugstore to get some ice cream, for my mother was having some kids in for ice cream and cake—and as I was coming back from the store Dick de Graffenried came up on horseback. And he parked right in front of the Opera Bar; they had two posts and a pole across them, where they'd tie the horses.

No, De Graffenried was in there; he was running the saloon, I guess. I was just a little kid of six then, so 'm not sure. And Billy Green came up and tied his horse there. And before I got up to the Buckingham Hotel, where the bar was, Billy Green came out, doubled up. De Graffenried'd shot him and hit him right in the brisket; and the bullet went right through the Presbyterian church, too. So I dropped the ice cream and went home without it, you see.

I think the fight was caused by jealousy more than anything else. They were both tough, and I don't think they wanted to take anything from each other. I don't think there was any real feud between De Graffenried and Green.

There was five of the Green boys: John, Ely, Al, Zach, and Billy. Billy and Zach were both punchers. Billy'd been punching cows on the place of a fellow called Lynch, but then he got married and started a little restaurant on Bridge Street [the chief business street of Old Town]. And while he was there, he got in

118

trouble with the Silva people [the gang, active in the 1880's and '90's, led by Vicente Silva] and the White Caps [rival brigands of the same vintage].

You see, a judge in New Town—Judge Thomas Smith—had deputized Billy, and he was acting as a police officer. The judge told him, "When I send you after a man, I want you to bring him back, and it's up to you whether he's dead or alive." Billy brought in some alive and some dead, and that's why he was in trouble with these gangs.

One time the justice of the peace of Old Town, who was in with the gangs, was trying to arrest Billy Green. There had been a law passed in the territory allowing JP's to issue warrants for arrest, regardless of the sheriff; and they could appoint their own deputies if they wanted to. So these deputies were about to arrest Billy, when a friend sent a message to Judge Smith in New Town; and the judge asked the help of some troops that were in Las Vegas. There was a railroad strike on the Santa Fe, and they had some troops stationed in back of the freight office.

Just when the deputies from Old Town thought they were ready to take Billy, a squad of soldiers arrived. Then Lopez, the Old Town marshal said, "You have no authority here."

And a young lieutenant who was in charge said to one of his boys, "Take care of him, Charlie."

Then Charlie used the butt of his rifle to ram Lopez, and that was the end of the argument. So Billy Green got out of that.

But he had an even closer shave. Pablo Herrera got killed west of the courthouse. He was an outlaw who'd come to town demanding merchandise from different people. And he had Billy Green down, by George, and he was going to stab him, you see. But this Nicasio Baca was the sheriff then, and by George, he shot Herrera just when he was about to bring his knife down, and that was the only thing that saved Billy Green.

His luck ran out, though, finally. There were seventeen convicts escaped from the Colorado penitentiary at Trinidad in 1899, and they sent here for Billy Green to go up there and help round 'em up. But the convicts caught him and killed him and burnt him.

But nobody knew about that for a while. That's why Ely Green, Billy's brother, went up there to see what he could find out.

119

You see, they didn't know what happened to Billy Green and the rest of the posse that went after the convicts; but later they found out by a pile of ashes and human bones. And there was a ring or watch or something that identified Billy.

A fellow called A. C. Smith used to make the Mora territory as a salesman. And years later he and a state cop—they used to have state cops that dressed in gray uniforms—went into Tom Walton's hotel, that used to be quite a place up there, to get something to eat. The cop went to take off his coat and hang it up in the hall; and this Oviedo Martinez, who was one of the fellows that escaped from the Colorado penitentiary, was looking in Walton's window. Smith noticed him while the state cop was hanging up his coat.

When he did that, a pair of handcuffs dropped out of his pocket. And when Martinez saw 'em, he beat it, and I don't believe they ever did catch him. I knew Oviedo Martinez myself, because I used to be a pretty good friend of his cousin, Felix Martinez, and sometimes Oviedo would drop in while I was there.

Colonel Fountain and his boy got killed down in southern New Mexico seventy or so years ago, and by George, they don't know who killed 'em yet. [Appointed a special prosecutor in a district rife with rustlers, Albert J. Fountain and his nine-year-old son, Henry, disappeared in 1896, leaving no discovered trace.] Or they do know who killed Fountain, but it's too late to go to bed, as the old saying went. Although some don't believe it, most thought it was Oliver Lee that did it.

I met him in 1901, I guess it was. My brother and I and my younger sister went down to Las Cruces to stay with my aunt, my mother's sister; and Oliver Lee was down there at Three Rivers, where my Uncle Charlie Armijo had a ranch. I was out there, hanging on Charlie Armijo's coat tail; and he had his goats in one corral, and calves in another, cows in another, and horses in another. And there was an old goat that had his tail sticking out just about two inches between the logs of the corral.

Oh, the distance from where we were standing might have been twenty feet or so; and Lee said, "Charlie, let me shoot that goat's tail off."

Charlie said, "Go ahead."

120

And, by George, Lee cut that goat's tail off just as pretty with a pistol, you see. That soaked into me, and I'll never forget it.

I used to meet Oliver Lee in Santa Fe; I had a lot of relatives there. After I got to be twenty or twenty-one years old, I went up to him once—it was when they had Governor Otero's Rough Rider banquet. Oliver Lee was there, and, by God, he knew me! He said, "Ain't you the young fellow that was down at Three Rivers with Charlie Armijo?"

I said, "Yes." And after that he was very nice to me, but everybody says he killed Colonel Fountain.

Those fellows down there were all cattle thieves. And the big men got rich at it, only they couldn't prove it on 'em. The Colonel was on his way back to Las Cruces from Lincoln [the county seats of Lincoln and Dona Ana counties, respectively], where he'd gotten indictments against something like thirty people. Maybe Oliver Lee didn't kill him himself, but he could have had men that killed him; an article I read one time said there were three men in on it. And they killed the Colonel's boy, too.

Lee was tried and acquitted, but he always expected somebody to try to kill him in revenge for what they thought he'd done, whether he did it or not; and to his dying day he wore a six-shooter wherever he went. A man that called on him at his ranch said that when he knocked on the door, he could see a hall through a little window in the door. And when Lee stepped out of a room into the hall, he didn't walk down the middle but on one side of it. And when he opened the door, he had a six-shooter in his hand.

That's about all I can think of but, well, Governor Otero, I think it was, though I don't think he was governor yet, once told me about a doctor in Santa Fe that was called out to an Indian village for something. And about the time he'd attended to that, he was told of an Indian woman that was about to have a baby. So the doctor delivered the child, and it was a red-headed baby. And he asked this woman if her husband had red hair.

And she said, "I don't know—he had his hat on."

13
A METROPOLIS IN THE BUD

"The Republican, in the old days, of course, had a job shop, and that paid the way."

CHARLES A. STAUFFER, Phoenix, Arizona

As a youngster Mr. Stauffer came to the Phoenix area when Arizona's capital was no more than an isolated rural village. Almost as numerous as the whites, the local Indians had in theory been confined to reservations but in practice ranged with a freedom which suggested they themselves were unaware of the fact. As for the farms which formed the area's basic industry, they were being wrenched one by one from grassland and forest purlieus, irrigated by a river controlled by no more than the brush dams which each new freshet swept away.

Now that same region is a diversely industrial one, with a population of almost a million. Among the very few observers throughout the extent of this stupendous transformation, Mr. Stauffer was peculiarly qualified to follow developments because of his chosen profession of newspaper administration. An unusual feature of the history of Phoenix is that two of its pioneer journals faced down all subsequent competition and remain the city's only dailies. And it was with Mr. Stauffer at the helm that they eventually came to flourish under one management.

How did a fledgling city pave its streets? What was the chief commodity sold? Why were longhorns banned from local rodeos? All these things are touched upon by a man who early recognized the value of pioneer recollections and has done more than his share toward preserving them. With this phase of his activities, indeed, his reminiscences begin.

HIS CONTRIBUTION

I frequently had occasion to meet old-timers who had been here in the '70's, and some in the '60's, when this region was first being settled. Naturally I would, being in the newspaper business. I was business manager of the Arizona *Republican* before being made general manager in 1921, and publisher in 1929.

During the first World War I was a great friend of an old pioneer who came here in the '70's; his name was Holmes. I had met him frequently on a stagecoach, back when that was the only means of transportation between here and Mesa and Tempe.

As business manager, I didn't think the paper could be put to bed if I wasn't there to check things. So I was always there after working hours for other people, the *Republican* being a morning paper; and old Holmes had a son who came in every day during the war, when, of course, people were anxious to know how things were going.

One day he began to talk with me about the old-timers who were beginning to pass away, and he said to me, "Why don't you get interviews with them? It's going to be too late, one of these days, to get the original stories of the experiences they've had."

As business manager, I wasn't quite in a position to direct editorial work. But when I stepped up to general manager in 1921, I arranged to do what we'd talked about by sending reporters to locate and talk to old-timers.

I worked with Mr. Dwight B. Heard, who was owner as-well-as publisher of the paper then, but whose office was not in the *Republican*'s plant, as he had other business interests. In one of our conferences I told him what we were doing in this way, and he said, "Charlie, let's have a reunion of the old-timers who are still well enough to get around."

So we started the Arizona Pioneers Reunion, holding the first one in 1921. They'd tell stories of old events, and of this murder and that murder; and we gathered those stories in a special section of the *Republican*'s issue of April 19, I think it was. There were six or eight solid pages of stories by the oldest living pioneers.

Every year, for many years after that, we did the same thing; we had storytelling hours and reporters interviewing old-timers. It seems to me that as late as 1947 we had one man who'd been a beaver trapper. And we had old stage drivers from the days when there'd been no other kind of transportation.

But they didn't always agree with each other at these reunions.

125

Sometimes after one man had told a story, another would say, "You're mistaken about that; I was *there*." Things like that, you know.

And now I'm an old-timer being interviewed myself. My parents came here in 1892 and landed in Glendale. They came from a little place in Kansas called Sedgwick. I was born on a ranch near there—my people were farmers—in 1880, so I was nearly twelve when we got here in February of '92.

I happen to have this slip about the growth of the population, starting with the census of 1890, which was only two years before I came here. Phoenix only had a little over three thousand people in the city limits, but, of course, they were much smaller than they are now. But the figures for Maricopa County tell the real story. With Tempe, Mesa, and Glendale, as well as Phoenix, the county had less than eleven thousand people. And the total for Arizona Territory was but 56,620.

There were lots of Indians around, when I got here. I have this picture, taken in 1895, of an Indian parade in Phoenix. As shown by this picture, what was interesting about the Indians at that time was that they all had long hair. An Indian was disgraced that had short hair, and it wasn't until some years later that they began cutting theirs.

We lived near the desert, when they were opening the country west of Phoenix, and the Indians would come there to run their horses. The Indians all had horses—the bucks particularly—and they'd be out with bows and arrows, and they'd chase rabbits. I never saw them kill one, but I suppose they did, as they were pretty smart with their bows and arrows.

I remember when all the land around our ranch in Glendale was gradually being put into cultivation. They'd put in wheat or barley for the first year or two; then they'd put in alfalfa as soon as they could, because it enriched the soil.

In the wheat fields particularly, the Indians would go out with their families in wagons. And when farmers were reaping the wheat, there'd be a lot knocked down and not picked up, when the harvesting machines turned corners. Then the Indians would pick up what the machines had left and load it into their wagons. And

126

they'd take the wheat and trade it for watermelons. That new soil grew wonderful watermelons, and the Indians loved them.

They'd go around to houses, halfway begging but more for curiosity than that, for they'd look in houses. I know they'd come up to our house and look in windows, and it would frighten my mother. But they were only curious, and I don't think settlers ever had any difficulties with those Indians. They were Pimas and Maricopas, and not like the Apaches.

The Indians liked to come to town, but Phoenix had a law that they had to be out of town by sundown. They used to come in from their reservations—they were all on reservations by that time—and sit down on the street in front of stores and sell their pottery and baskets.

There were lots of cowboys in town; this was quite a cowboy country, for there were cattle ranches all around, when Phoenix was first settled. And they had rodeos—horse races and cowboy events, but not by professionals.

When I was in Glendale, every boy had a saddle horse, and we boys would get together and come to Phoenix to see the rodeos. They had a racetrack where they held them, bordering Central Avenue and the Salt River. And I've seen them throw steers so hard that horns would fly up twenty feet in the air. That only happened with longhorns, so the legislature passed a law that they couldn't rope and throw longhorns; they had to use other kinds of cattle.

The reason they had so many cattle ranches hereabouts was that there used to be lots of good grass. And there used to be a lot of trees, too. Northwest of Glendale, between Agua Fria and New River, there isn't a tree now. But there was then a solid mesquite forest there, two or three miles wide.

Mesquite was wonderful wood for fuel, and our firewood was almost entirely mesquite, though some cottonwood was used, too. A great many Mexicans made a living out of the mesquite forest by cutting mesquite for firewood and hauling it on their rickety wagons. And then they'd go up and down the streets yelling, "*Leña! Leña!*"

When the farms were being laid out and opened up, there was a great mass of cottonwoods along the Salt River. People would go down there and get cottonwood posts about six or eight inches thick and put them in the ground when the sap was not flowing. And those cottonwood posts—they weren't cuttings—put out roots and grew into trees. Nearly all the borders of the old ranches were marked by cottonwood trees that were put in as posts.

In this dry country they couldn't have farmed without the river, of course, but it could cause trouble, too. Before we had regular dams to control it, farmers would build brush dams to divert the water into the irrigation canals, but every spring they would be swept away and would have to be rebuilt.

The river would run over its banks in places every year, but Phoenix was only bothered by the great flood of '91, when the waters came up to the Commercial Hotel. Some of the best houses in Phoenix were under water then, and East Lake Park was flooded.

That was a great place, you know. The flood was a year before my time; but there was a covered natatorium, where I used to swim, and there was a summer theater and other amusement spots.

In January of 1897 I left Glendale and went to Mesa, on the other side of the Salt River, to work on a ranch. Some friend said there was a job open, if I wanted to go over there, and I needed money to pay my way through the Territorial Normal School at Tempe. So I wrote and said I was a grown man. I wasn't quite seventeen, but I'd been on a ranch all my life and knew the work.

The place where I went was a regular one-hundred-and-sixty-acre farm south of Mesa, and I remember going over to take this job. We went over in a buckboard to what was called Wilson's Crossing. That was about halfway between here and the stock-yards [or about half the some thirty miles between Glendale and Mesa]. We stayed all night there, and the next morning we drove the horse and buckboard from there over to Tempe.

The road was no road to speak of. Outside of Phoenix none of the roads had any foundations, and when it rained, there'd have to be five or six roads going to the same places.

This one ended at a saloon called the Foreman House. From

there we drove down along the river to Hayden's Crossing, right where the present highway bridge is. And when we got there, we drove the buckboard on a wooden flat, you know.

The way they crossed the river was on a platform half as big as this house—maybe it was twenty-five or thirty feet long and ten feet wide. And they had a cable across the river at Hayden's ferry, attached to concrete monuments. The current supplied the power, and they had levers that angled the ferry upstream part of the way across and downstream the rest of it.

That was the only ferry, and the river wasn't crossable by it all the year around. Because there were no dams to control the spring freshet, we couldn't cross from some time in April or May until the water lowered again in June.

In the fall of 1897, which was the year they changed the course from three to four years, I went to Tempe [or the normal school there, now Arizona State University]. Tempe then had a population of two or three thousand, of whom a third lived in what was called Mexican Town [originally a separate settlement known as San Pablo]. There were no dormitories, so four or five of us bached together.

When I was in school there, a man named Curtin Miller owned the Tempe *News;* and for some months he had me come down and swing the crank of the press, as he turned out his little paper. Later I worked in the Tempe agency of the old Phoenix *Herald*. When the *Republican* bought out that paper in '99, they gave me the circulation agency, and that was the real start of my newspaper career.

The *Herald* was started by the McClintocks, and the Phoenix *Gazette* [like the *Republic,* as the *Republican* is now called, a surviving pioneer newspaper] by the McNeils. It's queer, but they were both from San Francisco.

I was very friendly with Colonel James McClintock, who was a writer [a valuable history of Arizona was his chief work] and a correspondent for the Los Angeles *Times* for a good many years. His brother started the *Herald* in '78 or '79, and the Colonel came to Phoenix because his brother was here, I guess. He graduated at the Territorial Normal School in the first class [that of 1887], and he was a reporter on the *Salt River Valley News*, now the *Tempe Daily News*.

The *Republican* was founded in 1890 by a political group at the state house, or territory house, as it was then. They had a race to see who would set the first column—it was all done by hand then—and McClintock won.

After I graduated from the Normal School in 1901, I was the *Republican*'s circulation manager. We had a circulation of two thousand and four carriers. There were only three people regularly in the office: the secretary, the bookkeeper, and a man at the counter to answer questions and take classified ads. I solicited advertising, as well as circulation, and got the carriers out in the morning.

When I started to work in Phoenix, the office was in a one-story building with an iron ceiling and roof; and as there were no coolers, the heat in the summer was something. But we were healthy and used to it.

The only air cooling we had then was in the restaurants. The principal restaurants were run by Chinese, and they had fans strung across the rooms and motors to work them. They'd have half a dozen curtains six feet long and several feet wide that the motor would wave, and you'd hear, "Whush, whush."

In the summer nobody slept indoors before they had coolers. You couldn't sleep indoors, though we tried all kinds of things, like hanging up wet blankets and running electric fans against them. Some houses had screened dormitories on top of them, and you can still find an occasional old house with one of those. But most people didn't have them, and we—women as well as men—took our beds out into the yard.

It was perfectly safe. People were safe on the streets then, too. There were no robberies, and as nobody had any idea that there would be, we never locked our doors.

There were almost no industries, you know. In all the villages, like Phoenix, Tucson, and Prescott, the main business was saloons. And every saloon had gambling in the rear. But gambling was not illegal; Phoenix was an open town. So all the saloons had roulette

130

wheels, and up front there'd be a ham and bread, and you could help yourself, if you bought a ten-cent glass of beer—or I guess it was five cents then.

There were cement sidewalks, but for many years we didn't have a foot of paving on the streets. In 1909 I was elected to the City Commission, and I represented it on the Citizens' Paving Committee. Mr. Heard was chairman of the Paving Committee, and he and another man and I went to San Bernardino, California, where they were making paving that was used in some of the larger cities. It was hot over there, so we thought that we'd find about the same summer conditions as in Phoenix.

What they had was called oil paving, a coat of surface-saturating oil that might have been two or three inches thick. It would buckle in the kind of heat we have here, though; but in El Paso somebody had invented a process of grinding up certain types of stone and mixing them with tar. That paving was maybe three and a half or four inches thick; and it answered our problem, for some that was laid then is still in use.

We started the paving at Third and Washington. As it wasn't a municipal project, we laid it according to the order in which the contributing property owners had signed the authorizing petition for paving. Colonel McClintock's place was served first. But there was one man who didn't sign the petition, so there was a big break in the paving in front of his place.

I forgot to say that the *Republican*, in the old days, of course had a job shop, and that paid the way. For the paper itself was often in the red. And we still had the job shop when Mr. Heard bought the *Republican* in 1912 and took me in as business manager.

That was the year that Arizona became a state, and governors were elected instead of being appointed by Washington. As a very prominent citizen, Mr. Heard ran for governor a couple of times on the Republican ticket, though Arizona was then a very heavily Democratic state.

There was an old man named John O. Dunbar, who was the owner of the *Gazette* in the early days but who later started what he called *Dunbar's Weekly*. I think he came here from Tombstone [where he'd been co-owner of the *Epitaph*-opposing *Nugget* in

131

that silver town's violent era]. Dunbar was a Democrat, and he didn't care what he said. When Mr. Heard ran for governor as a Republican, Dunbar fought him the whole time and damned him for everything he did or said. Well, it was politics, and he was running a political paper.

The funny thing was that our job shop printed it; and, of course, Mr. Heard owned the shop along with the rest of the plant. He was a wonderful man and never felt bad about being attacked, though Dunbar would get pretty sharp, that old man would.

It worried me more than it did Mr. Heard, and one day I asked him, "Do you want to keep right on printing his paper?"

And he said, "Oh, sure; it's going to be printed somewhere, so we might as well be the ones that get paid for it."

14
THE LAW AS ADMINISTERED

"During the trial I kept the gun in my pocket, and I demonstrated to the jury with it."

CLARK J. GUILD, Carson City, Nevada

When Judge Guild was nearing the end of his long career on the bench, he was startled to find that Carson City's historic mint— dating from the years when neighboring Virginia City was a national byword as a silver producer—was about to be sold by the United States Government. The purchaser of the monument turned out to be a group of which the Judge was quarterback, determined to use it as the previously lacking home for Nevada's pioneer mementoes and other exhibits illustrative of its history. The outcome of what began as a flash of intuition is the fine Nevada State Museum, of which Judge Guild is still a daily on deck officer.

In back of this enthusiasm for the promotion of his state culturally lies a spread of here recounted activities in other lines. He grew up in one of the bustling, if now largely dormant towns, of which fabulous Gold Canyon was the hub. A precocious mining venture showed the bent for engineering, albeit along other lines, which he originally meant to exploit. To float his schooling in that direction, he worked for railroads in several Western states until disaster waylaid him in one of them and insisted on a career calling for less physical action.

Then came the blend of politics and laws which occupied the time intervening between his railroad days and his State Museum ones. A district attorney part of the time, the Judge tells of murder cases won and lost—and of what happened when Big Bill Haywood fell afoul of a small-town marshal.

HIS CONTRIBUTION

I was born in Dayton, Nevada, in 1887. My father and mother were both immigrants who crossed the plains in the early days. They met in Dayton, married there, and had eleven children.

134

I mostly grew up in Dayton; I spent all my boyhood there. It was a mill town and lumber-distribution point. They brought the wood that was cut in the mountains down the Carson River in the spring of the year to Dayton. They took it out of the river there and hauled it to the mines of Virginia City, Gold Hill, and Silver City. And from those points they hauled ore to the mineral mills.

They processed both silver and gold there. The process was stamp mills plus plates and pans. The ore was crushed, and the particles were flushed down through copper plates, on which they poured quicksilver to catch the gold as it floated by. Well, some particles would get away in this process, and the remainder would go into pans, where it was stirred around in a fashion that would gather in these finer particles of gold. In the bottoms of the pans were also plates to catch the even finer flakes of gold.

The process worked with silver as well as gold. Then in later years they had cyanide pans to do over these fines—they would get more of the finer gold that way.

My father was one of the amalgamators of what was known as the Rock Point Mill for many years. In 1893, during Cleveland's depression, most of the mills were shut down, so many of those mill men went placer mining. They prospected along the Carson and up Gold Canyon—leading from Dayton to Silver City and Virginia City—where the early immigrants discovered the placer which finally led to the discovery of the Comstock Lode.

Most of the mill men went mining with the old-fashioned sluice box. And my brother and I, who lived across the creek from where some of them were prospecting, decided we'd do a little mining, too. An old blacksmith there in Dayton made us a windlass, a carpenter made us a sluice box with riffles, and the miners staked us to a little quicksilver, so we felt all set.

We had a four-by-four shaft down about fifteen feet, a little ways from where we lived, when Mother come over one day to see what was going on. My brother Henry was down in this hole, and I and a friend of ours were on the windlass. She almost fainted, and when Dad come home that night, she said, "Do you know what these boys are doing?" Then she told him and said, "One of 'em's going to get hurt if a rock falls on him, and I won't stand for it any longer."

Well, he went over to the shaft and looked around and said, "I'll fix 'em up, Mama; I'm going to let 'em come over here in the yard and dig a shaft where you can watch 'em."

That was all right with my brother Henry and I and our friend, so we pitted the shaft out in the backyard, where we had our outhouse, a Chic Sales. So we got a six-by-eight bore down about twelve feet, where we thought the pay gravel would be; then we were going to move our sluice boxes and start processing. But when we went to school one day, Dad got some help and moved the shanty over on top of our hole.

Oh, we were a couple of mad boys! I cried, and so did my brother Henry. But Dad said, "Well, now, boys, you did a good job, and I don't want you to lose by it. I'm going to give you three dollars apiece for your work." So that pretty well satisfied us.

But I liked fieldwork, and I wanted to be a civil engineer. So I started courses at the University of Nevada [located at Reno], but after going there about a year, I was out of money, so I went railroading to earn more.

I went to work for the Carson and Colorado narrow-gauge line; I first was firing, and then I was a brakeman. I was brakeman on the route that standardized the narrow gauge all the way from Mound House to Hawthorne. I left that line to go on the location work on the Western Pacific Railroad, which I wanted to do, because I thought it would be good experience for an engineer. I worked from Battle Mountain east to Beowawe and west of Battle Mountain to Golconda.

We were then transferred over the Fredonia Pass in California, where the Big Meadows now are. There we got snowed out of work in December—I had missed that semester at the university— and as I had a sister living in Idaho, I decided to go up there during the next few months and come back to the university in September.

So I started braking on a shortline running east and west out of Pocatello. That went from Pocatello east to Soda Springs, where it connected with the Union Pacific running into Ogden. And it went west to Huntington, Oregon, through Glens Falls and that territory.

136

In 1908 I was on the work trains that built the yard extension from Twin Falls to Buhl, west of Twin Falls. In early July, I was acting as rear brakeman, and they were sending us a large number of cattle cars to take up what we called the Shoshone Branch on the Oregon shortline. And one day we were sidetracked at American Falls on account of a train.

It used to be customary to get one of the operators at the depot to close the gate behind a train when it went out so it could get a run up the hill across the big bridge at American Falls. But I didn't know that, and I didn't realize our train wasn't going to wait for me to close the gate until it got halfway by me. Then I waited to jump for the caboose, but unfortunately I caught the head of the caboose instead of the rear end. It threw me under the truck and crushed my leg.

I was taken to the hospital at Salt Lake City, and they had to amputate above the knee. And one day Mr. Bagby, the general counsel of the Union Pacific, came to the hospital and said, "Young man, what do you want to do now?"

"Well," I said, "my career is through, I guess. I wanted to be a civil engineer."

He said, "Why don't you study law? You've got a good head on you."

I said, "What do you know about it?"

"Well," he said, "you're always reciting to these fellows here in the ward; I know what's going on. And they all tell me that you're a good orator. I'm going to give you a job in the claims department, and you can study law under me three nights a week."

When I got out of the hospital, I decided to go home for a little visit with my parents. Dayton was then the county seat, and I had a brother-in-law that was running a newspaper there, the old *Lyon County Times*, that's now the *Mason Valley News* at Yerington. He was chairman of the county Republican Party; and though nothing was said to me while I was in Dayton, three or four days after I got back to Salt Lake City he wired me, "You have been nominated on the Republican ticket for Auditor and Recorder of Lyon County. Will you accept?"

I took it in to Mr. Bagby, and he just threw up his hands. "Oh,

137

Clark, *don't* get into politics. You're a young man, and you'll make good in law. Aren't you happy here?"

I said, "Yes, I am, sir."

But about an hour afterward he come back where I was and said, "I've been thinking about that. You go home and run for that office. If you're elected, you can still study law with your district attorney and others back there. If you're not elected, come back here, and we'll go on as before."

So I cast my first vote in Dayton for myself as Auditor and Recorder of my county in 1908. Luckily I was elected, and I studied law, too. I recited law three nights a week to a man who was formerly president of Baldwin University in Ohio and who come out to Yerington—the county seat had been moved from Dayton to Yerington by then.

He was the parson of a Methodist church who'd been admitted to law in Ohio. I sang in the choir—I love to sing—and one day he come to the office and said, "I want to refresh myself on law so I can be admitted to the bar in Nevada. Why not come over to the parsonage three or four nights a week and study there?" I did, and I was admitted April 6, 1914.

A couple of years later I was elected district attorney for eight years, and after that I was elected district judge. I'd served twenty-nine and a half years when I resigned. I had a year and a half to go; but I had five counties, and it was just too much for one man. I had Storey, Ormsby, Lyon, Douglas, and Churchill counties—one judge taking care of them all—and I held court in every one of those counties every day of the week.

During the depression I had all the closed banks in my court here in Carson City, but it's quite a long story, going back to years before World War I. The first financial trouble that we had here in Nevada was the State Bank and Trust Company in 1907. That was a receivership that lasted about six or eight years, and the poor damned depositors only got about fifteen cents on the dollar. The history of it was that the building and Exchange Bank and the State Bank and Trust Company here in Carson City had branches in Goldfield and Tonopah, which were on the boom in those days.

I don't know that it was mismanagement altogether. But when they started banks in Goldfield and Tonopah, too, it drew away

138

from their local trade, so they didn't have much left to go on here in the way of depositors. The real cause of the failures of the State Bank and Trust Company and the Building and Exchange Bank was that while they were stretching resources too thin, other banks had sprung up in Tonopah and the other mining camps of Nevada.

It was during the boom days down there, and they had labor troubles in Goldfield; they had to bring in troops and so on. The I. W. W. [Industrial Workers of the World] moved in, and they caused a lot of trouble, because the miners coming out of the mines were compelled to change their workclothes [for more on this subject see contribution of Mrs. Miles, number 16] and walk through a big open space and put on their streetclothes. They objected, as they were highgrading [pocketing rich chunks of ore]. Or most of 'em were.

The mine-owners put a stop to it, but I. W. W.'s got pretty vicious, and they had to run 'em out of the state. That was Big Bill Haywood's outfit [for more on Haywood, see Dr. Catlett's contribution, number 15]. He was astir in Nevada, and I had an experience with him myself.

While I was district attorney of Lyon County, he come in to what was known as the Ludwig Mining District in that county; it was a copper-mining vicinity, and a smelter was running there. He started to stir up some trouble, but the chief of police of Yerington arrested him, and Haywood sent for me.

I told him, "I can't do you any good. I'm district attorney of this county, and as you were arrested by town police on no charge that's been referred to me, I have nothing to do with the case. I can't be your attorney, and I'm not your prosecutor, either."

But things happened, and I'll never forget this as long as I live. I had a neighbor who was my wife's uncle, that lived a block from where I did. I was downtown that evening and things were awful quiet. There was nobody in front of the drugstore and in places where fellows would sit on porch steps, reminiscing. And this fellow Archer walked home with me that evening, clean to the corner.

So I said to my wife, "Something's going on here; I can smell it. Charlie Archer never walked clear home with me before."

The next morning Governor Boyle called me on the phone and

139

he said, "What went on there last night, Clark?" And when I told him that I didn't know, he said, "Well, if you'll find out, I'd appreciate it."

So I went downtown and went into the drugstore, where I found a very fine friend of mine, and I said, "Dan, what went on here last night?"

"Do you want to know as district attorney?"

"No, I just want to know as plain Clark J. Guild."

"Well, then I'll tell you," he said. "We decided that this man Haywood was unfavorable to the community, so we took him out of jail and sent him on his way. We got about halfway out to the Carson River, and one of the leaders stopped and said, 'This is far enough; let's string him up right here.' But we talked 'em out of it and took him clear over to Hazen and told him never to come back."

So I called Governor Boyle and told him what had happened, and he said, "Well, I'm awfully sorry. It's good to be rid of him; I wish he was in the Pacific Ocean. But I wanted to put somebody on his tail that'd make sure he'd keep agoing." Well, that was the end of Big Bill Haywood in the state of Nevada.

The governor was Emmett D. Boyle. He was a mining engineer, and his father before him. He operated in the mines of Gold Hill and Como, and afterward he was the General Manager and Superintendent of the Blue Stone Mine at Yerington. He was a brilliant man, and he was an honorable man, too: a wonderful character.

While I was district attorney, I had a couple of interesting murder cases. There was a man by the name of—Rice? That doesn't sound right, but he was a gunman in the Goldfield area who'd come from Arizona. And after the trouble he got into at Goldfield was settled, he went to the little town of Silver City and had a few drinks in a saloon there. And he got into a scuffle with a couple of young men—one of 'm named Calhoun.

The quarrel didn't amount to too much, but he went back to his hotel and perhaps had a few drinks by himself. Anyhow he come back to the saloon, and this boy Calhoun was laughing. And Rice—it was a short name like that—drew a gun and killed him; shot him in the back.

140

Well, they sent for the sheriff, and old Bill Donnelly, a deputy, come and got the man. And on the way to jail Bill said to him, "Did you have that gun on you when you had that first scuffle in the saloon?"

And the fellow said, "Sure I did."

What Bill was getting at was that it made the difference between premeditation—if he'd gone for the gun and come back with it—and shooting in sudden anger because he thought Calhoun was laughing at him when he come in the second time. But when Bill told me that, it gave me the biggest clue to prosecution I ever saw in my life. I investigated Rice's career—or whatever his name was—and found out that he'd been committed for rape in Arizona. I had a transcript of the case, so I really wanted to convict that man.

Pat McCarran, who was afterwards of the Supreme Court of the State of Nevada and a United States Senator, was hired to defend the fellow. During the trial I kept the gun in my pocket, and I demonstrated to the jury with it. I said, "I want you to take particular notice of this. He said in his testimony that he had his gun in his back pocket, if you'll remember. I'm going to show you that in a scuffle—and I'm not going to do any real scuffling—what would happen." And I walked to the jury box with this gun in my pocket and jumped up and down a few times, and out the gun dropped.

Then I turned around and looked at the fellow, and he was as pale as a ghost. I'd caught him in a lie.

But I only got a hung jury—two men hung up the jury. So we had a new trial, and he was convicted the second time. The jury just found him guilty of manslaughter, though; but anyhow he went to the penitentiary and served his time.

Another murder case I had was interesting, too. A man by the name of Farley, who lived in the town of Mason, killed under the unwritten law. There was a man that was a pimp for the line [marking off the red-light district] that got monkeying around with his wife; and Farley stood behind a power pole as the pimp was coming down the street and shot him.

Farley went to Grant's Pass, Oregon, but they caught him and brought him back, and the grand jury indicted him. I felt sorry for him. I thought he did the right thing and still do. But I couldn't tell the court and jury that; I had an oath to live up to and had to prosecute whoever the grand jury told me to. But just the same I used to send magazines down to the jail for Farley to read.

Well, the jury convicted him of second-degree murder and I called up Governor Boyle. World War I was on, and I said, "This man doesn't belong in the penitentiary. Governor, you're a native Nevadan, and so am I, and we don't think this fellow was wrong. Why don't you grant him a pardon and let him enlist in the United States Army—that's what he wants to do."

"By God, I'll do it if you say so, Clark!" And the governor did.

And that man went to France and lost his life in the war over there. But he was grateful. Before he left he came to see me and the tears rolled down his cheeks as he said, "I want to fight for my country—I want to redeem myself before God."

Well, there's the opposite of two cases: one that I didn't want to prosecute and won; and the other I was glad to prosecute and succeeded so little.

15

THE DAY OF THE DYNAMITERS

"Sheriff Robertson said he wouldn't resign, until he noticed somebody had a rope."

MALLORY CATLETT, Denver, Colorado

The life of a man committed to office work, in the West of the nineteenth century's salad days, could be as replete with rugged action as that of any follower of outdoor trades—rustling and general banditry included. As a young man, newly certified as a dentist, Dr. Catlett discovered as much, while practicing in the most prosperous and rampageous of Colorado's gold camps.

Among those present when bullets featured disputes between management and labor, he here displays a memory of the action as vivid as it is precise. Drafted to assist in the repair work, when high explosives strained the facilities of the local hospitals, he was able to be graphic about that aspect of the picture, too. His familiarity with the background of a trouble period, as-well-as with the personalities involved, are further contributions to a clear understanding of the Wild West, glimpsed from this unusual angle. His account of Cripple Creek's reddest-letter day is, indeed, a summation of it previously unmatched in print.

But Dr. Catlett's recollections of that gold field make it clear that all the violence didn't stem from labor troubles. They also include anecdotes of his professional life that were peaceful, if not necessarily routine. Some of these relate to Denver, where he attained eminence both as a practicer of dentistry and as a professor of it at that city's university. Retired from those activities, he yet functions in another important capacity.

HIS CONTRIBUTION

I was born on a plantation in Madison County, Mississippi, in 1876, and I landed in Colorado on October 1, 1900, coming directly to Denver. I got my degree of Doctor of Dental Surgery at the University of Denver in 1903 and practiced for sixty years.

About the time I was finishing dental school I became acquainted with a man from Leadville named A. B. Hunt. Originally he was a mule-skinner who hauled ore from the mines to the mint here. He and his brother-in-law, Trimble, made money out of a mine and organized the Carbonate National Bank; a very strong bank then, though it's no longer in business.

Hunt came to Denver because he was having trouble with his eyes. He was at St. Luke's Hospital, where my little sister was his special nurse, and I met him then. He seemed interested in me, and he knew a lot about the South. He once asked, "Did the panic of 1893 affect the South?"

I said, "Mr. Hunt, I never heard of that until I came to Colorado in 1900. There was a severe panic in every Southern state in every year since the War between the States, and we couldn't tell the difference between one year and the next."

He said Leadville would be a good place for me to practice, as there were only two dentists, and I could get five to ten dollars a day just by patroling the gambling houses and saloons for clients. But I told him I'd already arranged for an office in Denver.

Then he asked, "Have you money to buy all the necessary equipment?"

I said, "No, but I have some equipment, and I can arrange to get credit for what else I want."

He asked, "How much money will it take?"

Well, there's nothing like now. I stuck my neck out and said, "Five hundred dollars."

He said, "That isn't enough; you ought to have a few hundred dollars to tide you over the starting months. You may not be as busy as you think you're going to be at first."

Well, my sister handed him his checkbook, and he wrote me a check for a thousand dollars. He said, "Go on down to the National Bank of Commerce and ask for Dr. Dugan."

Dugan was a Leadville physician who was cashier of that bank, and Hunt called him and said, "There's a young man on the way down with my personal check for a thousand dollars. Let him have the money." And he said to me, "You'd better deposit that money in the bank. That's too much cash for a young fellow to be carrying around."

Well, within a year I paid him the last dollar. Of course, I worked during my vacation and did a little bushwhacking, as we used to call moonlighting. Then my business went well, because I had patients lined up that my brother-in-law, who was a physician, attended to.

I cherish a little note in Hunt's handwriting, complimenting me on my thrift. You don't hear much about him now, but he established a foundation to help the unemployed. Now neither Hunt nor Trimble had any heirs, and on the Hunt Foundation you'll see the name of a trustee he appointed. So I have no regrets about coming to Colorado.

Anyhow I began practice in Denver, and one morning, early in my career, I got a phone call from the Brown Palace Hotel. The clerk said, "There's a crazy man here—or he acts that way—who says he has a toothache. He says there was a dentist in New York that treated his tooth, but he didn't want to extract it, because it might be infected."

Well, extracting teeth under all conditions was the specialty I'd been trained for. So I said, "Have a bellboy bring him to my office. I'll have some breakfast and will come right down."

A large, fine-looking man came in. And when I pulled the tooth, the pus rolled out, so he collapsed from lack of tension. I put him in the restroom, and about noon—he hadn't had any sleep for two nights—he came to and asked, "What time is it, son?"

I said, "It's twenty minutes to twelve."

He said, "My God! I was supposed to have a meeting with the Board of Directors of the Great Western Sugar Company. My name's Havemeyer." [Henry Osborne Havemeyer, founder in 1891 of the American Sugar Refining Company.]

And one noon, as I was just going to lunch, I got a call from a Dr. Watson, who said, "There's a gentleman here who wants a tooth extracted."

So a big young man came in with a bodyguard, and the bodyguard came right into the operating room. I told him to stay out, but he wouldn't mind me.

With him looking on, I extracted the tooth, and the young man asked, "How much do I owe you?"

146

I said, "Five dollars. Can I have your name for my records?"

And he said, "My name is Harry K. Thaw" [the wealthy murderer, in 1906, of the celebrated architect Stanford White].

Actually I had two sisters who were nurses in St. Luke's Hospital. One of them married the physician I mentioned; and when he went up to Victor, Colorado, in the Cripple Creek district, I followed along.

Cripple Creek was a hard-rock-mining camp spread over six square miles, served by three railroads and two high-powered lines. There were strikes and wars and dynamiting, and a lot of people were killed right around me. That was in 1904.

The ore mined in the district was shipped down to Colorado City, where the smelter was. The laborers in the smelter went on strike for higher wages, and to compel the owners to comply with an eight-hour-working-day law that had just been enacted. The men in both districts belonged to the Western Federation of Miners, so the ones in Cripple Creek went on a sympathetic strike to shut off the ore sent down to the mill.

But some miners kept working, and some came in from idle camps such as the ones in Idaho. Then there were farmers from the adjoining states of Kansas and Nebraska, where they had a pretty good complement of laborers. Of course, the union workers resented the strikebreakers, so there was trouble until the national guard was called in under the leadership of General M. Bell, a former Rough Rider. Teddy Roosevelt said that if he had an army composed of only one man, he wanted Sherman M. Bell, who was the hero of San Juan Hill.

Well, the strike went along, and for a while after that nothing happened. I was living with my brother-in-law, the physician, then; and one night the phone rang, about two o'clock, and the operator said there had been a terrible explosion at the railroad depot of Independence. It was on the train bringing men off the graveyard shift, and they were notifying all the physicians and surgeons in the area from as far away as Grand Junction.

There were fourteen people killed and forty-two injured. My brother-in-law said I had better go along, as I frequently gave anesthetics for emergency operations. I gave one man chloroform

147

—which was the only anesthetic we could use at nine thousand feet: ether was so volatile you couldn't find it—that two surgeons operated on. Dr. Cunningham amputated his right leg at the hip and Dr. Mackenzie the left leg below the knee.

Well, I gave anesthetics at the hospital till about one-thirty in the afternoon. Then I looked out the west window and saw a crowd that had gathered in a vacant lot there and went to see what was happening.

All the officers of Victor had been recalled. [Previous to the dynamiting, which had also blown up popular sympathy, the Western Federation of Miners had controlled Cripple Creek politically, so one reaction took the form of ousting town and county officials owing allegiance to the union.] Gibbons, who ran the Senate Saloon and Gambling House, was an alderman. Tom Callahan, a plumber, was an alderman. Jerry Halloran, a mule-skinner, was an alderman. And Mike Tobin, a bartender for old man Doucet, was an alderman. Because of suspected complicity with the dynamiters, they were all put in the hoosegow.

Sheriff Robertson said he wouldn't resign, until he noticed somebody had a rope. He later said, "That answer wasn't worth the contest."

Ed Bell, who was a brother of Sherman Bell, had been sworn in as sheriff. He made a little talk to the crowd; I guess there were about seventy-five there. "Go home and put up your arms," he said, "or I can't protect you."

One little squirt that I knew, Tommy McManus, said, "We don't need your protection; we'll protect ourselves."

Well, two men got on a big float there, standing by the right wheel. One was the district attorney of El Paso County, and the gist of his remarks was something like this: "The time has come when everybody who has a card in the Western Federation of Miners is an enemy of law and should be put over the hill."

That started the fireworks, and a couple of bullets were stopped by that wheel that the speaker and the district attorney of Teller County were standing by. The astute men disappeared. I don't know where they went, but they got off that wagon.

Let's see; I saw a billboard against a wall I could get behind, so I ran for it. A fellow stuck his head out and said, "There's no room back here, Mallory." This was Damon, the county clerk.

Well, the shooting stopped and I went back to the wagon. There was a man named McKean lying dead. There was a man shot above the kidney and paralyzed. There was a man who'd had his jaw shattered. And Spud Murphy, the fire chief, was writhing in pain.

The miners who'd fired went to Union Hall, on the seventh floor of a building. When they were ordered out they said, "Come and get us."

The hospital was on the fourth floor of a bank building nearby. I went up and brought the stretcher down and helped put a man on it that the gunmen were still beating. He was shot through the heart, and he was dead.

Because things had been quiet up to that day, most of the national guard had left, but some of the soldiers had remained. There were two in my office and two in the dressing room. And when I looked out toward the hollow square before Union Hall, I could see where others had cut loose on the building with thirty or forty Krag-Jorgensen rifles. The bullets'd go through the building, and they made a lot of flesh wounds.

The miners got a bellyful of that in a little while and stuck out a white flag. There were twenty-two of them wounded. Our hospital was the biggest one there, and we got about twelve of them.

I noticed one fellow; the seat of his pants was pretty bloody. They put him on a table and pulled his breeches down, and there was a hunk of flesh knocked out of each part of his rump. An orderly had a jar of iodine, and he sponged the raw wounds.

The fellow squirmed, and I said, "Tommy, it don't look like you protected yourself."

And he said, "Go to hell, you little scab son of a bitch!"

Well, the officials of the Western Federation of Miners—Charles H. Moyer, George A. Pettibone and Big Bill Haywood—were in the district, and they were charged with planning the dynamiting. They retained Harris, Hawkins, and Richardson from Denver, and Clarence Darrow came out from Chicago to assist them. He con-

149

vinced Judge Frost, of Victor, that the accused couldn't get a fair trial there. So they got a change of venue to Grand Junction, and after a short trial, they were acquitted.

Then a union man named Harry Orchard [who later confessed that he had dynamited the train at Independence] had a different idea. It seemed that Governor Frank Steunenberg of Idaho didn't stand in very good grace with the Western Federation of Miners. [Out of office by then, Steunenberg had earned the enmity of the Federation by asking Washington to send troops, when violence attended strikes in the Coeur d'Alene region in 1899.] So Orchard went to Lewiston and located Steunenberg's house; and as the governor went jauntily through its front gate, he was blown to smithereens.

Because he had been seen loafing around that gate, Orchard was arrested just as he was about to leave town. He was supplied with a high-powered legal staff, but they got up against a keen young district attorney named William E. Borah, who later went to the United States Senate for several terms. It was a long, vicious and acrimonious trial, but the jury finally returned a verdict of murder in the first degree.

There was no capital punishment in Idaho, so Orchard was sentenced to life imprisonment, after the high courts sustained the decision. The union's leaders were then brought from Denver and tried as accessories [in 1907], but they were again found not guilty.

Orchard could have been paroled two or three times; but he was afraid to leave prison because he might run across some of his old enemies, and they would cut his throat. He died in the penitentiary when eighty-eight.

To show why he was afraid, one man, who used to be marshal of Victor, returned to Denver, and his body was found out in an alley behind a hotel at Seventeenth and Arapahoe streets. That was about 1906, while the riot and all happened in 1904.

That wound up the Western Federation of Miners in the Cripple Creek district. They were about the same thing as the I. W. W.'s [The Industrial Workers of the World were organized by Haywood—whose activities are also cited in Judge Guild's contribution, number 14—in 1905]. Anyhow they were all rounded up, after the shooting I told about, and the country settled down.

I was up through the Cripple Creek district this year [1967] over the Fourth of July. There were millions of tons of waste and rock, and not a mine running.

The miners were paid in gold when I lived there; five-, ten-, and twenty-dollar pieces. Gold was twenty dollars and sixty-five cents an ounce. With that we had a national treasury surplus of twenty-two billion dollars. But Franklin Roosevelt put a stop to this. He ordered everybody in the nation who had any gold in his possession to turn it in. They built Fort Knox as a safe place to keep it, and they gave sixty-two cents in paper for it.

But I remember when I did a bunch of work for a big Swede who had a good mining lease at Victor. His bill was two hundred and ten dollars, and when it came due his wife gave me ten twenty-dollar gold pieces. It was the most money I'd ever held, and it was beautiful money, fresh from the Denver mint. It gave you a sense of security.

I practiced in Denver again after I came down here in 1907. I've been both secretary and president of our dental society. I was on the state board of examiners for dentists for six years. And I had the chair of dental pathology at the University of Denver for about eighteen years.

But it was quieter here than at Cripple Creek, where labor troubles weren't all that was going on. There were often four or five thousand dollars in gold on the gambling tables at Victor, where there were twenty-eight saloons that had roulette and crap tables.

Billy Sexton had a gambling house in Victor, and he or somebody in his crowd bought the old Down and Out Saloon—an old gambling house—to play a little dollar-limit poker. And they played there for about six months. Then one night two of them lingered a little longer, after the game broke up. And one said, "Henry, I haven't seen you win any money in this game."

And Henry said, "I haven't. Have you?"

And the first said, "No, and I think that old bewhiskered so and so is a crook."

So they watched Billy, and after a while they found him dealing from the bottom. The day of the funeral the priest was telling of what an exemplary character the deceased was, and that he never gambled and never drank and always gave his paycheck to his wife. So his widow jumped up and said, "Father, I don't believe you know who's in this box."

WOMEN OF THE FRONTIER

16

THE LAST BONANZA ERA

"You can't see one stick or stone today to let you know there ever was such a place."

MRS. MYRTLE TATE MILES, Reno, Nevada

On the staff of the Nevada State Historical Society, Mrs. Miles lived through many of the events she is now engaged in preserving for the record via the accumulation of period documents and testimony which include writings of her own. She was born when the towns which sprang from her state's first mining boom were still flourishing. She saw them flicker and fade—some of them to be for a time restored to health by the second wave of gold and silver excitement which the birth of the twentieth century bestowed on Nevada.

Of those new boom times Mrs. Miles was an active participant. She was in Tonopah and in even more glittering Goldfield in the days of their noisiest glory. When Manhattan began to rise above troved treasure, Mrs. Miles was among the stampeders. Then she saw all these, like the first generation of Nevada camps, subside from metropolitan promise to village pokiness—and in some cases to less than that.

All Western archaeology, as is now being realized, does not consist of finding the old abiding places of Indians. The science of investigating pioneer ghost camps is yet in its infancy; but the first step is the location of all-but-forgotten Ninevehs, among them being some whose story had the brevity demanded of wit. One of those engaged in this important work, as she here makes interestingly manifest, is Mrs. Miles.

HER CONTRIBUTION

I was born in Grantsville, Nye County, Nevada, in 1886. It was a mining camp discovered in 1863 or '64. It had quite a little boom at that time, and then it deteriorated. But in the 1880's it came back into prominence as a producer of gold and silver. That was true of

156

most of our camps that produced both gold and silver; and a great deal of money was taken out of the area at one time.

My father was a mail contractor—he had a contract from the government and ran mail and passenger stages. He had a stage route which ran from Austin to Grantsville; the distance was fifty miles at least and possibly farther. It was a day's journey by stage, and the mail stages usually traveled that distance in a day, with a change of horses midway.

The mail came by train as far as Austin in my time, but not when Grantsville was first discovered, because that was before the Central Pacific was built. In 1881 a spur railroad came to Austin from the Central Pacific called the Nevada Central. The mail was picked up at Austin and carried by stage to Grantsville, to the southwest, and to Belmont, a little to the southeast. To Belmont from Austin was nearly a hundred miles, and that was a two-day trip.

When I was three months old, we moved to Smoky Valley. The old station out there was named for my father: it was called Tate's. That was a stage station, and my father had a cattle ranch where he kept his horses, et cetera, across the valley.

Then there was a station which he established in 1886 for the purpose of putting in a branch stage line to Oval Canyon, five miles to the southwest of the Toyabe Mountains, where mining also had a little comeback at that time. It, too, had been a camp of the 1860's, and this little line that he put in from the station he'd built ran two and a half miles south to what is now known as Millet's. It connected with his main line between Austin and Belmont, which he ran for twenty-eight years.

My father's name was Thomas Tate. He was a Canadian who came to Virginia City in 1867 and traveled all over the West. He was in the boom days of Eureka and Pioche [silver camps, both established in 1870], and finally at Belmont and Austin. These were the county seats [although Austin is still one, Belmont was rated a complete ghost town by the census of 1960] of Nye and Lander, adjacent counties of central Nevada.

I went to a county school between our stage line and what is now known as the RO Ranch in Smoky Valley. It wasn't called

Millet's when I was a little girl; the Rogers' Place, we called it. Sometimes we rode horseback from our station to the school there, but usually we drove a team. We had a place to tie the horses, and a manger was there for the hay, which we took along in the back of the little wagon. And we took a big keg of water, and we poured that in a little trough to water the horses at noon. We had a well at the school, but it didn't prove to be very good, as the squirrels and chipmunks fell into it, and the lizards. So we carried our water.

The school didn't have many pupils. There was our own family, which would be my brother and I, and later my little sister. Of the Rogers family there were about five children; and then, in order to get a little federal money, we had a few Indians going to the school. They were Shoshones, and I think we had three Indian children—possibly four. The government would pay a certain amount for each Indian pupil that was taken by a school, for they were wards of the government, of course.

Otherwise our school was county-supported, and the teachers were mostly girls that were educated in the ungraded school at Belmont and took county examinations to become teachers. And some of them were very good indeed. They had no high school; it was an ungraded school that they attended, but what we would now call a grammar school.

For entertainment the families in the county visited back and forth. You'd load everybody in a wagon, and you'd go to stay for several days when you visited someone's ranch; and vice versa they'd come to visit you.

Then we had country dances. We'd go forty or fifty miles to a dance; but of course, if we did that we made arrangements to stay with friends or in a hotel overnight. That was frequently done, and all the children of any family went, too.

We lived at Tate's fifteen years, and moved to California in 1901. Our home there was at Big Pine, in Inyo County, right across the California line. But my father still had business interests in Nevada, and he came back when Tonopah was booming.

Then shortly after that rich ore was discovered in Manhattan Canyon, and the town of Manhattan was started. That was gold ore mostly, though there was silver, too.

My father moved there and had a livery stable; and my mother and I had a boarding house there for a little while, though it was quite accidental. Some of the people coming down from Austin were old friends that we had known years before. So we just got into this business more or less by accident, and we maintained it for five months, I think. Then we sold out during the boom.

My father built a house there, and we lived in it for several years. Then we returned to California, but after I was married, I came back to Manhattan and lived there for another couple of years. Manhattan was quite a producer at that time, and this was before placer was worked there; this was deep mining. A few years later they started to work placer in Manhattan Canyon, and that, too, was very profitable.

Manhattan is between Tonopah and Austin in the Toquima Range. *Toquima* is a Shoshone word. The Indian legend says it means "Black Backs" and was due to the fact that a very warlike California tribe fought with the Shoshones, and they called their enemies Toquimas. My own feeling about the word is that the first part of it refers to mountains, because both the Shoshones and the Pai-Utes use the word *toi* to mean mountains. For instance, there are the Toyabe Mountains on one side of Smoky Valley and the Toquimas, which originally might have been *Toiquimas,* on the other.

There is an error in history books concerning Manhattan. Many writers claim that it is a revived old town of the mining boom in the 1860's. That is incorrect. There was a Manhattan Mine, for which the canyon was named, and which was operated by an Eastern syndicate in the 1860's; but that was in another part of Manhattan Canyon, though I've never found anybody who knows exactly where. The town of Manhattan as we know it today was a new discovery of 1905. Ore was discovered there by John Humphrey, a cattle man, when he was riding after steers.

They claimed five thousand people at the height of Manhattan's boom. Today I don't suppose there are more than fifty. There is still a school there and a post office and a little store. But there is a lot more of the old town still standing; and the people living there don't like for it to be called a ghost town, although it's pretty close to that.

It was established in 1905, and before the end of 1906 there were nearly five thousand people there—a real boom. It was a good town until 1908, '09, or '10; along in there it deteriorated. Then a man called Drywash Wilson discovered placer down in Manhattan Canyon, and it was very good for a number of years more.

Jim Butler discovered the ore at Tonopah in May of 1900, and the town started that fall—about October of 1900. Tonopah was the first of this century's mining boom camps in that area. But there were very many of the old camps that were still inhabited; and the fact that mining started up again thereabouts gave a little general impetus to mining, and some of the old mines were re-opened. Old mining dumps were reworked, too, because they had better means of saving some of the ore that had been thrown out.

They claimed for Tonopah ten to fifteen thousand people. I would say that it might have been upward of ten thousand at its peak. A few years after it was discovered, it was around eight thousand and a very lively camp.

But Goldfield was the big one. It was discovered later than Tonopah. I was there in 1905, and it was booming then; but in 1906 it had its big boom. The ore there was discovered by two men—Will Marsh and Harry Stimmler—who left Tonopah to prospect.

I don't know how big Goldfield got to be, for that's been so exaggerated. They claimed probably more than they had, but it was a large and very lively camp. There's very little there now; for I was there last week [in April of 1968], and by the last count there were only a hundred and fifty people. But it's still the county seat of Esmeralda County, and the courthouse is fully staffed and maintained.

That was where Joe Gans and Battling Nelson had their famous fight in 1906. And there were strikes in Goldfield, especially in 1907 and '08. Theodore Roosevelt was president then, and Governor John Sparks [cited in a different capacity by Mr. Batt in contribution 3] asked him to send troops in, which he did. And there was quite a bad time for a while. Men like George Wingfield went to Utah and secretly brought back strikebreakers. Federal troops were stationed in Goldfield, as I said; and Governor Sparks started the state police and national guard to help out at that time.

160

The strikers were what was called I. W. W.'s. [For more on their activities in Nevada, see contribution of Judge Guild, number 14.] The regular mining union was not affiliated with that one; they were a more conservative group.

One of the big troubles in Goldfield—the mine-owners claimed it and rightly so, for it was done—was that the miners were stealing the owners blind: highgrading. So they built change rooms and insisted that before the miners went off shift they must change their clothes. And of course, they discovered a great deal of gold and gold samples, some of them worth a great deal.

There were assayers over there who acted the same as what they call a fence does with robberies, and a lot of them made a lot of money. That was one cause of trouble, and the miners' wages was another.

Tonopah had no real strikes or mining trouble. Oh, there was a little of it, but very little. But in Goldfield bad trouble lasted for quite a while. There were two or three killings and shootings on the street and so on, and it was quite exciting at times.

The miners would take the ore to the back door of the crooked assayers—of course, there were legitimate ones who would have nothing to do with that sort of thing—at night. I recall when a house next door to the one my husband and I were renting in Tonopah was raided by officers because highgrade was hidden in the cellar of the house. That was in 1908 or '09. The highgrade came from Goldfield, and they found it stored in this house. That would happen, that the highgrade could be taken to an outlaying place and hidden, and it frequently was.

The only real trouble they had at Tonopah was about clearing out the Chinese by the anti-Orientals, you know; just as in Virginia City they had trouble in the same way because of cheap Oriental labor. And so when the twentieth-century mining boom came to Nevada, many of the camps that were started up said they would not have Chinese. But the Chinese came [for more on this subject, see Mr. Keleher's contribution, number 10].

I can't give the exact date, but I think it was about in 1908, some of the citizens got together, and they put some of the Chinese out of Tonopah. One Chinaman was killed, and some of them were

161

taken below town and turned loose on the desert, to make their way the best they could to other points.

But if some camps would not tolerate Chinese at all, others were friendly and Chinamen ran the restaurants in them [see Mr. Stauffer's contribution, number 13, for a similar report on Arizona] and did the laundry work. In the early times each camp had a Chinatown, and you'll find Chinese cemeteries in them. Pioche has a very interesting one, and an old undertaker over there told me about a big furnace down in the Chinese cemetery. He said that when a Chinaman died, they'd leave him buried for three to five years; and then they'd dig him up, burn the flesh off the bones in this furnace, box the bones, and send them to China. And this old undertaker told me that this was part of his business and that he had regular boxes for that sort of thing.

Originally, Chinese in great numbers were brought into this area of the West when the Central Pacific Railroad was being built. It was cheap labor, so I think the big four of the railroad—Crocker, Huntington, Stanford, and Hopkins—encouraged the Oriental labor.

The Chinese were feared and looked upon as enemies by the Indians when they were building the Central Pacific in Nevada. The Indians were used to white men by then, but they felt that the Chinese were a foreign race who had no business here, and they didn't like their customs.

There was a great deal of claim-jumping in most of the camps. I can recall that in the boom days of Manhattan there was a great deal of gunplay over that. Men were ordered off property and out of the shafts at gunpoint.

Besides claim-jumping, and especially around Goldfield, there was lot-jumping. You see, a great deal of money was made on townsites. The minute a new strike was made, somebody would rush in and start a townsite and put the lots up for sale. And in some cases that was the only money made. Town lots were sold, when ore was discovered, but it was in such small amounts that mines were never sunk, and that was the end of that. It frequently happened that way in these little fly-by-night cases.

But of the places that did come to life, there is an amazing number of them of which you cannot now find a trace. We came past a place the other day, on the highway from Austin to Reno, where there isn't the faintest sign of a town which lasted about a year. You can't see one stick or stone today to let you know that there ever was such a place as Carroll. That was a camp near Carroll Summit, about 1908 or '10.

The early mining camps of the 1860's will be much easier to trace later on than the twentieth-century ones because the buildings of so many of them were of native stone, whereas the camps of the early 1900's were composed of timber buildings. And the timber buildings, of course, deteriorated or were hauled away when new strikes made new places. That happened very frequently.

There were some cases of trouble in the early camps because the Molly Maguires operated here. In the 1870's [the murderous Molly Maguires were broken up following Pinkerton investigations of their Pennsylvania mining activities in 1873, hence the westward flight of remnants] they were still operating here, though they were never very powerful in Nevada.

But there was a case in Belmont where two men who were labor agitators were supposed to have been Molly Maguires. The history of that whole thing is so mixed up with legend that it is hard to tell which is which. Anyhow, there were two men in prison because they were supposedly labor agitators, and the mine-owners, of course, were very much against that. One of the two was a man of about forty and the other a boy of twenty or twenty-one; and they were accused of being Molly Maguires, but whether they were or not, nobody now knows.

But an aunt of mine was a girl of fourteen or fifteen, in Belmont at that time, and she remembered the incident very clearly. The prisoners were about to stand trial when a vigilance committee visited the jail and hanged the two men. And it was the mine-owners and the merchants sympathetic to them who formed this vigilance committee and did the hanging.

There was quite a story about that. It was before the courthouse was built; but Belmont was the county seat, and the jail was downstairs in what was later known as the Overholt Saloon. And these men were hanged in that jail; and it was supposed to have put a curse upon the town, because the blood stains never came off. The blood spurted, you know, when they were decapitated. [Decapitation and hanging not being the same, except in the case of Black Jack Ketchum, cited by Mr. Powell in contribution 24, there were evidently two traditions as to how the victims were disposed of, which time has cheerfully mated.] I have seen these stains many times, but whether they were genuine bloodstains or whether someone used a paintbrush, I couldn't say. But that is the legend, and the old-timers maintained that it was absolutely true.

The lynched men were not buried in a respectable cemetery. They were put out there in a canyon between the town of Belmont and its old cemetery. They are under a pine tree, with a big rock at the head of the grave; and you have to know where to look or you'd never find the place.

But whether because of the curse or not, Belmont [which had an estimated peak population of eight thousand] is a ghost town now. It was the second seat of Nye County—Ione City was the first, lasting about three years. Then Belmont was the county seat from 1867 to 1904 or '05, when it was moved to Tonopah.

17

PUPILS OF ALL AGES

"They buried my great-grandfather wrapped in blankets and they poured barrels of whiskey over his body, and coal."

MRS. FABIOLA C. DE BACA GILBERT
Santa Fe, New Mexico

Mrs. Gilbert had the unusual experience of teaching in frontier schools where instruction was complicated by a foreign-language problem. There were differences of opinion as to which language was alien, however, for an influx of homesteaders had brought English into a region where Spanish speech had been native to all.

That was true of Mrs. Gilbert herself, descended as she was from one of the landed and historically prominent families that had helped to govern New Mexico for a century and a half before the fortunes of war turned it into an American territory in 1846. That for long made little difference to prosperous Hispanic families far removed from their new country's centers of influence. They continued to conduct themselves as they always had and to teach their children to do likewise.

It was Mrs. Gilbert's generation, maturing a half a dozen decades after the American conquest of New Mexico, that determined to bridge the gap between the two cultures. For her the first step was to attend the New Mexico Normal University—also the alma mater of Messrs. Henriquez and Charles Barker, contributors 12 and 20. Emerging equipped to teach English, she began the career here described.

Somewhere in the course of it, she wrote a book titled We Fed Them Cactus. *Interpretative of vaqueros rather than cowboys, it is important to the comprehension of the one Western state in which two currents of tradition remain prevalent forces.*

I was born in my grandfather's hacienda, eighteen miles east of Las Vegas. I lived there until I was five; then we came to Las Vegas, so I could go to school.

At that time Las Vegas was the most important town in New Mexico. Santa Fe was—well, the capital, but a small place, and Albuquerque was even smaller and not growing. But Las Vegas was the trading center for all the eastern plains. The Hispanos had herds of cattle and flocks of sheep below the mountains; they were very big cow- and sheep-ranchers. They brought their wool and their livestock to trade in Las Vegas—that's what made it an important trading center to begin with. Then after 1879, when the railroad came, that made it more important than ever.

Las Vegas was on a land grant which belonged to my great-great-grandfather. It was given to him by the Spanish, and later the Mexican Government confirmed my family's ownership. But people began to settle in Las Vegas without permission because it was a stopping place for those traveling on the Santa Fe Trail.

So there was litigation about the grant, and the people didn't want to leave. In about 1835 the settlers made a petition to be allowed to stay, and the heirs of my great-great-grandfather felt that they had a vested right. So the government made an agreement with them. They said, "If you will let the settlers keep the land they are on, we will give you acres elsewhere."

So my family got several pieces of property in return, and they are still called Baca Locations. Number one is Valle Grande, over by Los Alamos, which is a beautiful place. Number two is where the Bell Ranch is now, which is close to our ranches here; for we still have ranches in this vicinity. Number three was La Trinchera, mostly in Colorado, but a little bit in New Mexico. Then there were two in Arizona, about six miles from Nogales. So everybody was satisfied. The town was given a community grant, the Las Vegas Grant, but when my ancestors had it, it was called Las Vegas Grandes, or the Great Meadows.

My grandfather was born in Peña Blanca, on the Rio Grande between here and Albuquerque. And my grandmother on that side of the family was from Santa Fe; their hacienda was sixteen miles from here. His brothers-in-law, the Delgados, owned the whole plaza of Santa Fe. So my grandfather went to work for one of his brothers-in-law, who had a big store.

His father-in-law, who was my great-grandfather on my mother's side, owned practically all of Santa Fe. I can say that, because I still get an enquiry of title about any property that is sold here in Santa Fe, when they open up the different new areas. So he must have owned a lot.

I will tell how he died. He was a big merchant; he had stores in some of the mining towns, as well as stores in Santa Fe. And he had wagons that went to Chihuahua, Mexico, and also to the States, as they used to call the United States. And one time he decided he would go back East and see the big markets over there. Usually the *patrones* didn't venture on such trips and sent men that worked for them. But my great-grandfather decided to go and took one of his grandsons, Román Romero, who was a very prominent man in Las Vegas later.

They went to Kansas City, Westport, and all those places, but coming back there was an outbreak of cholera; and my great-grandfather caught it and died on the way back. One of the men he had taken with him was named Josano Lela. My great-grandfather didn't have real slaves, but he had bond slaves, and the Lela family belonged to him in that sense. So Josano Lela was one of the men with the outfit that went East, and he used to tell us how they dug a great big grave on the Kansas prairie.

They buried my great-grandfather wrapped in blankets, and they poured barrels of whiskey over his body, and coal [to repel burrowing animals]. Then they closed the grave and brushed away all signs of it, because in those days Indians would scalp any corpse they could find.

But Josano Lela was a regular scout, and he said he knew just where my great-grandfather was buried. They couldn't bring him back at first, because it was summer. So they waited until fall, and then Josano and others went and brought the body back to Santa Fe.

One of his sons had gone to live in Las Vegas and opened stores there, and my grandfather decided to move to Las Vegas, too. So that's how he came to move back to a place which his family had originally owned by land grant. And that's how I came to be born over there instead of here.

But while I was still a child, that town began to lose importance. When the Rock Island Railroad came through—in 1901, I believe—that's what killed Las Vegas. It came through the plains south of the town, and the ranchers, instead of coming as far as Las Vegas, began shipping their cattle and wool to the Eastern markets on the Rock Island. Before that they had to come a big distance by wagons up hill to Las Vegas [elevation 6,400 feet]. But this way they were close to the shipping points, and that started the downfall of Las Vegas.

The first railroad to come through, the Santa Fe, made Las Vegas [for a report on the town when it was a great market center, see the contribution of Mr. Henriquez, number 12], and the competitor broke it. Then another thing that helped overthrow Las Vegas, so to speak, was the coming of another element to take up the lands. The country around had all been parts of land grants, but the government took over [see Mr. Keleher's contribution, number 10, for report on why this happened] and opened it for homesteaders. That certainly hurt the sheep and cattle industries of the earlier people who were ranching there, for what had been open range was chopped up; because the homesteaders were taking one hundred and sixty acres first and later three hundred and twenty. That helped to ruin Las Vegas, because the ranchers who lived near enough to keep on trading there were losing out.

But it was still a lot bigger than it is now, when I went to school there. I went to school at the Sisters of Loretto, a grammar school; and I went to what is now Highlands University for my high school. When I finished high school, I went on to college work there. I took education courses, because it was a normal school then, so I was trained to be a teacher.

We didn't have dances at the normal school, but we had parties and quite a few clubs. The glee club put on some programs, and I belonged to that. As a matter of fact, I didn't learn to dance until I got away from school. My father didn't like for us to go to dances.

169

He was a very aristocratic person and didn't like us to just mix with everybody, so I didn't go to dances until I was out on my own, teaching school. Then sometimes, with his permission, I'd go. You see, the first school where I was teaching was only six miles from our ranch.

The normal school was the largest in the territory, though New Mexico became a state the year before I was through; I graduated in 1913. After that I taught in two rural schools in Guadalupe County. The schools then were different from those we have now. I was a teacher trained where we had all the advantages of equipment. But when I went to teach in a rural school, it was in a very poor district, where the taxes were paid by the railroad, and they didn't have the facilities I was used to.

There was one teacher for all the eight grades in most places, though the one I taught in first only had six grades. At that time the homesteaders had come into that part of New Mexico. The homesteaders' children came to school to me, and there were some Spanish-speaking children, too. So it was a mixed school, but it was enjoyable.

At that time they had some readers that were one-part English and one-part Spanish translations, and we used them. They were very helpful, and people have certainly lost an opportunity to teach Spanish-speaking children today without using them. It was easy to start them learning English with those readers.

And the children of the homesteaders learned Spanish from them. It was only a seven-month school, but after seven months the English-speaking children were speaking Spanish, and the Spanish children were speaking English; they would converse with each other in either language.

Of course, I taught definitely in English. I think one of the hard things for the Spanish-speaking children was pronunciation, and grammar for the English-speaking children.

How did I handle them all? Beautifully; I was young! With all those children and classes, I didn't have time to think that anything was hard. It worries me now that teachers complain about the facilities and other things that schools have now. Well, we didn't worry about those things then; we just worked with what we found.

170

I don't know how the money of the county was apportioned; but anyway you sometimes couldn't get paid, because there was no money in the treasury. So they gave you some kind of paper, and you had to wait until they had the money. I happened to have a father who could pay my expenses, so I didn't have to worry about that. They would pay you at a discount on the warrant, if you cashed it somewhere before the county was ready to make good. But if you waited long enough, you could get the full amount. I did, because I was lucky enough to have my father in back of me.

I rode to the rural school on horseback sometimes, and then we had a carriage. If I took my horse with me on a Sunday evening to the place near the school where I boarded, then I'd have a horse to go back home with on the following weekend. But if not, my father or my brother would come for me in the carriage. But horseback was the usual way, and my father had beautiful horses.

There was some trouble between the various ranches at that time. I wrote a book, you know, called *We Fed Them Cactus*, and that tells about the feuds.

My father had both sheep and cattle at first, but he always resented sheep afterward. You see, he got rid of the sheep and went in only for cattle, for that Las Vegas area is cattle country.

You know, sheep eat too much grass; they crop it down to the roots almost. So it's best not to have them in cattle country. Even horses eat more of the grass than a cow; but we did have a lot of horses. My father had them until the big blizzard of 1918; and before that we had a long drouth. That happens to ranchers, you know; they either have drouth or get ruined by some other kind of weather. So after that blizzard my father got rid of the horses he had left.

We Fed Them Cactus tells of those times and of the earlier days, and how the coming of another culture and another people helped to make Las Vegas the poorer town that it is today. You know, there are actually two towns in Las Vegas. There was Old Town —the original town, settled in about 1820, I suppose. And then New Town grew up around the railroad station.

But I have some more things to say about the schools, when I was growing up and began teaching. I never had the experience

171

myself, because I belonged to a different social scale; but the rural schools in New Mexico sometimes only had three months of school. And sometimes they had teachers who hadn't even finished the eighth grade. They used to say there was a law, though I don't think it's true, that said anybody could be a teacher who could read and write.

New Mexico was a poor territory, but I don't think it was that so much as politics. You see, the government was in the hands of the few that had the money and influence, and education for the people as a whole was terribly neglected. As I said, when I started, they were having seven-month sessions in most schools. It wasn't until well after statehood that they began to have the full school sessions of nine-months.

I taught rural school for a couple of years. After that I taught in Santa Rosa, which is a fair-sized town, you know, and the seat of Guadalupe County. There I only had one grade, the first grade; because I had really been trained as a primary teacher. To my surprise, the first day I went there to teach, I had seventy-five pupils.

But they managed somehow to divide the room, you know. And they got another teacher, which was hard to arrange in those days, for money was hard for the county to get.

Still, they did get another teacher, and I taught in Santa Rosa for four years. And I used to teach Spanish there also. You see, the primary grades were dismissed at eleven in the morning and at one in the afternoon. So that gave me one hour in the morning and one in the afternoon to teach Spanish in the seventh and eighth grades, and in high school.

But I decided I wanted to teach home economics, though not to children—to the grown people of rural New Mexico that needed to know about those things. And after going back to college—this time to the agricultural college at Las Cruces [a couple of hundred miles down the Rio Grande from Albuquerque], which is now New Mexico State University—I went to work for extension.

I pioneered in extension, as a matter of fact; I was one of the first home-economics demonstrators sent up to the mountainous northern parts of the state. When we started out, the people in those

172

rural regions didn't know how to preserve fruits and vegetables, or so many things that farmers in other parts of the country knew how to do. They didn't know how to dig wells; they carried water to their houses in barrels filled from the nearest stream—sometimes miles away.

But the people didn't always want to be helped or to change their ways. You had to be able to take abuse and put up with suspicion to get along with them; and above all you had to have a sense of humor.

And there were no roads when I started in; you just drove your car over wagon trails, where a flash flood might hold you up for a couple of hours while you were waiting for the water to drain out of a wash. That's why I called it pioneering. But extension was the greatest work in the world, and I wrote a book about it called *The Good Life*.

18

RECOLLECTIONS OF THE
FOURTH ESTATE

*"I remember that Mr. Fitzsimmons trained down below
the state prison on a big ranch there."*

MRS. LUCY DAVIS CROWELL, Carson City, Nevada

*On both sides of her family Mrs. Crowell was involved with
frontier journalism. In the course of marrying two newspapermen,
her mother became a reporter herself. The second of those mar-
riages allied her with Mrs. Crowell's father, in the person of the
redoubtable Sam Davis. His also here remembered younger
brother, Robert, is perhaps best known today for having co-
authored a biography of O. Henry titled* The Caliph of Bagdad.

*Long overshadowed by a man who took his talents to New
York and published many books there, Sam Davis is now beginning
to get some share of countrywide attention and may emerge with
quite a bit more. One that early thought him a significant short-
story writer was no small authority on the genre, his name being
Ambrose Bierce. And when there has been further examination of
the papers now in Mrs. Crowell's possession, posterity may confirm
that contemporary judgment.*

*Meanwhile Mrs. Crowell offers attractive glimpses of a colorful
and witty member of Nevada's newspaperdom, in the days when
there was a fluid exchange between it and California journalism.
Then, in addition to other pioneer fourth-estate data, she tells of
how a heavyweight championship focused the national spotlight on
Carson City, a subject which she illuminates with details not commonly found in chronicles of America's prize ring. Included, too,
are quotations from perhaps the first woman to cover such an
event.*

HER CONTRIBUTION

My mother came from the State of Maine, where she'd known
Henry Rust Mighels, first editor of the Carson City *Appeal*. When
he left their home town in 1860, he said, "I'm going to send for

176

you when I get settled somewhere. I'm going to marry you." She was then sixteen years old and thought that was a joke.

But the Civil War came along. He served in the war, was badly wounded, and was discharged before the end of it. He came West then and settled in various places in California, but he was eventually hired to come to Carson City and act as the editor of the Carson City *Appeal*, which was first published in May of 1865.

He enjoyed Carson City and decided that this was where he was going to live, so he sent for my mother. Finding he wasn't joking about that, she decided to join him. There was no transportation then except by boat to the Isthmus of Panama, across it by a narrow-gauge railroad, and by boat again from there to San Francisco. He had gone from here to San Francisco to meet her in Hank Monk's stage [a driver and vehicle frequently cited in Western annals]. They were married and came by stage to Carson, where my mother arrived on August 22, 1866.

Henry Mighels went on editing the paper until he became very ill. He finally died of cancer after a lingering illness. At that time there were no hospitals, so my mother took care of him at home, but he still wanted to write his editorials. He was a brilliant editorial writer, and he had a type setup at home. He'd had a small room built in the yard in back of the house as a studio, because he was very artistic and painted lovely pictures. So when he got ill, he had this type setup installed there—the kind you picked up and put in place by hand, you know. He wrote his editorials, and my mother set the type and rolled off a proof. And if she made a mistake, she heard about it. He was pretty critical, but of course, he was ill and suffering.

Although it is now an evening newspaper, the *Appeal* was then a morning one, so a lot of the work was done at night. So my mother would take her font of type, after she got the editorial set, tied up with a string and tucked under her arm. And she had a big white English bulldog, and he walked beside her down to where the *Appeal*'s office was. And when she was ready to come home, nobody's dog or anything else ever came near her. It was a perfect protection.

When Mr. Mighels died in 1879, it was arranged that she would

177

inherit the *Appeal;* his half interest in it, that is. She hired one man as editor who was not satisfactory; then she finally called my father, Samuel Post Davis, who was a friend of Mr. Mighels' and of hers. He was working for the *Territorial Enterprise* [the Virginia City paper for which Samuel Clemens was working when he first used "Mark Twain" as a pseudonym] and free-lancing for various other newspapers, mostly in California.

She asked him to come down and edit her paper. He did that, and they got along so nicely that in 1880 my dad and mother were married. So I arrived in 1881, and they had six children altogether.

My father was born in Connecticut in 1850. Dad's brother Bob—Robert H. Davis—wrote that whole shelf of books up there. He traveled the world over for the Munsey Publications [for which he had been fiction editor when they formed O. Henry's principal market] and wrote whatever he felt like wherever he happened to be. Then what he wrote in later years was published in the New York *Sun.*

He came here because my grandfather was an Episcopalian clergyman who was called to be the rector of the Episcopal church in Carson along about '76 or so. There were three boys and a sister. Sam Davis, my father, was the oldest of the group, and Bob was the youngest.

He worked for the *Appeal,* but though he was somehow later listed as the editor of the *Appeal,* he never was. He was only about ten years old when he first came here, but he soon got a little job carrying the paper and doing odd jobs around the office. Then he finally became a compositor and interested in newspaper work generally. But he left here as quite a young man and went to San Francisco and went into the writing business professionally there.

I remember the old Washington press that they turned by hand at the time they worked for the *Appeal,* and all it could do was to turn out one paper at a time. I remember how it looked, standing up on a platform. The old office was down opposite the capitol in the middle of the block. Then my mother gave the paper to her oldest son—my stepbrother—and he bought a stone building on the corner. And on that building the University of Nevada put a plaque honoring Robert H. Davis when his widow left his estate to the university.

My father stayed with the *Appeal* until 1898, and then he was elected state controller [an office he held until 1906]. It was while he was controller that my mother turned the paper over to her son, Harry Mighels. And she eventually gave it to him, so Dad never went back to the *Appeal* again.

But he was still with it in 1897 and covered the Corbett-Fitzsimmons fight, which was held here then. [On St. Patrick's Day of that year Gentleman Jim Corbett, heavyweight champion of the world, battled Robert Prometheus "Bob" Fitzsimmons.] I remember that Mr. Fitzsimmons trained down below the state prison on a big ranch there; and he used to run the two miles up to Carson Street for exercise.

By that time my Grandfather Davis had retired, and my father thought it was too bad that he had nothing to do; he was just sitting around and had given up. So Dad had a bill sent through the legislature to arrange for Sunday service in the state prison. And my grandfather was appointed for three Sundays a month and a Catholic priest for the fourth.

As long as he lived, my grandfather went down to the prison. We lived on a ranch by that time, and I used to drive in with a little horse and buggy and pick him up and take him down there. My grandmother played the organ, and she had a lovely voice. I thought I could sing a little, too, so we were the choir.

We were in a little alcove, with the dining room below us, where the prisoners sat. There was a man with us sitting with a rifle across his knees, and there was a small organ to one side, leaving just room for three or four people.

So Fitzsimmons heard that we had these services and asked for permission to come in and attend service at the prison every Sunday. He did, and he and I sang off the same hymnal. So that was my personal interest in Mr. Fitzsimmons.

Well, of course, they had a big period of training, and there was a good deal of national interest in what was going on here. My uncle Bob Davis was appointed by the New York *Sun* to come out here and be in Mr. Fitzsimmons' camp and to keep in touch with everything that was going on. And I'm sure he wrote an article that's in one of his books, about the story of Mr. Fitzsimmons and his wife, called *Ruby Red*, or something like that.

179

Mr. Corbett was the handsome "Gentleman Jim." Mr. Fitz-simmons was happy-go-lucky, freckle-faced, red-headed, with a small head for a big body, and his arms were awfully long. Not handsome at all, but cordial and genial and friendly with every-body. But nobody hardly dared speak to Mr. Corbett, who had a different attitude. We were living on the ranch, as I said, and he was at the hot springs only a mile away; but we never saw him.

When the time came for the fight, one of the papers from Chicago, though I can't think of its name right at the moment, wired my father, asking him to report the fight for it. When he wired that he was sorry but that he'd made another engagement for that, they telegraphed back, "Do you suppose your wife would do it?"

Well, Dad propositioned Mother about it, and she could write and was used to newspaper work. But the idea of going to a prize fight—nice ladies did *not* do anything of the sort then. But Dad finally talked her into it, and she went, almost hiding her face.

Mrs. Fitzsimmons and the wives of the different managers—a handful of women like that were there with my mother. But though she watched the fight and wrote it up, she did not see the famous solar-plexus blow, as Fitzsimmons' back was turned toward her. Fitzsimmons hit him in the stomach, just barely high enough not to be below the belt. Corbett slumped down then, and Mother couldn't see why. She didn't see anything very exciting about it, and when she got home, she said, "Why, I've seen my boys out in the back yard fight as good a fight as that."

But she wrote it up, and her account was published; and I believe they paid her fifty dollars for it. But she did not sign "Nellie Davis" at all—she signed her maiden name.

I have some clippings about that. Because my mother lived to be a hundred, the Carson papers ran articles about her every now and then, and I'd like to read a part of one at this point.

"She covered the Corbett-Fitzsimmons fight for the Chicago *Tribune* but didn't see the solar-plexus blow that felled 'Gentle-man Jim,' who, by the way, was not so gentlemanly as the freckle-face Fitz," she recalled. "I was so afraid somebody would get hurt,

I was just petrified. Women didn't go to fights in those days, but the Chicago *Tribune* wanted me to cover the fight for it, so I did. It was in the fourteenth round, and they were clinched. Fitzsimmons' nose was bloody, and he kept wiping the blood on his glove and smearing the gore on Corbett's back. Corbett was a sight.

"I was for Fitz and had a bet on with William Woodburn [later attorney general of Nevada]. Fitz broke one arm away from Corbett's embrace, they told me later, and hit Corbett in the solar plexus. Fitz's back was turned toward me. Corbett just sank slowly to the floor. Fitz let him down easy, and Gentleman Jim took the count.

"But Corbett was no gentleman at his training camp. He swore at his trainers and was disagreeable in general, which is why I happened to bet on Fitz. Mr. Woodburn, who was a Carson City attorney, was saying what a clumsy clown Fitz was and that anybody would be crazy to bet on him. He bet me the best pair of gloves in town, but Mr. Woodburn never paid that bet. Every time I saw him after the fight, he said he hadn't found a pair of gloves good enough for me."

There's an anecdote about the time my father was associated with Sarah Bernhardt which has been run two different times in slightly different versions in the *Reader's Digest*. But first I should say my father was a great teller of funny stories. His jokes weren't dirty, but he could keep people laughing for hours. He often went to San Francisco, taking the sleeper; but after he got talking to somebody, the man would start laughing. Then others would gather around, and they'd forget to go to bed.

Dad did a lot of writing for the San Francisco *Examiner*, as well as his own paper; and when Sarah Bernhardt came to San Francisco in 1893, he and half a dozen other reporters were scheduled to meet the train at Tiburo, I think it was, and escort her into the city. She didn't speak English, and Dad and the rest didn't speak French, so there was an interpreter, naturally.

While they were going down the bay, Dad was sitting there with the rest of the gang, telling stories as he usually did; and everybody was laughing. And she called her interpreter and said, "What's that man talking about?" So he explained, and she said, "Tell him to come up here, and you interpret the stories for me." And when she'd listened a while she said, "This is the man who can act as my reporter, and the rest can go home."

And that's the way it was all the time she was in San Francisco. Dad was paid very generously by the *Examiner* to escort her around and give her a good time—and of course, turn in plenty of exclusive copy for the newspaper.

Here's the gist of the anecdote about Dad and Sarah Bernhardt that the *Reader's Digest* ran. When she bade him farewell, she kissed him on one cheek and said, "That's for the Carson *Appeal*." The other cheek was for the San Francisco *Examiner*, and then she said, "On the lips, Mr. Davis, for yourself."

He said, "Madame, that's very nice, but I represent the Associated Press, with about four hundred and eighty newspapers."

I worked for a year or so in California myself. My husband and I were divorced then, and I was living in Berkeley. The best job I could get in San Francisco started me at sixty-five dollars a month, and out of that I was paying rent, hiring someone to take care of my two children, and commuting to San Francisco. So I wasn't very affluent, but my father was generous and we got by.

But Mother was quite insistent that I come back to Carson City, so she talked to the man who was the head of the Public Service Commission—they called it the Railroad Commission then—and arranged for them to hire me at a hundred dollars. So I took the telegram that Mother sent me about that to my employer, who by that time had raised my salary first to seventy and then to eighty dollars. He was a mining engineer, and coming from Nevada I understood mining; and I thought I was good office help generally.

I told the man I'd stay if he'd meet what I'd been offered, but when I showed him the telegram, he said, "No girl in the world is worth more as a stenographer than eighty dollars a month, so you can go to your home in Carson City. Please arrange to have somebody take your place, though; I'm too busy to do it myself. But be sure she's middle-aged and plain."

I understood what that was: the background of his needing a

middle-aged and plain woman. And I saw its application to me. I was thirty-six years old, but he considered me middle-aged and plain. But that was all right; I was unhappy and not sleeping nights, and I guess I looked like a real old lady.

So I found him a woman who had engineering experience and came back here a couple of months later. That was in 1917, and soon after I got back here, my father suffered a stroke while he was attending a business meeting in San Jose, California.

When she got word, Mother sent me down there to see what could be done. The resident doctor of the hospital was away, and the young man in charge didn't know how to take care of the case because of the condition of gangrene in my father's foot. So I got Dad to Berkeley and took him to a hospital there that the family knew about, and it ended with an amputation of his right leg at the hip.

He only lived about nine months after that. He regained his speech, but he was never out of bed again.

My father left a tremendous lot of stories and poems in manuscript. He never published anything himself except this two-volume history of Nevada. Then way back when, Mr. Ambrose Bierce, who was very friendly with my father, gathered up a lot of pieces and published a little book of them [*Short Stories*, San Francisco, 1885].

And that's all that were ever published in book form during his lifetime. [Since then Mr. Davis's *The Typographical Howitzer* has been anthologized and is by way of being recognized as a Western classic.] He wrote more for the fun of writing, not with the idea that he was going to make a lot of money. He'd think of something, and he might write it on the stiff cuffs of his boiled shirt, which was the way men dressed then.

Finally he'd say to Mother, "Nell, what happened to that shirt I had on yesterday? I had some notes on the cuff."

And she'd say, "I sent it to the Chinese laundry."

Nobody could read his writing, and sometimes he couldn't himself, so she never could tell whether his notes were important or not. But anyhow when she said that, he'd laugh and think his story or whatever it was over again.

183

The place where he died was the ranch he'd established about two miles north of Carson, when he imported the first Holstein cattle ever to come to the state of Nevada. I helped my mother take care of my father out there at the ranch, where I was living then, too.

But about a year afterward I left the Railroad Commission for a better job on the staff of the State Supreme Court. Deciding I was going to be here permanently—I worked for the Supreme Court for forty years, as it turned out—I moved into town after I got that job so I wouldn't have to drive the children to school before going to work. Not liking the idea of paying rent, I bought this house in 1919. Dating from 1884, this is an old house; and with its high ceilings, several floors and big yard, gives a pretty good idea of what the whole town looked like when I was growing up here.

19

TALES OF A STAGECOACH
STATION

"The best way to keep it open was a shotgun at night, and they used to do that."

MRS. AGNES WRIGHT SPRING, Denver, Colorado

As the author of some seventeen volumes of Western Americana, Mrs. Spring will need no introduction to many. A native of Colorado, she spent much of her youth in the valley of Wyoming's Little Laramie. There she was one of the permanent dwellers in a bustling stagecoach station, with its forever changing shifts of transient boarders. Hailing from all sections of the country, these fared from a railhead on the Union Pacific to mines in the mountains and back.

Of this fluid microcosmos Mrs. Spring relays fascinating details. She also spells out what it was like for a girl to grow up where the most poignant attachments were for outdoor experiences in a land but little removed from wilderness.

The direct connection between her early interests and her emergence as an official gatherer of frontier data form another part of her memories. For in addition to being a chronicler, she became the state historian of Wyoming and of Colorado, to which she returned in time to meet many colorful pioneers and to get first-hand reports of others.

She here relates how she unearthed the career of Wild Bill Hickok's previously shadowy partner. She furthermore deals with the Tabors, the man and two women who were actors in the West's great natural morality play. In sum the facts were that after a tycoon divorced the wife who had seen him through hard times so that he could wed the youthful mate of a man paid to step aside—but the upshot is best told by Mrs. Spring.

HER CONTRIBUTION

My mother and father went from Iowa to Delta, Colorado, in the early days, and I was born over there. Then we went to a small town called Minturn, and then on to Wyoming. I think I must have gone there about 1900.

My father had a ranch on the Little Laramie River and ran a stage line—it was Gordon L. Wright's stage line—up to the mines. They were the mines around the Rambler—the Keystone and the New Rambler—in the Snowy Range.

It was twenty-three miles into Laramie, and from our station the line went fifty miles on up into the mountains. So Dad's line was about seventy-five miles long. Then we had a swing that went over into Centennial, a little town in the Snowy Range. It was named that because a mine was found there in 1876.

There was a steady flow of people going back and forth through our station. Some of them were big-money men from the East, some of them were miners; we had every kind of person. The girls on most of the ranches were isolated, but we weren't. We lived in just like a little world there, with all the people coming and going. We always had about forty people at the table.

When the railroad [a spur of the Union Pacific] came, we had the graders. I used to help my mother at the table, and I never saw men eat so. Then we used to have the Swedes that my father hauled in the stage, that were tie hacks. They'd cut ties for the railroad way up in the mountains. They used to work up there all summer and ski down in the fall; and they'd leave the skis—beautiful homemade ones—with us. My father used to haul the tie hacks back to Laramie, and he said they drank straight alcohol. One of them gave him a drink one day while he was driving, and he said he never got his breath for five miles.

Our next door neighbor in one direction was a Civil War nurse who had come out in '65 and gone up to Virginia City, Montana; but her husband died and she married a buffalo-hunter named James Doherty. Across the way was an old fellow who was born in a covered wagon, and he told us he'd fought at Adobe Walls [a fight between buffalo-hunters, assembled in the ruins of a Texas trading post in 1874, and Comanches led by the celebrated Quanah Parker]. His name was Lew Porter.

Then up beyond him was a moonshiner called Hunt. We could see the smoke from his cabin, where they'd cook the mash.

One character we had was named Felix Dearlove, who was a little bit different. His mother was a cousin of Queen Victoria, and they lived on a ranch below us. But she died and the old man [Felix's father] got to reading the *Heart and Hand* magazine. We used to get that ourselves; and there would be women advertising for husbands and so forth. So he brought a woman they always called Miss Rose to the ranch and married her. But she got him to sell the ranch and go to the West Coast.

One morning a year or so later my mother heard somebody at the door, and there was Felix, who said he'd come back to Wyoming to live. He said his father had got fed up with Miss Rose and kicked her in the slats. But Miss Rose got the money, and the old man died. So Felix and his brother came back to Wyoming and herded sheep for years, living in a little tent up on the side of the mountain, when they'd had a lovely ranch down below.

The neighbors were mostly people with cattle who cut their own hay—we had very fine hay. And when a big irrigation ditch was built through the ranch to help grow it, we learned how to keep a headgate open.

The best way to keep it open was a shotgun at night, and they used to do that. People down below wanted water in a lake, I think, so they wanted it diverted. But the ones who didn't have any water wanted to keep the gate open, and they did. I remember one man who stayed there. I forget how many nights, but he had a shotgun to keep the gate open and get the water through.

My father had four daughters and no sons, so he used to let me do some of the things a boy should, I suppose. I once drove a freight wagon with him up to the mines with a load of dynamite. I drove one team, and he the other.

There was a funny town in the mountains called Holmes. That was where the miners lived, and when they got teed up, they'd do the most unbelievable things. They'd climb up a straight pine tree and build a platform, and then they'd carry a cook stove up. And they'd carry a dummy cook up there. It was just their fun.

The town was high, about ten thousand feet. My father used to take me up there in the stage, and we'd go there in a sled in the winter. But there's not a trace of Holmes now. I tried to take my husband there ten years ago, to show him what I thought would be a wonderful old ghost town, and we couldn't find anything. The CCC and the Forest Service had cleaned out every remnant.

After my father died, my mother visited us on a fruit ranch we used to have in Fort Collins, Colorado; and night after night she would sit up with me, and I'd write down her descriptions of the people who used to come through our stage station. She would tell me about Booker Smith and other promoters going through to the mines. They were gold and silver mines; also copper—the New Rambler was copper. They boomed for a while and then they faded.

I know my father took an awful punishment. He would haul tons and tons of freight, and the mining companies wouldn't pay him because they would go broke. But he'd pay his men and have to buy horses and everything.

I don't think my father had any trouble with bandits, but I remember that once a man shot and killed Sheriff Bath up on the Woods Landing road, which came very near us. That was after the railroad came; I think perhaps in 1915 or '16. They found his saddle blanket out on the Laramie Plains, about eleven miles from Laramie, but they never did catch him.

I remember one night when Lew Porter—the one who'd been in the Adobe Walls fight—came into our house and said to my mother, "Well, they got me, Mrs. Wright."

And she said, "*Oh*—why?"

Then he said, "You know I have a deer all the time hanging in the shed."

He lived on game, and nobody paid any attention, because when he killed a deer, he ate it—he needed it. But some new forest ranger, or one of the game men, arrested him and gave him a summons. He had dinner with us that day and talked about his arrest with a laugh, because he knew he had broken the law. But most people condoned hunting for the pot.

As the mountains were quite a resort in the summer, we used to have thirty or forty people a day going through to fish. But we had lovely trout near the ranch, too. I remember I came rushing in one day with a trout that must have been over two pounds; and there

189

was a man from Denver who said, "Little girl, I'll give you a dollar for that."

You weren't supposed to sell trout, but I didn't know it; and as a dollar was big money to me, I gave him the fish. But I drew an outline of it first upon a board and kept the board to show people.

Just the minute the dishes were done and the beds were made, I had a fishpole on my shoulder. It was the outdoors that I loved. I used to walk up and down the river alone, and suddenly I'd see a duck come from under the weeds with her brood. Or I'd see a rabbit, a prairie dog, a squirrel, or a badger coming out of his hole; and once in a great while a deer or an elk.

The Little Laramie wasn't very wide, but in some places it was quite deep and swift. I remember I pulled an old man out one day; he had been drinking and couldn't get up. Omar Barker—no, Bennett Foster [the one a New Mexico poet and short-story writer, the other a novelist from the same state]—claims that I fished him out of the river there when he was ten years old, but I don't remember it.

I didn't go to country school, though there was a little log one at the edge of the ranch and my older sister taught it. As my father had this stage line, I used to ride the twenty-three miles to Laramie and go to school there. I stayed with my grandmother in town during schooldays and then rode back and forth on weekends.

We had great county fairs at Laramie, and the cowboys would come in from the ranches as rodeo-riders, and we knew them all. One of the rodeo-riders was the brother of Thurmond Arnold [author of *The Folk Lore of Capitalism* and a native of Laramie]. He used to tie us up by our pigtails in this teepee we had. We dressed up like Indians at the fairs—they didn't have any Indians at Laramie, so we took their places. We'd wear comic dresses and moccasins and get painted up and do our crazy dances out in front of the stands. Someone had been to Fort Washakie [on the Wind River Shoshone Reservation] and had learned one of the dances.

At Laramie I saw them ride Midnight, the marvelous bucker—in 1906, I think it was. No, not Midnight; I'm thinking of the old, old one, the worst bucker they ever had—Steamboat! I saw them ride Midnight, too, and Five Minutes to Midnight, but that was later, when I was in Cheyenne; about 1918.

I have a collection of pictures of some women rodeo-riders. I saw Prairie Rose and some of those girls ride. They used to have relay races and change their saddles, and many of them got hurt. They had to jerk the saddle off and put it on the next horse and fasten the cinches and go on. But later they had the horses all saddled, when they changed.

When I was older, we went to all the dances; but we were always in groups, never alone. Oh, the fun we'd have! They'd get somebody outdoors and turn a goat—no, not a goat, a buck sheep—loose; and he'd chase the fellow up a pole and keep him there for a while.

There was no drinking at the dances. There might be fights outside, but most of the men saw to it that there was none around the women. They were very gracious to the ladies in our part of the country.

My father didn't think we could go to the university [that of Wyoming, located at Laramie] because we couldn't afford it. But my older sister and I got positions there. I went through two years of prep school, working in the library, and then was assistant librarian during my four years at the university. Dr. Grace Raymond Hibbard, who wrote many Western books, was the librarian, and that's perhaps the way I started to write myself.

She told me one night that there was a D. A. R. prize of fifty dollars for the best essay on a place in Wyoming worthy of a monument. And Dr. Hibbard told me that South Pass would be a good place to write about. She gave me an armload of books, and I stayed up all night and wrote the essay. I got the fifty dollars, but I don't think there was another contestant.

That must have been about 1911. From then on I discovered that there were lots of essay contests, and as nobody else wanted to work for them, I got the prizes. I remember I wrote a piece for the *Tribune* of Cheyenne about Fort Laramie. Its buildings were falling down, and nobody was paying any attention to it; but I said it should be made a historical place.

I guess I was always interested in history because my father would stop the stage and point out the old Overland Trail. It crossed our ranch, and in the spring, when the new grass was coming, you could see the ruts.

191

There were two branches of the trail, of course. There was the one that went up by Casper and Fort Laramie—that was the original Oregon Trail. But this Overland Trail came up from Denver. It ran through Fort Collins and up across the Laramie Plains, over Elk Mountain and into Fort Bridger.

My father used to tell me that was the old trail that my grandfather had crossed on when going to California in 1861. And he used to tell me stories about Delta, Colorado. He was in Delta when the McCarty boys [Bill, Tom, and George] held up the Merchant's Bank [in 1893] and killed one of the tellers.

Because my father had this yen for history, we used to take one of the stagecoaches that ran on the old line [the Central Overland] across Wyoming. We'd pack supplies in a freight wagon, people would ride the old stagecoach, and we'd go into the Snowy Range, camping. I remember one time we'd been camping for four days without meeting a soul, and suddenly we saw people who'd come out from the university. But now you can't go anywhere without finding people.

So many people today don't know what we had in the early days: they don't know what freedom we had, or how few of us there were. When I graduated from the University of Wyoming, we had about fifteen in the class, and each of us had about ten jobs offered. We knew everyone in Wyoming; they used to say that I knew all the cats and dogs, too. You knew where the other students came from, and their whole families. And now they have—oh, twenty thousand students, half of them from out of the state.

When it came to the automobile era, my husband—well, the first time I saw him he took me from the ranch to Laramie. He had a Ford, and you had to change your own tires and pump up the inner tubes. He had, I think, fifteen punctures between the ranch and Laramie, and he never swore—he would just get out and fix it. And I said to myself, "If a man can do that, he must be pretty good."

He was from Boston, but he came here to the School of Mines and loved it. So he never went back to Massachusetts—it was always Colorado for him.

He was a geologist. He was once working in a silver mine in

192

Mexico, but Villa's men chased him out. He was in Chihuahua, and they told him to get out because Villa and his men were coming. He and another young man got a hand car and started for El Paso. They came to a gully where the ties were burnt out, but the rails held. He always told how the hand car swished over that gully, and the trestle didn't break.

I came back to Colorado because I married a geologist whose work took him to mining towns in various parts of the state. I remember a man they used to call the Gum-shoe Kid who used to tell us wild tales of the doings at Aspen and Goldfield, and how miners would highgrade [cited, too, in contributions of Judge Guild, number 14, and Mrs. Miles, number 16]. They would mine gold ore and put a rich specimen in their lunch bucket or something and sell it. Miners made a good deal of money that way. They'd bring ore to the Gum-shoe Kid, and he'd set up a market for it.

The Gum-shoe Kid was a great friend of H. A. W. Tabor's wife, Baby Doe, and the first Mrs. Tabor. And one day, when he was getting ready to move to California, he gave me two liquor jiggers that had belonged to Tabor; and then he gave me a beautiful black vase that Tabor had given to Augusta [his first wife]. He knew Baby Doe while she was watching over that mine [the one the broken tycoon urged her to retain on his deathbed; for further details, *see* contribution of Mr. Rhodes, number 22], and he was one of the few she'd let in. But she never made a cent out of it. They found her frozen on the floor, and Augusta got the millions.

Here's an interesting thing in studying the history of the West. The men came to Denver, and then they went to Central City, and next maybe they drifted to Georgetown [towns that stemmed from the "Pike's Peak or Bust" Gold Rush of 1859 through 1862]; and after that to Virginia City—the one in Montana—or to the Black Hills. Wherever there was a rush, off they went; and in reading about different parts of the West, you could follow these same men. They were like friends every time I'd see their names.

I just sold a book on Charlie Utter, Wild Bill Hickok's pard'. Everybody's read about the headstone he placed for Bill—"Goodbye, pard', we'll meet in the Happy Hunting Grounds"—but nobody seemed to know anything about him.

But I'd keep meeting him; everywhere I turned, I'd run into

little Charlie Utter. He was a very fine, reliable temperance worker who turned into a big-time gambler. He went to the Black Hills, and Wild Bill was killed in his camp.

I had a terrible time tracing him, because—you know how it is—you can't find anything about men if they're good. And Charlie never shot a man and was never mixed up with the law. But I trailed him through Colorado and Wyoming, and he ended up in Panama as a doctor. I don't know why he went there, but he may have had a medicine show, and some writers say he did. Anyhow they came to him one day in 1913 and said there was a very wealthy woman who was expecting a caesarian operation. They'd planned on bringing in a big-name doctor, but an emergency arose and they couldn't wait for him, and somebody decided that Charlie was a doctor.

Well, Charlie used to be a hunter, of course, and knew what the anatomy looked like, I suppose, and how to cut and everything. So when they went to him and asked him to operate, he did. He was successful, and after that he was called the American Indian Doctor [doubtless owing to his medicine-show entrance]. And as Dr. Charles Utter, he practiced from then on.

OF ASSORTED
PIONEER MATTERS

20

A VARIEGATED CAREER

"We only made about fifteen miles a day, so we were about a month and a half on the road."

CHARLES B. BARKER, Santa Fe, New Mexico

Perhaps nobody now living, other than Mr. Barker, has had a career which so perfectly illustrates the extremes of the pioneer epoch—through beginning by confronting a wilderness and ending as a citizen of urbanity. Back in the 1880's countless youthful readers of adventure stories about the West dreamed of faring along frontier trails toward an untried region. For young Charles Barker that imagining of other boys was a here rehearsed reality.

Arrived in a country which was just being homesteaded, he had the experience of helping to clear virgin land and of eating the inimitable crop that sprang from it. He helped build the region's first mechanical contrivance, too, launching it industrially.

Learning in the midst of rawness is a phase of pioneering which didn't overlook him. Yet although he graduated with the first class of a territory's first institution of higher learning, the initial outcome was to turn him from ranching to mining. Working both as a hard-rock driller and as a processor of ore, he understood, and describes with clarity, the whole business of making natural treasures available for use.

But mining turned out to be training for field work of another sort, which pushed him into court as a presenter of cases. Then as that led to the desire to practice as a lawyer, the transition from rugged outdoorsman to prominence as a professional man was achieved by one who meanwhile had become a forwarder of a unique Western cultural project.

HIS CONTRIBUTION

I was born in Burnet County, Texas, in 1878. Where we lived was on the Colorado River; I think it was about sixty miles up the river from Austin.

I was three years old when we moved to Shackleford County. There we lived about two miles east of Moran—a very little village on the Texas Central Railroad that ran between Cisco and Albany, which was the county seat of Shackleford, as Cisco was of Eastland County. I think Cisco and Albany were about thirty miles apart, and Moran was about midway between them.

I wasn't quite eleven when we came to New Mexico. One reason we moved from Texas was a drought that was starving us to death. That Moran country was very dry the last couple of years that we were there, and the range wouldn't support enough cattle to keep us going. Then my mother had had asthma quite bad for many years, and it seemed to be getting worse. And my father had an idea, or he'd heard from someone, that a high altitude might be good for it.

So that's what we were looking for, but we didn't have any definite destination in mind when we left Shackleford County. Father had communicated with somebody in New Mexico—I forget who it was, but it may have been Dr. Spark, who used to live near our ranch—so he had a general idea of where we were going.

My parents had eleven children in all, but only eight had been born at that time. Four were small and just rode in one of the three covered wagons that carried our belongings and supplies. My father drove the ox team that pulled one, my mother drove a horse team, and my two sisters older than I drove the other horse team. I rode a horse all the way, and so did my older brother, Benjamin, who died, I believe, in '91.

He and I drove a little herd of cattle. We had fifty-six head of cattle, and I think we had eighteen horses. We drove the stock right along with the wagons. It was no problem; after a day or two they got acclimated and just took off every morning.

We left Shackleford County on the twenty-second day of August in '89. We only made about fifteen miles a day, so we were about a month and a half on the road. We had some trouble in finding water, but very little; for we had some information, usually, as to where water was. I think we made maybe two or three dry camps; that was about all.

199

We had a barrel, and we filled the barrel with water, so we had water for our camp; and we would try to arrange for the stock to have water. We would figure that if they could have all the water they could drink in the evening, they wouldn't give us any trouble during the night. And when the morning came, they would be about as anxious to go on as we were, so usually it was no trouble.

I don't believe we had any trouble with animal predators, but a couple of times we had stampedes. The first was on the Salt Fork of the Brazos. It wasn't too far out; I guess it was in Haskell County.

Where we crossed the Salt Fork of the Brazos, it was just a very small stream, but it flooded quite a lot—you could see signs of that. The water was supplied mainly by a spring that bubbled out of the side of the bank. And the water was flavored by—well, we called it gypsum, but I don't know whether it was gypsum or alkali; it was one or the other. And there was salt in that water, which is the way the stream got its name. That water was terrible. It wasn't so bad if you'd drink it cold out of the spring, but after it had set awhile, it had enough sulphur in it so you could smell it. It actually smelled awful.

So the stock drank that salt water, and it didn't do 'em much good. We pulled out of the river bottom and up on to the bank about a mile, I guess, and made camp. But the next morning, when we stirred the cattle out of their beds—you see, the cattle would lie down at night; they'd do that right along. But this time, when we stirred 'em out and got 'em going, they were thirsty; and they broke and ran back to the river.

That was one place where the cattle broke loose; the other was where we crossed Palo Duro Canyon. That's on the Prairie Dog Town Fork of the Brazos—no, I believe that's on the Red River, the Prairie Dog Town Fork.

We knew there was a canyon there, but we hadn't been told what it was going to look like. We came upon it all at once, and here was this canyon, and the road was steep down into it. But we went down and made camp there.

Well, that was a very beautiful spot. The grass was up, oh, a foot and a half high; and there was a little stream running through the canyon, with pools here and there, and catfish in the pools, and wild ducks. The banks were bluffs covered with wild grapes. Of course, the grapes made good jelly, but you couldn't eat them raw—there was too much acid in them.

Well, we were running a little short of food, and it was only, I think, about twenty miles to Amarillo. We weren't going through Amarillo, so father took off for there to get supplies. We wanted the stock to rest a little while, so we stayed there and waited two or three days. And when we left there, that was one of the cases when we figured on a dry camp. We knew where to look for the next water, but it was quite a long pull to get to it. So instead of leaving directly from the camp in the canyon, we pulled up on the bank for I imagine two or three miles and made a dry camp.

And the cattle for some reason—oh, I know. That was getting along close to the first of October, or the latter part of September anyways, and what happened was that there came up a Texas norther. Well, when the norther struck, the cattle pulled out for cover down in the canyon. Of course, up on the bank there that wind was terrific, and it was cold—very cold compared to what it had been. And we were not able to get the cattle back till the next morning.

I think those were the only two times when the cattle really got away from us. Well, then we came to the Canadian River and followed that into New Mexico. And when we got into high country, we just happened to find a chap who had a ranch up in the mountains north of Las Vegas [see also Mr. Elliott Barker's contribution, number 6]. It was at an elevation of about eight thousand feet in Sapello Canyon. That's the first canyon south of the town of Mora. This fellow had homesteaded the place, and Father paid two hundred dollars for the relinquishment.

We landed on the ranch and took up our abode there on my birthday, October 12, 1889—the day I was eleven years old. Sapello is a comparatively narrow canyon. The soil is very rich, but there isn't much of it. We had pretty good luck for a while, though. Providence, I think, intervened for us.

We hadn't been on the place but about three weeks when there came a snow three feet deep. That wasn't so good for the stock;

being Texas cows and horses, they never saw snow and didn't know how to take care of themselves in it, so we lost most of 'em. But where it helped was that the ground had not yet frozen. It was early in November when it fell, and the snow coming that early covered the ground and kept it from freezing at all.

To get the oak, aspen, and sometimes big pine trees out—well, if the ground hadn't frozen we couldn't have done much good. But the ground was covered with snow, and as it was mostly hillside, it was no problem to shovel it out of the way and grub at the growth, whatever it was. We cleared up, I think, about ten acres by planting time.

We planted potatoes, for the most part, on the land we cleared of timber and brush. And we got two cents a pound for our potatoes. They were beautiful—just as white and smooth, and from new ground, you know—so we were able to sell 'em at two cents a pound in Las Vegas. The first year we made a thousand dollars out of our potato patch, and a thousand dollars in those days was a lot of money. So with that thousand, or a part of it, Father bought the next ranch below ours, so we had three hundred and twenty acres.

And later on—I forget the year, but I think it must have been about '94 or '93—my father bought a little sawmill. And he built a waterwheel—well, we boys helped him, of course. It was an over-shot waterwheel, twenty—no, I think that wheel was twenty-one feet in diameter. It didn't furnish enough power, though. Well, you could saw with it, but you had to saw pretty slow.

We had a lot of beautiful timber—just a lot of fine pine timber. The trunks would be maybe thirty, forty, or fifty feet with no branches, which meant you got clean lumber. And we could sell as much clean lumber as we could cut. We could cut up to thirty inches in width, and we could sell it in Las Vegas for thirty-two dollars a thousand board feet. If you could get that kind of lumber today—you probably couldn't but if you *could* get it—it'd cost about three hundred a thousand.

Everybody worked, and we managed to live, if we didn't live very well by today's standards. And we managed to get some sort of an education.

There was a Presbyterian mission school not too far away. My two older sisters attended that school one winter, and I attended it two or three years. Then my father would get a tutor to live with us and teach us kids, and he built a little school building for us and the whole neighborhood at his expense.

The last tutor we had was a distant relative of my mother's; William S. Spear was his name. He was from North Carolina, and so was she, though she'd married Father in Virginia. He was a very wise man, a man of real parts. He was a philosopher, and he'd been all over the world. He was Lincoln's Minister to Zanzibar, and he had published a newspaper and written several books.

Father got him out here in—I have to figure back. I think I went to Las Vegas to school in '96 or '97. But I got the idea from William Spear. I was just as green and ignorant as a kid could be. But I caught on a little about what life was like from that old man.

He had a few sayings that he was constantly hammering into me. He'd say, "Don't forget that difficulties are opportunities."

Then he'd try to teach us public speaking, and he had a rig-marole he'd go through. And I was just at that age—sixteen or seventeen, I guess—when I was very impressionable. I was just hungry for knowledge. I got the idea from him—he didn't stay all winter—that as soon as he left I was going to go to Las Vegas and see if the high school would take me in; which they did in the ninth grade.

Then what they called the New Mexico Normal University, which is now Highlands University, was established. There were seven or eight on the faculty, and they didn't have too many students. That school opened on October 3, 1898. The building wasn't finished, but Dr. Edgar Hewitt, who was the president, was determined to open the school. It was getting a little cold, but he got some canvas curtains and hung 'em where the doors should have been, and we started classes. Dr. Hewitt—that was the same one who was later famous as an archaeologist—insisted that sixty-six degrees was the right temperature, whether your teeth were chattering or not.

I completed the course at the teachers' college, but I never did teach. Why I don't know—I just drifted into it, I guess—I started to work in mining camps; sometimes in the mines, sometimes in the mills.

About the time that I got out of college my mother died, and I'd gone back to the ranch to pull my father through his crisis or to help anyway. But with younger brothers to help my father, there was nothing for me to do at the ranch, and there was a chap in the vicinity that I got acquainted with who was a miner. And he taught me quite a bit about the art of hand mining—how to use a doublejack, and so on—and I became quite an expert, or thought I was.

Twining was a copper-mining camp at the head of the Hondo River, about twenty miles north of Taos. And this other chap and I went there together in June of 1903. We got my brother-in-law, who had a buckboard, to take the two of us up to Twining. I think that between us we had thirty-five cents in our pockets, but a guy hired us right away. We got there one afternoon and went to work the next morning.

The pay was about three dollars a day, and they charged a dollar a day for room and board. But I didn't do much mining there. Most of the work I did was incidental to the operation.

The installation had been put in with a great many faults. It was not operable, and the job that was being done was to go over the machinery and make necessary adjustments. For instance, the mine was up a very steep hill from the mill that operated there. They had put in an air line that carried compressed air for the machines up to where the ore was being mined, but the guy that installed that air line hadn't put in any expansion joints.

Of course, a real engineer wouldn't do that; but an old man who had a considerable interest in the property was the big boss, and he wasn't a technical man. So a lot of things had to be done over, and that was one. We had to cut the air line and put in two expansion joints, because before we did that the pipe would crawl down the hill about three or four feet every day. Metal expands when it gets hot, and it goes downhill and won't go up. Well, anyway, we got this thing going.

But the whole operation there was done without the proper

technical advice. Mr. Fraser, the old man that was the manager, had had some experience with what we called the Wilfley table in mines where the thing had worked well, and he didn't understand why it wouldn't work at Twining.

This table was built of tapered slats, linked, and with ore and water pouring over them. A jig motion was supposed to shift the heavier material to the upper edge of the table and dump it into a launder, where it was saved. And that material was supposed to be concentrated ore, while the tailings were sluiced away down the lower side of the table.

That type of mechanical concentration will work, providing the metal you are concentrating is heavier than the gangue rock. But it happened that most of the ore we mined there was copper carbonate. Well, the specific gravity of that mineral was the same as the gangue rock. There was a little sulphide ore there, which we could concentrate with the Wilfley table, because it was heavier than the rock. But this other ore we couldn't process that way. You can see how much concentration you'd have; you didn't have any.

I commenced—and the other men, too, more experienced than I—to see the symptoms of bankruptcy. What I learned at mining camps was that when finances start to go bad with a mining operation, you could always tell it by some sixth sense. If you stick around too long, you're going to have maybe a month's wages owing you that you're never going to collect. So when I and my pal satisfied ourselves that the Twining operation was bound to go bad, we got up and left.

I went from there to Jasper, Colorado, a terribly cold place up on the Alamosa above the town of Del Norte. Jasper didn't have any rich mines, but it had some gold. I worked there a while and at Tres Piedras, New Mexico, where there was lots of prospecting in those days but very little production. Summit was a famous gold-mining camp in Colorado, and I worked there, too.

Then in 1905 I went to Cripple Creek [just a year later than the troubled times there described by Dr. Catlett in contribution 15]. I had married in the meantime, and I had a little child, born in 1904. In Cripple Creek I at first worked in several different mines, none of them very satisfactory, though I'd learned to operate a drilling

205

machine, and that paid a dollar-a-day-better wages. That paid four dollars a day, and hand work earned three.

But we fell in with a delightful family. Their name was Richmond, and we got acquainted because we were living close together in Cripple Creek. The man was bookkeeper for the Joe Dandy Mine, a very rich mine. As he knew I was just knocking around here and there, working wherever I could get a job, he got me a job on the Joe Dandy Mine, where I worked two years.

The vein of the Joe Dandy was phonolite, or clinkstone—it really clinks—in a country rock of basalt. It was a vein about eight feet thick with quite a steep pitch. Toward the end of the second year I was there we had gotten to the point where we were searching the edges for a little ore that we had overlooked; and that's what we were producing, though we finally got down to where we weren't producing much.

So the powers that were shut down the mine. But they retained me and another chap, because with our machines we'd gone in a hanging wall of solid basalt. It had seams in it, and these seams had considerable gold.

We had gone in, using square sets of posts and crosspieces. The sets were about six feet high, one on top of the other, and I think we were three sets high when this thing happened that I'm going to tell about.

By then we'd gone in and shot down a lot of that hanging wall with dynamite, because we knew the value of those seams. But the rock broke in such great big pieces that we couldn't handle 'em, so we had to shoot the fragments and break 'em up.

This chap and I had two little compressed-air machines that you twisted like a brace and bit. Then we'd put a little plug in a great big chunk of rock and shoot it. We were working there merrily one day, with this great hanging wall over us, when we heard a noise.

I think I was a little faster than he was. When I heard that noise, I tore out of there as fast as I could. And a big rock about a fourth the size of this room [a high-ceilinged office roughly sixteen-by-sixteen] had slid out onto the square set and punched a great big hole in it. And this other chap fell down the hole.

206

Well, I didn't get hurt at all, but he was permanently injured; his ankle had been crushed. But anyway I loaded him into a car, pushed him out to the shaft, took him up to the top and called a doctor.

When I got through with him, I just automatically started to call the cage to go back down. I wasn't going to work anymore that day; but miners used to have blacksmiths make candlesticks out of worn-out files. We used candles while working, and the candlesticks had both a point and a hook. You could stick one in a crack somewhere or you could hook it on something, and all those miners kind of—well, they became attached to their candlesticks, which was nonsense.

I had left my candlestick down there when I brought the boy up. I remember sticking it in a post by the shaft for the cage. So I said to myself, "I'm going down to get my candlestick." Then I said, "I'm on top now, and I believe I'll just stay." So I never went back, and I never did any more mining.

When I left Cripple Creek, I went back to the ranch; and I knocked around there, doing a few odd things like building a lime kiln in Las Vegas. Then in the spring of 1909 I saw a notice in the paper—the Las Vegas *Optic*—that on St. Patrick's Day the General Land Office would give practical miners examinations for jobs as contract inspectors and investigation work into mineral or any sort of land claims.

So on St. Patrick's Day of 1909 I got my little pony, or Father's rather, and took the examination and rode home the same day to Sapello Canyon. And about the first of May I got notice that I had passed and was hired, so I came to Santa Fe.

Well, I stayed with that job five and a half years, and I liked the work. But I had accumulated three children, and I had to be away most of the time. Our practice was to take off about once a month and be gone maybe three weeks on investigation work, and then come back to the office and make our reports. And I got to thinking to myself, "My children are growing up, and I'm getting practically nothing out of them; and they certainly don't get anything out of me. So I'm going to get out of this damned situation."

207

In the mean time I'd been admitted to practice law before the Interior Department; I had not been admitted to practice before the courts at that time. But friends told me that I should get admitted to the bar, as I had the right sort of mind for it, and in 1914 I started reading law. Going to law school wasn't necessary then.

And that's my pioneer-period story, except for my connection with the School of American Research. I'm not so clear about the date, but that was started by Dr. Hewitt, who had been working to organize it ever since he came to Santa Fe in 1906. But it hadn't got going when I came here in 1909.

I remember, though, that Frank Springer, who was a paleontologist as well as a very wealthy man, was sort of the father of the School of American Research. He was one of the men who took the Maxwell Land Grant [subject of a book written by Mr. Keleher; see contribution 10] to the Supreme Court. He won the case, and for his fee got a large slice of that grant.

He was a great friend of Dr. Hewitt's, and their interests were much the same. And I think Frank Springer furnished most of the money, if not all, to build the Art Museum here. I believe that was completed in 1917; and that was the beginning of the activities of the School of American Research. And my connection with it originally was that when the organization was formed, Dr. Hewitt asked me to act as secretary.

Now they conduct that school for graduate students in archaeology and allied subjects. So it's really quite an asset to Santa Fe, and attracts scientific people and others who are interested in that branch of science. Today I think—in fact, I'm sure that I'm the oldest member of the board of directors. But since I got crippled a year and a half ago, it's all I can do to keep up with my law practice, so I haven't attended recent board meetings.

21

INDIANS HERE AND BANKING THERE

*"There wasn't any attempt to rob my bank, but there
was a faro bank right next door to me."*

GUY LA VERNE EMERSON, Denver, Colorado

*When fresh out of a university, Mr. Emerson went to Muskogee,
the administrative center of what was then the Indian Territory. In
that period of steam power and unfenced range locomotives were
equipped with a fending device known as the "cow catcher"; and
as this was a busy instrument in what is now Oklahoma, he had the
task of finding out what kind of cows were actually caught, as
opposed to the claims put forth by injured owners.*

*Joining the Indian Service next, Mr. Emerson was given the
assignment of closing a chapter of Western history that began
when the Cherokees were moved across the Mississippi in 1828. He
was instructed to find and relocate, that is, the last tribesmen to be
moved to the Indian Territory from points East—a tour of duty
from which he emerged with an astonishing array of dusky godchildren.*

*When he repaired to Colorado, after shutting that book, he
functioned as a financier on both slopes of the Rockies. Failing in
his bid to become mayor of booming Silverton, he gained a more
prestigious post when the state's bankers elected him president of
their association.*

*Nearly sixty years have now elapsed between then and the time
of the reminiscences that follow without interrupting his activity.
When interviewed, he was in his office at the Midland Savings
Building, where he was not only occupied with financial affairs but
other interests represented by his tenure of the presidency of the
Denver Mining Club.*

HIS CONTRIBUTION

Born on a farm in Dixon County, Nebraska, in 1876, I was taken as
a child to Missouri and was brought up in the Ozarks. I went to a
preparatory school in the little town of Mountain Grove. After I

finished, I got a job in Butler, Missouri. I was a bank clerk there during the industrial depression of 1893—worse than the one we had in 1933, which wasn't comparable.

From the bank I went to the University of Missouri in Columbia, after which, in 1897, I was offered a job as clerk for the Missouri, Kansas and Texas Railroad. And I was admitted to the bar to do special work for the Katie.

We were always hitting thoroughbred Hereford cattle, and I got appointed by the federal judge in Muskogee as a lawyer to take these so-called commissioner-case damage suits for Hereford cattle. They just knew the name down in that country at that time. They were longhorns, with horns five feet long, but they turned out to be Herefords after they were hit by the engine.

Then I got a job as a law clerk with the United States Indian Service, and I was with the Five Tribes [Cherokees, Choctaws, Chickasaws, Creeks, and Seminoles] Commission. That commission prepared the rolls on which the allotment of lands in the Indian Territory for the Five Civilized Tribes was arranged. I was acting secretary of that for a year; and I was sent by the Government from Muskogee to Meridian, Mississippi, to round up some Choctaw Indians who were left behind when the tribe was moved after the Treaty of Dancing Rabbit Creek [made in 1830].

There were still some Choctaws in Mississippi, so in 1900 or 1901 I had that assignment, and I found it very interesting. That was a long time ago, so I don't know that I could tell how many there were; but I spent a winter in camp on the Pearl River in Mississippi, because we couldn't get the Indians to come into Meridian to make their claims. They didn't believe they'd get any land. They had been misled in the early days, or their forefathers had, and they wouldn't come in. So we had to go right out and get them.

What they had to do was to prove that they had a Choctaw ancestor living in Mississippi at the time of the Treaty of Dancing Rabbit Creek, and that he didn't come west with the tribe. And if they could prove that their ancestors stayed there, they were entitled to acreage in the Indian Territory, and quite a few of them came out West.

Our best interpreter was a full-blooded Choctaw, a very smart

211

Indian named Oscar Billy. When I met him first, he appeared before the commission in Meridian. He wore overalls, a hickory shirt, and was barefooted, but he was so smart and active and quick that I engaged him as interpreter.

Before that I had had an old Indian preacher by the name of Isham Johnson as interpreter. Isham was a very good Indian and a Methodist preacher, but he was slower than the seven-year itch. I'd ask a man questions, starting with, "Did any of your ancestors live in Mississippi and remain there when the Treaty of Dancing Rabbit Creek was made?" And old Isham would look around the room, and then he'd look at this other Indian a while before he started something in Choctaw. I used to get so *provoked* with him.

A peculiar incident that I remember involved a young Indian about eighteen years old. We examined him, asking about his parents; then I asked him if he had a wife, and old Isham asked that in Choctaw.

Old Isham seldom smiled, but he cracked a smile that time much to my surprise and gave the answer: "Had one but somebody took it away from me."

One day a very old Indian came in; he was white-haired and didn't talk much English. I asked him the usual questions, and he said yes, he went out to this new country when the army took Indians out there and dumped them on the plains—just dumped them in what was Indian Territory then and let them shift for themselves.

Many of them struggled to get back to Mississippi, and some of them did. He told me a very interesting story, and when he described it, I could just see this transaction. He said these Indians had ponies—or some of them did—and they used these ponies to cross the Mississippi River. He said that one Indian would ride the pony, and another would get hold of the pony's tail; and he said, "We got back that way."

Closing the rolls of the land claims—by then we were back in the Indian Territory and holding meetings down at Tishomingo in the Choctaw Country—was an interesting experience. The people who were on the roll as of a certain date were entitled to allotments of land, and that land was valuable. So we had to put on the roll all

212

the babies who were born up to that date. But when mothers would bring them in, sometimes we'd find that they hadn't named the babies yet. [Indian infants were often called nothing until at length they suggested a name themselves by some act or quirk of character.]

Well, we'd name them. I had a pal I had an agreement with when that would happen. If it was a boy baby, and the hearing was before me, we'd call him William Oregon. My friend's name was William Oregon Beall—he was related to the former Senator Beall from Maryland. Then if a woman came before him, and her boy hadn't been named as a baby, he'd call him Guy La Verne after me. And we each had stenographers, so we'd name the girl babies after them.

They'd come in with an Indian surname like Walking Stick or Rattling Gourd, and Guy La Verne Rattling Gourd would result. My pal, William O. Beall, who stayed in Muskogee and later became an attorney for the Sinclair Oil Company, came to visit me twenty years after we used to hold those meetings. And he said, "Guy, you'd be surprised how many Guy La Verne Walking Sticks and Rattling Gourds and Swervers are available down there now."

I don't remember how many godchildren I once had; but this was a serious business. I forget the amount of land each Indian got; it varied as a matter of fact. The land was supposed to be allotted on valuation, and a man allotted the high land that was pasture would get many more acres than a man that was on the Verdigris River bottom or that of the Arkansas River or the Red River of the south. I thought it was too bad that some got only the pasture land while others got the rich bottom land; but, by George, when the oil came in, most of it came in on the high lands, so it evened up.

Insofar as I know, the Choctaws were the last Indians which the government moved west of the Mississippi. And if they didn't get in by a certain time, the land was all allotted, and they were out forever.

I left the Indian Service in the fall of 1902, because I got an offer of a position as assistant cashier of the Mercantile National Bank at

Pueblo. I had been to Colorado before, while on vacation in 1898. It was very hot in the summer in Muskogee, you know, so I went up Pike's Peak in a straw hat and a seersucker suit; and they had a snowstorm. But anyway, I liked Colorado. I came back to Denver and stopped at the Brown Palace hotel. It was a palace to a man who'd lived in the Indian Territory, and I wondered if fortune would bring me out here again.

Much to my surprise, though, a friend of mine who was a banker in Muskogee bought control of a bank in Pueblo, and he knew that I had had banking experience in Missouri. So I got a telegram from him while we were in Tishomingo, closing the rolls of the Choctaw Indian land claims. Before going with the Indian Service I came out to this country for the Katie railroad to take a deposition, and I became very sold on Colorado. So as soon as we'd finished up at Tishomingo, I left to take the job that had been offered me.

I stayed in the Mercantile National Bank of Colorado as assistant cashier for three years. While I was in Pueblo I belonged to something similar to the Chamber of Commerce. I've forgotten what we called it, but anyhow we had a meeting one time.

Pueblo had a steelworks and three smelters, so we were very optimistic, and we decided we ought to have a slogan for the town. We held a meeting that was very well attended, and some people suggested our slogan should be "the Pittsburgh of the West." Well, we'd just got it nicely incorporated in a promotional campaign when the Cripple Creek strike came on. [For details of that event, see Dr. Catlett's contribution, number 15.] That closed the smelters. Then the steelworks shut down, and in a year or two there wasn't any smoke from Pueblo, so the slogan didn't go over very well.

By that time I was getting itchy feet and wanted a bank of my own. So I went up to Silverton in 1905. By Gad, you'd have to elbow your way on Main Street, and I thought it was going to be the biggest mining town in the world. I was firmly convinced of that, so I organized the Silverton National Bank.

And things went on nicely until October of 1907. In that month I went down to work one morning and got a telegram saying that the Knickerbocker Trust Company of New York had failed. That was before the Federal Reserve System, and the Knickerbocker Trust Company was the biggest financial institution in the country at the time. So there was no money in our New York bank, our Chicago bank, or our Denver bank—money was just cut off, right like that.

When we got the word, we had a big payroll coming up. A power system was being put through, and the account was in my bank. We were in a terrible fix. I went in and counted all the money on hand, and we had just about enough to meet the payroll and darned little more.

So I called Henry Hine, the electrical contractor, at Colorado Springs, and I said, "Mr. Hine, we have this payroll coming up, and you usually send us a check on your bank there. Then we credit your account and turn the checks loose. But as we haven't enough money to meet the payroll, I wish you'd send us cash instead of the check."

"Mr. Emerson," he answered, "I'm sorry to say that we can't get any money here. But I don't think you should worry too much about it, as a lot of the men are working near other towns and will cash their checks in saloons in those places."

Well, that comforted me a little bit, but there were two or three mining payrolls coming up, and those fellows lived right in town and would be in for their money. So that worried me.

Now, this was an interesting experience. We had a company in Silverton called the Old Hundred Mining Company, and I went to the manager and said, "You're shipping gold bars to the United States Mint [at Denver], and you're getting money deposited in your bank there." Gold had been selling at twenty dollars and sixty-seven cents an ounce, and I knew those bars were selling for only eighteen dollars an ounce at the mint. So I said, "I'll advance you fifteen dollars per bar, and when we get the settlement sheets, I'll give you the balance."

So I got them to bring these gold bars and shipped them to the mint, and within a few days we had fives, tens, twenties—beautiful gold money—coming in. Then I told the paying teller, "You stack that gold out here where people can see it."

In the gambling houses, you know, they have dollars stacked up, so I had the money stacked to the right of the customer as he came in, and he'd look through the glass and see this gold. And it was surprising how comforting and soothing it was to frightened depositors to see a lot of gold. So I never went through a panic, and people came in from all over the area and cashed checks at our bank.

There wasn't any attempt to rob my bank, but there was a *faro* bank right next door to me—the biggest gambling place in San Juan County—called the Hub Saloon. The place was owned by Jack Slattery, who was later a state senator and was a very good citizen. They held that saloon up every now and then.

One of the sensational robberies was pulled by the fellow who ran the faro game, I think it was. Anyhow, he was the principal gambler there, and he knew his way around. I can't recall his name, but I knew him well; and that was a spectacular holdup.

This fellow came in and ordered everybody to hold up his hands. He shot one man—Herman Stroebel, who was one of Slattery's helpers—and that scared everybody else. He frisked the place and then went over to where Slattery stood back of the counter up front, took everything in sight, and disappeared. And, by Gad, they never caught him!

They were pretty wild and woolly days, and the snowstorms over there were very bad. In the winter of 1906 they had very heavy snows; in January and February it snowed practically every day. Then the wind would come up, and the snow would break loose and create snowslides.

There was a mine about four miles from Silverton, very high up, and on one side was Cunningham Gulch. And there was a boardinghouse close to it, way up toward the top near the timber line. They thought it was a very safe place, but this tremendous storm came on, and on St. Patrick's Day the slides began to run. And one slide took that boardinghouse, and *men*, right down the side of that mountain—oh, gosh, it must have been fifteen hundred feet, at least—into Cunningham Gulch. There were twenty-one men, as I remember it, in the boardinghouse at the time. Four of them came out of it alive somehow, but they were never normal again. It was too much of a shock.

To get back to gambling houses, I was not too religious, but being a banker I thought I shouldn't go into saloons. So I was on pretty good behavior most of the time.

But there was open gambling there, you know—it was against the law by then, but officers just overlooked it—and the preachers of the community thought they ought to stop it. So they came to me and told me that they had a petition to close gambling, and that as a good citizen, I ought to sign.

So as a good citizen, I thought, I signed this petition. I didn't then realize that many of my depositors were gamblers, and that one of the biggest accounts I had was a gambler's. But in a few hours many of the gamblers invaded the bank and drew their accounts out, which really hurt business.

The preachers told me that I was a very important citizen, and I wanted to believe 'em, you know. So when this occurred, that the gamblers drew their money out, it irritated me, and I was ready to do something about it.

Then the preachers came back and said they were going to run an independent ticket for mayor of Silverton. "We're going to close gambling down," they said, "and you've been recommended to us as a candidate for mayor. You're one of the leading citizens of this community."

And I admitted it. I was dumb as an oyster then, but I felt very sure of myself—much more sure than I feel at ninety, ninety-one, that is. So I permitted my name to go on the ballot.

Well, the election came off, and I got so near nothing that I often say I don't believe even all the preachers in town voted for me. That was my first and only experience in politics.

Incidentally, I knew Alvah Adams, who was later governor of Colorado. I knew him at Pueblo, when he was president of the Pueblo Savings Bank, right across the street from the one I worked for there. And in 1908, at the bankers' convention at Colorado Springs, he appointed me Secretary of the Bankers' Association.

I took it seriously and built up the membership. And after I'd served two years and got pretty much acquainted in bank politics, I was elected president of the Colorado Bankers' Association at Grand Junction in 1910. Here I was with a bank of less than two hundred thousand in deposits, and I ran against presidents of Denver banks. But the country boys stayed with the country boy and elected me.

I served one term. And that took me up to when I left Silverton in 1911 and went to Chicago, not to come back to Colorado for twenty-five years.

22

THE SAGA OF A PROSPECTOR

"Oh, God, I'd go out for three or four months all by myself."

FRED RHODES, Prescott, Arizona

During his boyhood Mr. Rhodes made the acquaintance of about all the famous gold and silver camps in Colorado, in tow to a restless father. Later he was to know many of Arizona's mining towns, too, including those whose foundations were copper rather than one of the cited precious metals. More often than not, however, he was a prospector, coursing a desert's valleys and mountains for signs of ore of a high-enough grade to make filing a claim worthwhile. To follow his trail is to confront place names with which few among even Arizonans, are now familiar. For since the great age of his type of adventurer there has been nothing to draw visitors to many of the districts he explored.

In addition to knowing a country as only a sifter of its mineral resources can, Mr. Rhodes became himself a mine, in his case of information about those who followed his chancy profession. As a youngster he listened to the shoptalk dealing with notable Colorado camps, the lodes on which they were founded, and the personalities that peopled Western mining tradition. In Arizona he was the associate and competitor of the prospectors who made some of its celebrated strikes. And when laboring to stake himself, he worked in such storied mines as the last shaft to be plumbed in Tombstone, prior to the recent new discoveries of silver in that vicinity. Concerning the old lode, by the way, he explodes a myth of long standing.

HIS CONTRIBUTION

I'm called just Fred Rhodes. I was born in Pueblo, Colorado; then I went to the Western Slope.

That's where I was raised, around mining camps—all the Western Slope ones, you know, and some Eastern Slope ones, too: Leadville, Cripple Creek, Creede, Aspen, Gothic and all them places. In them days I was followin' the old man around. My father was a prospector and a miner, about like I am.

He never made no million dollars, though; he was too lazy. I never did, either, but I done better'n he did. My old man'd hear of a strike someplace, and up and away he'd go, you know. But he wouldn't stay there long enough to make anything. Then he'd go to another camp. That's the reason I got to go to pretty near all of 'em, when I was a kid.

This other stuff around the West—cowboys and farmers and all—I don't know nothin' about. Although I was born in Pueblo, I come to the Western Slope when I was a yearlin', and all I ever knowed was minin'. I was born doin' it, damn near. The first thing I remember I was on a minin' dump.

I went to school mainly in Telluride, where I stayed about six years. It was a lively town then. You see, we went there in 1890, and it was aboomin'. The mines was all gold with telluride ore; and it was as good a camp as there was outside of Cripple Creek, which produced a whole lot more.

But you take Telluride and Marshall Basin, Southwark Basin, English Basin, and all like that, there was good mines there. There was the Tomboy, the Humboldt, the Pandora, the Sheridan, the Shenandoah and—I can't think of 'em all now.

If I remember right, I was about fifteen when I left Telluride. I worked in the mines there myself. I mined and prospected ever since I was born, as the fellow said. I worked there in the Silver Pick Mine quite a while. And I worked in Marshall Basin. And from there I went to Goldfield, over on the Eastern Slope.

That mine that old Tom Walsh owned, the Urania, was a Campus mine. That's the only one there that produced anything to speak of, and that's where Evelyn Walsh McLean got her fortune, you know. Tom borrowed money to buy it; he bought it for three thousand dollars and made his strike in 1892.

Mrs. Walsh died—I know it was either two or three years after he struck it. He made millions out of it, but when he died, by golly, he didn't have nothin'—he was broke. But Evelyn, she had her home in Washington, and she still had that Hope Diamond, so she had somethin' left.

And I was in Leadville. That was a great silver camp—silver and lead. That's where old man Tabor [for more about him, see Mrs. Spring's contribution, number 19] made his pile—and lost it. Like the rest of 'em, he died a tramp.

When he went broke, I guess Baby Doe did, too. I don't know for certain, but I think she was still with that old Matchless Mine, and it was worked out. Tabor had a girl named Silver Dollar that died in Kansas City. They named her after that silver mine in Leadville. But I don't know which wife old Tabor had her by, as I can't remember when the kid was born.

We went to Creede [for more about this camp, see Mr. Bennett's contribution, number 11] when old Soapy Smith was there, but we didn't stay there very long. Bob Ford was there, and I guess Ford'd killed Jesse James somewhere. And Ed Kelly killed Ford right there in Creede.

The Kellys, you know, they run that Bucket of Blood on Santa Fe Avenue in Pueblo. And if I got it right, it was one of the Kelly boys that went down there and killed the last one of the James gang in that town south of Pueblo on the Santa Fe. I know the place—shucks, I've been in it—Trinidad.

I saw all of them fellows, because I was there, but I was just a kid, you know. The first one in Cripple Creek was old Wingfield Scott Stratton. He struck the Independence, and then she began boomin'. Jimmie Doyle and Jimmie Byrne had the Portland. Then old Mack had the Gold King, and Strong had the Strong Mine. I don't know who owned the others. I could've told you thirty years ago, but I can't now. But anyhow there was thirty-five mines in Cripple Creek that produced over a million dollars.

They had bad miners'-union strikes—one in Cripple Creek [described by Dr. Catlett in contribution 15] and one in Telluride. I know about 'em all right, but they happened after I left Colorado. I was in California a little while after that, and then I come here. I got to Arizona in September of 1900, when I was eighteen years old.

I come here as a miner and a prospector. I had to work as a miner for a while so I could get the money to prospect, you know. That's what I done right along.

I was lookin' for gold mostly, but at the same time there's a lot

222

of silver in this country. I prospected the Sheridan Range and down on the Harqua Halas and the Harcuvars. I was along the Bill Williams and down in the Fortuna Mountains, the Papago Mountains, the Big Ajos, the Growler Mountains, and the Babuquivaris. Shucks, I prospected about all over Arizona.

I was by myself *most* of the time; sometimes I had a partner. Oh, God, I'd go out for three or four months all by myself.

I never did use burros, you know, but lots of 'em did. But I'd get an old spring wagon, you know, and I could get within walkin' distance of anywhere I wanted to go with that.

That's the way I done it at first, but in later years I'd get a pickup. I had all kinds that I wore out, roundin' them hills. They don't last forever, you know; but then I made enough money to pay for 'em, so it was all right.

For quite a while I was down along the border, from just west of Nogales clean to Yuma. There's lots of ore in that country, scattered here and there in the mountains, you know. But the fields there ain't the biggest in the world; and if they are big, they're too low-grade.

Still my best strikes was mostly down in the Quijotoas by the Mexican border—the Quijotoas, the Sheridans, and the Comobabis. That was all silver, but later I had some tungsten mines down there, too. I worked 'em for a while; but when the price dropped from sixty-five dollars a unit down to sixteen, you know, why all the tungsten mines shut down.

Mostly, though, I'd prospect for mines that I didn't work. I'd get a good one and sell it. If a fellow made me a fair offer, I just took it. I didn't try to hold anything and make a million out of it. The claims I found wasn't worth it anyway.

But then I did make some money. I done better'n most of 'em; and they'll tell you the same thing down at Covered Wells and Sells, so I can't complain a damned bit.

Sells is where the Papago Agency is, and that's where my headquarters was for years. I'd prospect out of there and be gone a week or a month; and I shipped ore out of there. I got some mines down there yet—silver and tungsten. But I don't know whether the tungsten'll ever amount to anything again or not.

It's quite a job to open a mine alone. You've got to build a way to get in and out, you know.

Me and another fellow once had some properties down in the Castle Domes. One of 'em we could drive right up to, but from two more we had to pack ore—it was lead, silver, and a little gold—down between a quarter and a half mile to the road. Then we put it in a truck and shipped it to El Paso. But we come out on it all right till we run out of ore, as the fellow says. So that's the way it goes.

But mostly, as I said, I didn't work mines. When I made a strike, I took some ore out and shipped it [to assayers as well as potential customers]. Then I'd hold the mine until I found somebody that wanted it. I had one that I was goin' to throw up—quit—but a fellow wanted it, so I traded it to him for a house in Phoenix. That's how I got rid of *that* one. He done a lot of work on it, but he didn't make nothin'.

When I sold a mine, I'd just give a quit-claim deed to it. It was yours when you located one, and I never had any trouble with claim-jumpers. That was a time when some fellows'd jump claims, but they never done it with mine. I always had the work done, you know, and put it on record. If I *wanted* one, I didn't take no chances.

But once I had three claims down there; and one I wanted pretty bad, for that was a pretty good claim. I lost it because I got in two days late to pay the agency fee. There's a time limit, you know, so they wouldn't receive the money, and the claim went back to the Indians. That was the only claim I ever lost, but that was my fault for overlookin' it a couple of days.

I made more money prospectin' than I did minin', but still I had to do that every now and then. I worked for the old Fortuna Mine, the North Star, and the King of Arizona—some of them old gold mines that was found years ago.

Charlie Adams found the King of Arizona. He died a tramp, though he sold out for a hundred and fifty thousand dollars. I knowed him, but I don't know just when he sold. But I think it was in 1893, or else that's when he found it. Anyhow I knowed him down there in Quartzite in 1902, and he was flat broke—didn't have a dime.

Well, old Felix Mayer found the North Star. He sold for three hundred thousand, and he done pretty well. Oh, he died broke, all right, but he made his last a long time.

Old Bill Baer was down in that country and made three fortunes down there. The last mine he had he sold for I think it was twenty-five hundred dollars. That was the smallest sale he ever made, but he kind of kept that; and when he died, he had some money left. He got tired of bein' a tramp, you know.

I worked in Globe, Bisbee, and old Tombstone. I wasn't in Bisbee when they had that deportation [for description of that event, see Mr. Powell's contribution, number 24], as I was in the Sheridan Range, prospectin'. But I'd been there before, and I come back later.

I was in Tombstone when the last mine there was shut down—in 1908, I'm pretty sure it was. We took the shaft down to a thousand feet, but they got no more ore below six hundred. But they had a big body of silver before that. They took a few million out of there, you know.

They had lots of water in that mine. When we quit work there, there was thirteen number-nine sinkers in the bottom of that shaft and eight jackhammers. And boy, you talk about a roar! You couldn't hear it thunder.

And water! A twenty-inch volume was comin' out of there. The water come through the cracks in the rock from way up there at the two-hundred-foot level down all the way to the thousand-foot one. The farther you got down, the more water there was. You see, that mine's got a rock formation that don't hold water back much. There's a lot of difference in that. Lots of mines a whole lot deeper'n that one don't make a fifth of the water that one did.

Some people claim that the water drowned the mine out, but the fact was that it didn't have no ore at the bottom. That's the reason they quit. We went down to the thousand-foot mark, and Jesus! there was no ore in sight.

They thought the vein'd come in again, but it didn't do it. There wasn't a sign of ore at the bottom of that shaft. I was there when they shut down, and I know what I'm talkin' about.

And I was in the mine at Pearce. From Tombstone I think it was eight miles to the Pearce mine. That was a big gold mine, and I seen

225

a fellow with his head sheared off there. It was in a mill, and there was a flywheel that went around about once every minute. The spokes was three feet apart, you know, and you could poke your head through there and look at the belt to see that it was on, for it'd run off once in a while. This fellow poked his head in there and didn't quite pull it back quick enough. And it was right against a *ce*ment wall, so it just ripped off.

I never had any trouble with explosives while I was prospectin', and I got by pretty lucky in the mines. I never got crippled or hurt at all. But when I was diggin' around my house a few years ago, a boulder hit me on the hip and knocked it down a bit. That's why I'm limpin' now. That was the only accident I ever had, and I had no business gettin' hurt then. But I did, as the fellow says.

23
WITH THE OLD 101

"Of course, they say that the older a man gets, the bigger things was when he was young."

DAVID BIBBS, Las Vegas, New Mexico

When but fifteen, Mr. Bibbs began barnstorming in the Indian Territory and Texas as a rodeo performer. In time he joined contributors Higgins and Powell—alike well known to him—as one of the Southwest's legendary riders; and he still holds one world's rodeo record, of which he here gives the details.

But he had other widely noticed talents. A man who could pick up any musical instrument and play it as though he'd been doing it all his life, he was in demand as a member of frontier bands first, and later of cowboy musical teams that played for audiences elsewhere in the land. Gifted as a singer, besides, he became so renowned as a voicer of campfire ballads that collectors of frontier songs and the tunes that belong with them have been for many years appealing to him for authoritative information.

One of the reasons why Mr. Bibbs became learned in pioneer balladry was that he knew that patriarch of cowboy-song gatherers, N. Howard Thorp. Unlike many successors, Thorp was himself a frontiersman and rider of cattle trails. And he not only assembled ballads by other hands but wrote some that have since become anthologized favorites. With this pioneer literary figure, Mr. Bibbs deals both gently and uproariously, for a not yet mentioned skill of his is that of oral narration.

Of this a fine example is his account of an expedition into Mexico in search of steers big enough to meet the old-time rules for rodeo bulldogging. His tale of how he got back is an unhorsed cowboy's odyssey in brief.

HIS CONTRIBUTION

My name's David, all right, but I've always been called Dee for short. I was born in 1893 at Ardmore, which is in Oklahoma now, but it was in the Indian Territory then.

There was a fellow called Charlie something that was the city clerk or city attorney of Las Vegas when I moved here. Anyway, I voted the next election day, and here come Charlie. And he says, "Who are you, and what business do you have in voting in this country?"

It was the first time I ever voted here, and he was goin' to contest my vote, see? And he went through this long rigamarole about what all I'd have to learn to be an American.

And I said, "I can't count to a hundred, and I can't read or write. "How'm I goin' to learn all that stuff and go before the judge? I wouldn't know what to tell him."

Then Charlie says, "But you wrote that you were born in Ardmore, I. T."

I see he was all hopped up and didn't know what he was talkin' about, and I says, "Yeah, Ardmore, I. T. In 1893 that was in the Indian Territory; it didn't belong to the United States." He never did get over that.

I grew up in Ardmore, and I started rodeo ridin' when I was about fifteen, at the old 101 in Oklahoma. The 101 Ranch put on some of the first rodeos there.

We used to pass the hat, you know, when ridin' broncs in Oklahoma and Texas. Besides that there wasn't much to a rodeo but only steer-ropin' in them days; they didn't rope calves. Bulldoggin' was started by a fellow called Pickett that worked for the 101; then a few of us boys took it up right away. That was way back yonder in 1910, when I was just a kid.

There was an old fellow through here a while back named Charlie Press. We used to ride broncs in the Wild West show together, and he said, "Do you remember that I put you off on your first steer?"

"That was the 101 Wild West Show [also cited by Mr. Higgins in contribution 8] of the Miller Brothers. That was the best Wild West show I ever saw. Old Buffalo Bill had a good show, of course. I never did work for Bill, but I knowed him.

I started workin' for the 101 shows about 1910 or '11, and I stayed with it about thirty-five or forty years. We went everywhere—all over the United States. What did I do with the show? I done it all—rode broncs, roped; anything.

Before I went with the 101, Doughbelly Price and me was workin' for a little old one-horse outfit. Doughbelly Price was one of them little old roosters that weighed about a hundred and twenty pounds. Him and another kid and me got a dollar a time to ride those little old horses.

Doughbelly decided he'd get drunk one time, and him and this other little kid went over to an old drugstore. There wasn't any real whiskey in them moonshine days, but this old man said, "Yeah, I've got me some stuff here that's got a kick in it." And he let 'em have it.

They sat there and drank it, and then they got back to the old show ring. But the next mornin' they was about to die, so Dough-belly says, "Let's go back over there and get that old man to give us somethin' else."

They went back to the store, and the old man wasn't there; but his kid was there—his boy. And he said, "Yeah, Dad was tellin' about you boys drinkin' up all of his embalmin' fluid last night."

Old Doughbelly Price was one of these fellows that was flyin' on earth. He was a little bit of nothin', but he was a real bronc-rider. But his brother, Van Price, was one of the best bronc riders that ever was.

And there was old Johnnie Miller, now at Prescott, Arizona, at the RO Ranch. He had a lot to do with promotin' Wild West shows, and he was way up there with the ropin' himself. He's old as a big tree now, but I hear from him every Christmas and sometimes two or three other times durin' the year.

In 1909 I won a silver buckle for bronc-ridin' at Morse, Oklahoma. I've won lots of others since, but that was my first one. It was a long time and a long time ago, but I'm still ridin' broncs, and I broke a horse just last year.

I hold the record for bulldoggin' three steers, one right after the other. It's a lot different in bulldoggin' steers now. They don't give the steers no start these days, but we used to have a twenty-foot open-daylight rule before you could start after 'em. And under that rule I throwed three steers in twenty-seven seconds right here in Las Vegas.

And they were bigger steers than they use now. Of course, they say that the older a man gets, the bigger things was when he was young. But some fellow that was here the other day that'd watched me throw 'em told me that they was about the biggest steers he ever saw. They weren't fat like feedin'-pen steers. They was Mexican cattle that they'd had for four years and turned out to pasture, and, oh boy, they was *big*. These little old cows they have nowadays, lots of 'em won't weigh over five hundred or six hundred. But the ones they used to use weighed nine hundred or a thousand pounds.

Old Tex Rickard and Tex Austin, in those championship matches they had at the old Madison Square Garden, said that a steer had to weigh eight hundred and fifty pounds or they wouldn't use it. They weighed them cattle for them championship shows way back yonder.

I used to be in Texas a lot as well as Oklahoma. I rodeoed in Fort Worth and Dallas and El Paso and Amarillo—everywhere.

Forth Worth was where they started havin' the wild-bronc races. They'd put forty or fifty broncs that hadn't been broke in a place ninety feet wide and about a hundred and twenty long. You couldn't even use a hackamore when you rode 'em, and you didn't have no rope, either. You'd just go in there while they was runnin' around and grab one by the mane as he sailed by and climb on. But just catchin' a horse that way wasn't good enough. To be in the race, you had to steer the one you'd caught up to another wild horse and switch to him without touchin' the ground. And the second one was the horse you rode the race on.

I remember one wild-horse race when an old rodeo rider I knowed got run over by a lot of broncs. And he was good, too. I won't call his name, but they used to say that he was about the best rodeo rider and the meanest man that ever lived. But what happened that I started to tell about was that when he caught his first bronc, it stumbled and fell with him. Well, the rest of the broncs was bein' chased by other fellows that was tryin' to get in the race, you know, so they was runnin' all around the place. And when this fellow hit the ground about forty of them old wild horses was right behind him, and they run right over him.

Well, he got up and caught another bronc and run in the race, and everybody thought he was O.K. But it wasn't until a good twenty-four hours later, when he was in a wild-horse race again the next night, that he come to and remembered what'd hit him.

I like to play—I can play most any kind of a musical instrument. And I used to sing a lot, especially cowboy songs. One time, when I was in Forth Worth, I met John Lomax [compiler, with his son Alan, of *American Ballads and Folk Songs*], and he asked me to sing some things for him. That must have been about 1920, and he was just gettin' started on collectin' cowboy songs.

But he wasn't the first that done it; old Jack Thorp was. [Thorp's initial collection was published at Estancia, New Mexico, in 1908]. And he wrote songs, too; he wrote "Little Joe, the Wrangler," for one. [According to a note of Thorp's, this favorite was written in the course of a cattle drive across the Panhandle to Higgins, Texas, in 1898.]

He was N. Thorp, but everybody called him Jack. Nobody knew what the "N" stood for [Nathan, according to the betraying Library of Congress Catalogue].

He could talk six or seven languages, and he wrote a book called *Tales of the Chuck Wagon*. He was a *nice* old fellow. He lived in Santa Fe for a while, and he had a little old place way down yonder by Socorro. Some of them writin's of his kind of talk about Socorro.

We took him with us to a rodeo in Chicago one time. And when Jack got up there, he fell in with a bunch of honyonks, you know, and we never seen him anymore for three or four days. They were advertisin' him and introducin' him at the show—"*Tales of the Chuck Wagon* by Jack Thorp," you know—and no Jack.

They finally found him and got him back to the hotel. He'd been off with them honyonks or somethin'; I don't know who they were. But anyway we got hold of him, and he was flat broke and hadn't changed shirts. He was a terrible-lookin' old thing, drunk as a hoot owl, and just stayed that way.

Somewhere along the line he'd wired back home for money, and she—he had a little bit of a short wife—sent a hundred and fifty dollars to the hotel for him. Hell knows how much he'd already spent, you see. And when that money come, a couple of the rodeo riders took it away from him. They was all roomin' up there in the same hotel, and Jack was so drunk that he didn't know nothin' about it.

Well, when the train we was on got back as far as Wagon Mound, they gave it to him and said, "Here's your money that you didn't spend."

But he was goin' to meet his wife directly. He was a big fellow—weighed two hundred pounds, with a big old mustache on him—but he was worryin' about meetin' his wife, especially as he'd lost his hat.

And I says, "Well, hell, here's mine," and I give him my hat.

And the poor little old woman never did notice anything, see? When he got off that train, he still had that hundred and fifty dollars, and he'd sobered up some, and he had that hat on, and she didn't notice the difference.

That was the end of Jack Thorp for a while, except that he sent my hat back. And he'd had it all cleaned and pressed, which it wasn't when I give it to him. But now here's the part I was goin' to tell about.

I never saw him no more for about three or four years. Then I was goin' to Albuquerque one day, and it said on the side of the road, "Jack Thorp, Cowboy Writer," or somethin' like that. And there was Navajo blankets hangin' on the fence and around—for sale, see?

I had somebody with me that wanted to sell me some cattle or somethin', and I said to him, "Here's an old fellow I want to see."

So I pulled in there; and he was flat on his back, sick. And I said, "Jack—"

Of course, Mrs. Thorp was standin' there over him, and he give me the Sh-h high sign. The poor old fellow died in two or three months. But sick as he was, he didn't want no talk about Chicago or my hat, so he put his old finger over his mouth.

My old grandparents on my mother's side helped locate Douglas, Arizona. They went out there about 1895—before the turn of the century anyhow. I've been there and at Naco [cited also by Messrs. Higgins and Powell in contributions 8 and 24]. Ain't that some town?

One time, when I was in Douglas, I went across the border to look at some cows for the rodeo association that was a hundred and fifty miles below there. We started out about three o'clock in the mornin' and got down there and saw 'em. Then we started for home, and the car give out eighty or ninety miles from the border.

At that time you could wait all day down there without seein' another car. There was a railroad track—an old railroad went down through that country, but it only run one train a week. The hand cars—they carried the mail on hand cars—went every day; but I didn't feel like pumpin' one all that way. Well, I stood around there in that Mexican sun, and it was summer, you know, and I seen they wasn't goin' to get the car fixed. I wanted a place to squat until they give up, and I'd seen a spot where I thought we might get horses or somethin', when they joined me.

We was with a man named Alfonso Morales—his family owned lots of cattle in that country, and I said, "How can I get to that cow camp we saw a ways back?"

He said it was yonder, about fifteen miles across country, and I decided to walk there. By that time it was nine or ten o'clock, so I got over there at that camp about one or two o'clock.

There was twin mills there, and there was a caretaker, and all that old man done was to watch them windmills and keep the water runnin'. So that Mexican was sittin' there, and he kind of liked me.

I couldn't talk no Mexican, but I said, "How many people have you killed on our side of the border?"

I found that he'd been in Arizona, which is why I said, "How many Americans did you kill over there?" [A reference to Villa's attack on Douglas, cited in Mr. Watson's contribution, number 9.] He just kind of cut his eye on me—he never did answer me.

But we was gettin' along all right. He had a wife and a daughter —a daughter about ten years old—and three or four nasty old chickens runnin' around there. And they had a dove and a magpie for pets. And the dove could whip the magpie. Maybe he couldn't whip a hawk, but he'd tackle him anyway.

After a while I said, "Let's eat one of them chickens."

And this Mexican says, "O.K." So we just up and killed one and cooked him and eat him. I knew the three guys I'd left back there was starvin' to death—poor devils—but I couldn't help that.

We eat this chicken about four or five o'clock in the evenin'. I was just sittin' there, full of that chicken, when them other fellows come along. The car never had got fixed, so they'd walked, too. And they sat there and eat them old beans and water and tortillas made out of corn meal, and it wasn't very good. I didn't even tell 'em that I'd had the chicken. It'd just've hurt their feelin's.

When they'd finished, Alfonso said, "I'll get on a pony, and I'll cut across yonder and head a train off that's due this evenin'. You boys come on across to this other cow camp, twelve or fourteen miles away. It's by the tracks, and I'll have the train pick you up there."

So we started walkin', but we never saw Alfonso any more. But about the time we got to this other camp, here come a Mexican fellow in a pickup. So we stopped him and he said, "I'll be back in a while, and if you're still here, you can ride into town with me." Well, there was still no Alfonso and no train, and this fellow did come back, so we rode with him.

Now here's the part I was goin' to tell about. We got over there to Agua Prieta [just across the border from Douglas] just at dark, and this Jose, his name was, pulled up in front of his house; and he never come out, and he never come out, and he never come out. But some kids finally come around the pickup to look us over, and I used what little Mexican I could, talkin' to one of them kids, and I finally got him to go in and get Jose to come back out of there.

You see, we couldn't get across the border without somebody's help. We didn't have no passes, we didn't have nothin'. Alfonso was our affidavit, and we'd lost Alfonso.

You know Mexicans—they're gun-shy. But Jose finally showed up, and I said, "Hell, fellow, you can get us by that station there!" As he lived right there in Agua Prieta, I figured everybody knowed him.

Them Mexicans was standin' there with them tall guns at that port of entry, you know. But I knowed they'd let us get out of Mexico all right, and what I was worryin' about was gettin' back in the United States. When we had Alfonso with us, he just give 'em

235

the high sign, so we didn't have nothin' to show why we were in there. We was breakin' the law without Alfonso.

So I said to Jose, "Take us over there and tell them American officers what we told you about how we come to get in Mexico without tickets and we'll pay you or anything."

Finally he said he'd take us over, and we drove up under this old sign. You know how it is when you go into a country. And, by God! a fellow looked us over and said, "God damn, if it ain't old Dee Bibbs!"

He was the husband of one of my aunts, so I said, "For God's sake, get us out of here!"

He was goin' to shake us down for a pass, but I said, "We ain't got nothin' but a bad reputation."

So that's the way we got out of there. But it'll pay anybody who goes down in Mexico to have that little old card.

24
HOW IT WAS ALONG THE BORDER

*"I remember the names of some of 'em, but I wouldn't
want to tell."*

WILLIAM POWELL, Prescott, Arizona

*In the West that was, many men were known by pseudonyms too
informal to be taken seriously as aliases. They were nicknames but
with the differences that even friends didn't know the true ones
they fronted for. Such was the case with Mr. Powell, for two
decades of the border country of which Tombstone was the hub,
without being known by any name but Booger Ed, plucked from
the air as colors to fly when riding in a rodeo.*

*His skill at this sport, as it chances, earned him a reputation
throughout the Southwest. When other pioneers were being interviewed for this compilation, the mention of Booger Ed would
draw reminiscent interest—though he had to be so identified, as
Mr. Powell's formal name still wasn't known to most.*

*Not counting the drifting miners who swelled the populations of
some of its towns (see contribution of Mr. Rhodes, number 22, re
Tombstone and Pearce), southeastern Arizona was a sparsely
settled region where every dweller knew his fellows. And among
those living there while Mr. Powell did so were quite a few who
earned niches in Western lore. As a teen-ager finding work where
he could get it, he was in the employ of both Bill Greene and Cap
Mossman. He met Pancho Villa and the likewise redoubtable
Emilio Kosterlitzky. Jeff Milton and John Slaughter were among
the defenders of the law known to him, while his acquaintance
among opposers of it included Burt Alvord and associated robbers
of trains—some of them running on now-discontinued lines.*

HIS CONTRIBUTION

My name's William Powell, but I went by the name of Booger Ed
down in Tombstone. I used to rodeo a lot in the early days. They

asked what my name was the first time, and I finally said, "It's Booger Ed." I kept that name as long as I stayed down in that country. They know the difference now, but they didn't then.

I was born in 1886, west of Wichita Falls. It was all country then, but there's an oil town there now—Electra, I think.

I went to Tombstone in '98 or somewhere along in there, when I was about twelve years old. I ran away from home and was travelin' west with some people that was goin' to California, but when I got to Tombstone I figured I'd went far enough.

I worked around at different places, then a fellow by the name of Fred Bennett that was runnin' a big ranch there picked me up and I stayed there on and off for years and years. I punched cows around Tombstone until 1916, then I went over here to the White Mountains, where I punched cows and was a livestock inspector.

The Tombstone boom was just about over when I got there, and not long after that the town blowed up. Bisbee was boomin', and most of the miners went there. But Tombstone was still the county seat. They held on to it for a long time, but Bisbee finally got it [in 1929].

What we had was cowboy rodeos then. They wasn't professionals like they are now. We used to have rodeos around Tucson, Tombstone, Willcox, and other places. Cowpunchers done the ridin', and I've rode in many a horse race right up that main street in Tombstone [Allen Street]. Of course, it was just a gravel street then. It used to be quite a place, and there was lots of rustling down there. That was open country between Arizona and old Mexico, and rustlers could get through easy.

The rustlers was Americans—outlawed Americans. They'd hide out in Mexico, then they'd steal stuff on this side of the border and take it into Mexico and sell it. I remember the names of some of 'em, but I wouldn't want to tell. Some of 'em are still alive down there.

That's how come I got this leg cut off; I knew too much about 'em. In 1909 I got that leg shot off by rustlers. I run into a bunch of 'em that had a bunch of cattle rounded up and was drivin' 'em across the line and we had a little battle. There was five Mexicans

239

and three white men [a valid distinction, not a slur, as most border Mexicans are dominantly Indian as to blood]. I never did get a good look at 'em; they left when they seen they was caught. I had an idea who they was, of course, but I didn't *know*.

I had no other brushes with rustlers to amount to anything. But old Billy Stiles, and I can't think of them other names—they worked there for a long time. They was outlaws. Billy Stiles was married to a Mexican woman there on the border, and I guess he's still got a son there. Billy went into Mexico and stayed there for several years, and then he come back and went up to Salt Lake City. He was supposed to have been a deputy sheriff, and was killed there in Salt Lake. His wife went up there, and she identified him, so I guess it was the same guy.

Burt Alvord was around when I was there. Burt and his gang held up that train over by Willcox one time [September 9, 1889]. That brother of his—I know his name as well as I do my arm, but I can't think of it—he left there and went over into New Mexico and served five years in the penitentiary at Santa Fe. But after he got out, he come back to Tombstone and behaved himself pretty well and worked for a cow outfit for a long time. I worked with him on a roundup, and he was all right—a good fellow to work with.

I never worked with Burt, because he never worked; he was on the go all the time. I don't know what happened to him after he served a couple of years in the old Territorial Penitentiary at Yuma; I've been tryin' to think. When you don't talk about things for a long time, they get away from you; but I think I heard that he turned up in Panama.

I knew old Jeff Milton. We called him "the Chinese Rustler," because he worked for the Immigration Service, and they was runnin' a lot of Chinamen across the line then. Jeff was about the only border officer they had for a while. And he was express messenger for a long time on that Southern Pacific railroad that run from Benson into Nogales. We called it "the Burro Line." I knowed old Jeff Milton till he died. That was in Tombstone, and he's buried there.

Old Jeff got his arm shot off right outside Fairbank on that

Burro Line. Three-finger Jack [*nom de guerre* of Jesse Dunlap] held up the train, and Jeff got shot; but I don't remember what year it was, unless it was 1900. But I remember very well where Jack and some others held up the train. It was right out of Fairbank by Boquilla.

There was another old guy that I met down there a few years ago. I'll be damned if I can think of his name, but he used to run with them outlaws. He was just a kid and looked after their horses for 'em. He was in Tombstone two years ago; I was down there then. We've got a little association down there, the Southwest Pioneer Cowboy Association. We have a picnic in the Dragoon Mountains every year, but the last two years I haven't been able to git down there.

Now I remember the guy I was tryin' to think of, his name— Max Axford. He was there in the early days, and he used to go with Burt Alvord and Billy Stiles when he was just a kid.

Some of the old Clanton gang was still around when I was down there, but most of 'em cleared out after they killed a bunch of 'em in that shootin' scrape in Tombstone [the O.K. Corral fracas, in which the Earp brothers and Doc Holliday were pitted against the Clanton and McLowry brothers plus Billy Claiborne]. When Wyatt Earp left there, they was pretty well quieted down.

Jim Wolfe was a rancher in there; in fact he was a cover-up for them outlaws. And another by the name of Snake George did the same thing. That's what the Clantons used to do, too. After they left Tombstone, the Clantons had a ranch east of Springerville over in New Mexico at Spur Lake. It was the WH-Bar, and the ranch is still goin'; but the Clantons are all gone.

I was on the border during the Mexican Revolution, when Pancho Villa was makin' trouble, and I knowed him. When I was a little bitty kid, Pancho Villa worked over there at Fort Huachuca as a scout for the United States Army. Then the outlaws went over into Mexico and started that revolution. Well, it first started around 1909, but it didn't get good until about 1914.

Pancho made a raid on Columbus, New Mexico [for more about Villa's attacks on the United States, see Mr. Watson's contribution, number 9]. That's the only place he done any damage. But Villa

241

was in Naco, just across the line from Bisbee. Him and Carranza and Benjamin Hill [a Mexican general, the name notwithstanding] and that outfit was cooped up there, and they had a trench around their part of Naco in the winter.

Although I was livin' up in the White Mountains by then, I was visitin' in Tombstone when they had the Bisbee Deportation [in July of 1917]. Old Harry Wheeler was sheriff at that time. They [a posse mustered in the strength of two thousand] deported the I. W. Ws. [see also the contribution of Mr. Rhodes, number 22]. I don't know how many, but, by God! there was a trainload of 'em. They had a lawyer, and the deputies just went to his office and got all his books and loaded him on the train [of freight cars] along with the rest. I thought I'd always remember the name of that lawyer. He was a damned smart lawyer; and he's in Los Angeles now, if he ain't dead.

They took 'em [over a thousand wartime strike advocates] into New Mexico and sidetracked 'em. Years afterward some of 'em came back in there, but they never could go to work anymore.

The country around Tombstone was breedin' country, not beef country [the cattle were raised there but shipped elsewhere for fattening for the market]. When I first started in, I remember the cows was all the colors of the rainbow. Years afterward they got to breedin' up—Herefords mostly; but Bill Greene [a frontier tycoon also known to Wall Street] started raisin' Durhams. A Durham's not a rustler, and Bill found that he had to feed 'em. He had some good Durhams down in Mexico on the Greene ranch.

Through old Porfirio Diaz [for more about him see, Mr. Keleher's contribution, number 10], Bill got hold of a *lot* of land there. He had a *big* cow outfit, but, you know, they finally took it all away. All that's left of the old ranch is ten sections this side of the line.

I worked for old Bill Greene; I used to drive him around in a buckboard when I was a kid. He was a good fellow. He had a ranch there at Hereford, but after they found that Cananea mine [see contribution of Mr. Higgins, number 8, for details about it] Bill moved down there.

The Yaqui Indians tried to kill old Bill two or three times, but they never did git it done. They was against him because he had that Cananea mine, and at that time they didn't want anybody in there.

Old Bill lived up on a hillside there. And one time the Yaquis cut down an old cottonwood tree and hollowed it out; and they got bolts and nuts and everything they could get hold of. They was goin' to make a cannon—they was goin' to blow old Bill's house up. So they set their powder off, and, of course, it busted the cottonwood wide open and killed nearly every damned one of 'em.

And I seen old Colonel Kosterlitzky [Polish-born commander of the Rurales or Mexican rangers]. He was quite a character, that bird was. They was all afraid of Kosterlitzky. He didn't monkey with 'em, and he didn't ask no questions. He just stood 'em up against a wall and shot 'em.

He saved Bill Greene once. If he hadn't been there in Cananea, they would have killed old Bill that time. They was slippin' in there from the highways. But old Kosterlitzky got hold of what was goin' on some way, and he took his Rurales and met 'em.

When he got hold of it some way he come off that Yaqui River [seventy-five miles east of Cananea] and he had to come over a mountain. But he got there with his Rurales and met the Yaquis and killed a bunch of 'em, so they backed off.

John Slaughter [renowned for his bandit-hunting activities] was around when I was down there in Tombstone. He was the Sheriff of Cochise County, but old John's been dead a long time now. You know, he had a big ranch east of Douglas, the San Bernardino outfit. After he died, his wife lived for a while in Douglas, but I have an idea she's dead now, too, as she'd be close to a hundred.

Then there was another old John Slaughter, a nephew of the other one, who was quite a character. He was a horse-thief and everything else, but the sheriff never arrested him. He got killed down there a few years ago between Bisbee and Douglas in a car wreck.

He used to steal those Indian horses over there on the White

Mountain Apache Reservation and drive 'em off toward Montana. And I asked him one time, "John, what do you want to steal them Indian horses for?"

And he said, "Hell, they'd've been overstocked if I hadn't took 'em."

One time I was up in Montana and John was operatin' up there with a pretty tough gang called the Ryne gang. We gathered a remuda up there one spring to start a roundup, and the next mornin' we didn't happen to have a horse. So we trailed the men that took 'em to the Canadian line, and there was a basin in there right at the line. And they camped right at the monument [marking the international boundary] in this basin.

There was about twenty-five of us followin' 'em—ranchers and cowpunchers—and we waited till along in the night everything quieted down. Then we went down there and surrounded 'em. Well, the next mornin' these fellows—there was six of 'em—all they had to do was to step across the Canadian line. So we just rounded up the horses and went on back.

I talked to old John about it one time, when I come back to Arizona, and he said, "You know it's a good thing we didn't see you fellows; we'd've killed every one of you."

And I said, "Like heck you would—twenty-five of us against six."

I was up in Montana in 1905 and '06. I had an uncle up there that had a big ranch on the Missouri. I stayed two years with him and had all I wanted. It was rough ranchin' there in the winter, especially the last one I was there. It got thirty-five or forty below zero, and we lost half of the cattle. In them days we had no way of takin' care of 'em when there was deep snow, and the next spring on a roundup we figured we'd lost half. My uncle had about three thousand head of cattle, and he lost fifteen hundred.

There was a lot of horse-stealin' as well as rustlin' down around Tombstone. One time a bunch of horse-thieves come through there from around Clifton, and this old John Slaughter that I was tellin' about was in the bunch. A fellow there had a pretty good remuda, so they stole them horses and started to cross into

New Mexico. They camped out there on Mule Creek and hobbled their horses.

But this rancher was afollowin' 'em, see. So that night after they all went to bed, he slipped around there and unhobbled his horses and took 'em back home, and theirs, too. I used to tease old John Slaughter about bein' left to go afoot.

I knew Cap Mossman [Captain Burton Mossman]. When I was a little kid, I worked for Cap Mossman and old Ed Tovrea [later proprietor of a big cattle-feeding operation near Phoenix]. They had a little slaughterhouse at Don Luis, and when I was a little kid I herded beef for 'em.

Mossman was a nice fellow. They brought him into this country, the Hashknife outfit did, to clean it up. [Cleaning was necessary because the Hashknife, the brand of the huge Aztec Land and Cattle Company in northern Arizona, had hired some bad hats that couldn't be dislodged peaceably.] After he cleaned that up, they started the Territorial Rangers and got him in as captain.

I knew Joe Eagar. He lived there at Eagarville. [The old name, now just called Eagar]. And that sheriff whose name I called a little while ago—Harry Wheeler. He was captain of the rangers at the last. And there was another one of 'em—Rye Miles—that died down around Phoenix, I believe it was, several years ago. I used to know nearly all of 'em; but I think old Joe Eagar, who's dead now, too, was the last one.

The rangers was down around Tombstone a lot because of the border rustlers. But we had some rangers that wasn't too good theirselves.

There used to be a fellow down there named Billy Kean that was in the Rangers, and he had a brother that had a ranch by Willcox. They *stocked* that ranch. And there was another fellow down there in the Sulphur Springs Valley, McAtee, that done the same thing.

They broke the rangers up in 1909. There was still need for 'em—God, yes!—but though I don't know what happened, something blowed up. Then they had county Rangers; each county had two. They tried that out, and it didn't work.

There was one outlaw back then that I forgot to tell about. Black Jack Ketchum was in that country down there one time, too. They got him in New Mexico later, and when they hung him, it jerked his head off. But, you know, he held up a train in that part of Arizona one time, and they took all these mailbags and got away with 'em. They hunted and hunted and never could figure out what went with them mailbags. But a few years ago, when I was a livestock inspector, me and a forest ranger went out in the mountains east of Clifton, and on top of one of them peaks we found them mailbags, locks and all. They'd just taken a knife and ripped 'em open.

THE AUTHORS' ACHIEVEMENT

Abandoned times that youth agone has manned
Are hull down, by the norm, in misty seas;
The lamps by which a buried world was scanned
Are dim and distant as the Pleiades
When screened through scholarship, however probing;
The lens that's bent on vanished certainties
Today but radiates refracted now,
Misreckoning coins from prior mints by robing
Their values with an alien why and how.

But here, amid the Astronautic Age,
Itself about to breed new pioneers,
The old frontier bequeaths the printed page
The testament of voice anent careers
That nestle with the times from which they started
Effectively as cogs with wheeling gears;
Like crafty Faustus, wafting Helen forth,
An epoch's conjured up, its courses charted
From border to the south to border north.

Alumni of no other times today
Could mount a world a half as high and wide,
A demi-continent upon display
With all the parts and people it implied;
Their history and industries expounded,
Their jests, their feuds, their aspirations cried,
The crimes that sullied, gallantries that graced
Their bouts with solitude, the towns they founded,
Their commerce and their flights of culture traced.

And no symposium can be the match
Of this for news of liberated man
Till hatching frontiers open through dispatch
Of lightning bolts of passage, now in plan,
To novel wastelands—empty as the stages

That spurred Elizabethan wit to span
Their bleakness with immeasurable zest;
Or barren as the realm that fired the pages
Acrackle with the annals of the West.

Acknowledgments

Special Thanks for aid in compiling this work are due:

Mrs. Carolyn Kinney, Superintendent of the Arizona Pioneers' Home, Prescott, Arizona, for inviting me to that fine camping ground of old-timers hailing from all parts of the West;

S. Omar Barker, author and walking compendium of Southwestern lore, for guidance and transportation about twin-Las Vegas, New Mexico;

Robert Laxalt, author and director of the University of Nevada Press, for spreading red carpets in the Reno-Carson City area;

Fred Mazulla, Roundup Foreman and Tally Man of the Denver Westerners, for shunting his own business aside in order to attend to mine.

Other assisters in finding able contributors to this work gave leads, made phone calls in my behalf, or performed the also useful business of narrowing the field by reporting negatively on candidates and telling where it would be useless to look for any. In several cases, too, they drove an airborne visitor to their areas to the sites of distant appointments. With gratitude for all, they are listed in the order assigned by the alphabet:

Robert Armstrong, Special Collections Librarian, University of Nevada, Reno; Miss Maxine Benson, Colorado State Historian, Denver; Ray Busey, former Mayor of Phoenix, Arizona; Frank Connolly, publisher of the Tempe, Arizona, *Daily News;* Harry Connolly, sage of Payson, Arizona; Howard DeWald, editor of the magazine section of the Phoenix *Arizona Republic;* Donald V. Dotts, Alumni Secretary of Arizona State University, Tempe; S. John Downs, Western Americana buff, Tempe, Arizona; Bruce Ellis, Museum of New Mexico, Santa Fe; Mrs. Laura Allyn Ekstrom, State Historical Society of Colorado, Denver; Miss Marian Fletcher, recommended driver of Grand Junction, Colorado; Mrs. Alys Freese, Western Division, Denver Public Library; Mrs. William Graham, author and collector of frontier artifacts, Phoenix, Arizona; Al Look, footloose author of that pithy encyclopedia *Sidelights on Colorado;* Charles McGinley, squatted in Albuquerque, New Mexico, long enough to have homesteaded it; Forbes Parkhill, author of Western novels and nonfiction, Denver, when not elsewhere; Richard Stranger, but a friendly one, Grand Junction, Colorado; Miss Judy Taylor, dependable Reno, Nevada, chauffeur; Preston Walker, publisher of the Grand Junction *Sentinel,* among other Colorado papers; Mrs. Marion Welliver, Nevada State Historical Society, Reno; Mrs. Agnes Spring Wright [also a contributor] author and historian, Denver; Mrs. Marie Young, coordinator of pioneer reminiscences, Fruita, Colorado.

INDEX

254

255

257